Political Regime of Contemporary China

Zhao Hongwei

University Press of America,® Inc.
Lanham · New York · Oxford

4720 Boston Way
Lanham, Maryland 20706
UPA Acquisitions Department (301) 459-3366

12 Hid's Copse Rd.
Cumnor Hill, Oxford OX2 9JJ

Printed in the United States of America
British Library Cataloging in Publication Information Available

ISBN 0-7618-2226-7 (pbk. : alk. paper)

™ The paper used in this publication meets the minimum requirements of American National Standard for Information Sciences—Permanence of Paper for Printed Library Materials, ANSI Z39.48—1984

Contents

Foreword

This book presents a theoretical frame of the Multi-layered Centralized Regime that expounds and proves the modern Chinese political regime in various aspects. The volume covers (1) the changing process of the political regime from its origin all the way to its forming up in different time period from the Kingdom Era to what it is today, (2) the power structure, the policy making process and implementation throughout the nation and the society, and (3) the mechanism of the political regime alteration. As a comprehensive academic work on modern Chinese political regime, this book is the only one that appeared ever since *Politics in China* (Townsend. J, 1974).

This book includes the author's major research in *China's Multi-layered Centralized Regime and Economic Development* published in Japanese in 1998, as well as some additional research that he has been completed today. It is a comprehensive expression of his research. *China's Multi-layered Centralized Regime and Economic Development* received book reviews with high remarks from many academic institutions including Japan Association for International Politics, Japan Association for Asian Studies, and the Institute of Asian Economic Studies. As the Asian Economics, a Japanese academic journal, observed, "Today, there are few studies dealing with China's political regime from its very top level. The new concept of Multi-layered Centralized Regime presented in this book is a significant academic contribution, and therefore it should be highly evaluated."

According to Asian Studies, "The Multi-layered Centralized Regime" is a clear conceptual frame, by which the previous theories on political regime have been improved in terms of showing a three dimensions of analysis. The political regime as a power structure is a valuable discovery by the author. Therefore this academic work has the potential of being extensively adopted for studies in the field of political science.

For the purpose of introducing Japan's excellent researching achievement to the world, the Japan Society for the Promotion of Science granted the author the fund of Grant-in Aid for Publication of Scientific Research Results. This grant has made it possible to publish the book in English. The author appreciates the efforts of Japan Society for the Promotion of Science and its scholars who have involved in reviewing this work.

The most significant difference between this book and the research in Europe and America should be the fact that a lot of Japanese academic works have been cited. On the other hand, the author did not cite as many of the related English research in this book. The author believes that in the field of the China study, Japan and America are both standing at the top level in terms of the number of researchers and academic publication as well as the quality of the publication. Because of the language barrier, there are not many Japanese researchers known to the world outside Japan. This book marks the beginning of the Chinese politics studies in Japan being published in English. The author undertakes the mission to introduce Japanese China studies to the world. So with this consideration and his full feeling of appreciation to those Japanese researchers who have fostered him to become a researcher, the author has tried to cite and to introduce as many of the Japanese works as possible within the limited space given in the book.

Dr. ZHAO Hongwei, an expert in politics and diplomacy of China, is currently Professor of Political Science at Hosei University in Tokyo, Japan. He obtained his Ph.D. degree in June 1993 from Tokyo University. His major publications include two books: *A Paradox of China* (Koudansya Press, 2000) and *China's Multi-layered Centralized Regime and Economic Development* (University of Tokyo Press, 1998). A volume Dr. Zhao edited is *One China, One Taiwan* (Koudansya Press, 2000). In addition, he contributed chapters to different important books in Chinese political structure. For example, "The Power of the Provincial Party Committee" in *The Political Structure: Central and Local* (University of Tokyo Press, 2000), "The China—Hong Kong Relation & The China – Taiwan Relation" in *The Dynamism of the International Relations in the East Asia*, (Keizai Shinpo Press, 1999), "The Administrative Reform in China" in *The Administrative Reform in the World* (The Waseda University Press, 1999), and "The Meaning of The Deng Xiao-ping Theory" in China Yearbook (Japan Association of The Chinese Studies, 1998). In 1998, Dr. Zhao earned the Tokyo

University Press Publish Award for the Japanese version of the current volume.

Zhang Jie, Ph.D.
Associate Professor of Sociology
Director of the Center for China Studies
State University of New York College at Buffalo

November 12, 2001, in Buffalo, New York, USA

Acknowledgments

Upon this book's publication in English, the author thanks Professor Shodien Kikuchi (Deceased) and Professor Keiichi Tsunegawa of the University of Tokyo. To these two professors, the author owes a special debt for not only offering valuable guidance throughout his Master's and Ph.D. courses in the University of Tokyo, but also the steady intensification of the enthusiasm for the study of the Chinese politics. Special thanks are due the following professors for their valuable comments and criticisms offered to the research at on-campus seminars and various workshops. They are Professor Akira Ishiyi, Professor Takashi Inoguchi, Professor Masataka Wakabayashi, Professor Mitsuru Takahashi, Professor Yoritoshi Namigi, Professor Masayuki Yamauchi, Professor Akihiko Tanaka, Professor Motokazu Furuta in the University of Tokyo; Professor and President of Shimane Prefecture University Shigeaki Uno, Professor Tatsume Okabe of Senshu University, Professor Shoko Ota, Professor Kazuko Mori and Professor Satoru Amago of Waseta University, Professor Nario Nishimura of The Osaka Foreign Language University, Professor Ryosei Kokuben of Keio University, Professor Akio Takahara of Rikkyo University, Professor Yoshibumi Nakai of The Institute of Asian Economic Studies, Professor Liang Tang of Yokohama City University.

The author also thanks Dr. Zhang Jie, Associate Professor of Sociology and Director of the Center for China Studies at State University of New York College at Buffalo for his professional, academic, and logistic assistance in publishing this book. Our thanks should also go to Mr. Travis Sky Ingersoll of Buffalo, Dr. Zhou Li of Dalian Medical University of China, and Professor Yuan Guang of Capital Normal University of China. Without their assistance, it is impossible for the volume to be produced in the United States.

Note on Transliteration

The new *"pinyin"* Romanization system is applied to Chinese names of persons, places, and terms. The transliteration is also used for the titles of Chinese publications. Some popular names have traditional Wade-Giles spellings appearing in parentheses after the first use of the *"pinyin."* However, traditional spellings for a few names of prominent persons like Sun Yat-sen, widely known places like Taipei, and names of persons in Taiwan and Hong Kong are not within the *"pinyin"* system.

As a convention in this volume, total transliteration is employed for the Chinese personal names, in which surnames are in front of given names, exactly as they are in Chinese. For example, in the name of Deng Xiaping, Deng is the surname, and Xiaoping is the given name.

Chapter 1

Theory of Political Regime of Contemporary China

Introduction

During the last 150 years of Chinese history, the China issue has been a worldwide topic. Particularly at present, when China is the last great socialist state, and her political regime is in the midst of fluctuations, it is arresting the world attention. "A change of the political regime has an influence upon the life of millions of people, creating a spectrum of feelings from terror to hope" (Linz & Stephan 1978, p. 1, Yamaguchi 1989, preface). A change of the regime of such a big country as China would surely bring about a crisis or a point of change, not only to the country, but also to the world.

On February 19th, 1997, when the death of the strong man, Deng Xiaoping, was reported, the mass media worldwide started a media battle on how China would change. Deng Xiaoping, who once called himself 'a grand designer of economic reformation', advocated his opinion by stating "white or black, a cat who catches more rats is a better cat." He repeated his cherished opinion that the only criterion evaluating a political regime is whether it contributes to economic development or not (Deng Xiaoping 1992, p. 457, 1993, p. 213).

Then during the period of the economic reform which started from 1978 and is continuing to today, the Chinese leaders asked what kind of political regime would be needed for economic reform. And what is the origin of the political regime and the economical reform? And what is the origin of the political regime of contemporary China, and its process, and where it will go? The purpose of this book is to illuminate these points. The first chapter is composed of two paragraphs. Here I hope I can demonstrate my own frame of analysis, inquiring into the research done by Japanese and Americans into the political regime in contemporary China.

Section 1: Research on the Political Regime of Contemporary China

It has been a basic trait of the study of today's China to divide the political regime into two types: 'the regime of the Mao Zedong era (1949-1976) and 'the regime of the Deng Xiaoping era (1978-1997), calling the former a 'Totalitarian system' and the latter an 'Authoritarian structure'. Hereafter, this author will try to clarify the various relative views by dividing them into the Mao Zedong era and Deng Xiaoping era, but before that he will explain the political research on systems such as 'the democratic system', 'the totalitarian system', and 'the authoritarian system'. Also at the end of this paragraph, we will examine the political transformation of contemporary China, which is closely related to the research on the political structure of today's China.

Models of Political Regime

According to the postwar study of political science, political structure is classified into three types: 'the democratic system' 'the authoritarian system', and 'the totalitarian system' (Chart 1-1) the

Chart 1-1: Macro Perspective Models of Political Regime

	Authoritarian Regime	Democratic Regime	Totalitarian Regime
Policy Making Actors	Limited number of people or group	Individual or volunteer group	Only avant-garde political party
Policy making Procedures	Unclear, but there must be predictable pattern	Through legalization	Decision by the Party
Attitude Towards public participation To politics	Negative to pub participation or movement	Encourage pub. voluntary participation	Positive politic mobilization of public
Thought or Ideology Supporting Regime	Emotional Mentality as national unity or cooperation	Freedom of thought by individual or group	Refined systematic ideology monopolized by the party

Source) TSUNEKAWA Keiichi "Composition of Latin American Crisis" (Japan) Yuhikaku Publisher, 1996, p. 281

former two systems, in particular, have been classified into subtypes. There are many subtypes in the democratic system; for instance, 'the elite democratic type', 'the pluralistic democratic type' 'the multi-polar coexistence type' and 'the neo corporatism type' (Yamaguchi 1989, 2nd chapter). J. Linz, the originator of the classification, once presented seven subtitles on the authoritarian system, but he included the Italian fascism, German fascism, and undemocratic systems in the Soviet Union and East European countries after the Stalin era (Linz 1975, pp. 175-411). As a result, he came to reject all political regimes but the democratic and the authoritarian systems. We can adduce the works by Keiichi Tsunekawa and Masatake Wakabayashi who defined the authoritarian system more closely and categorized it based upon solid case studies. Tsunekawa discussed authoritarian systems such as 'civilian bureaucracy', 'military bureaucracy', 'military faction', and 'personal dictatorship' using case studies of Latin American countries. Wakabayashi extracted the quasi Leninist party state type from Taiwan case studies (Wakabayashi 1992, foreword).

The theory of the totalitarian regime was originally developed as a tool to analyze the Nazism and Fascism, and after the war, it was utilized as a specimen to distinguish the socialist states. However, the totalitarian type has not been categorized by dividing it into subtypes; if there are any, the type can be bisected into 'drastic' and 'conservative', and socialist states can be characterized as 'drastic totalitarian structures' (Townsend, translated by Kojima, 1980, p. 177-179). Therefore, as the diversity of the socialist states was made clearer by removing the fetters of Stalinism and by the Great Proletarian Cultural Revolution in China, the totalitarian regime lost its validity as a classifying type for analysis (Kokubu 'Nomura version' 1990, p. 65). As can be seen so far, it has not succeeded in forming the sample types with which we can categorize the political regimes of the socialist states, and by which we can explain political, economic, and social phenomena, and analyze the processes, mechanism, and directions of the systems. These are still left as unsolved problems. In this kind of situation, we have to say that the research on the political regime of contemporary China is greatly restricted.

Research on the Political Regime in the Mao Zedong Era

It was mainly American China scholars who typed the political regime of the Mao Zedong era. It was a general point in dispute throughout the 1950s whether the China of Mao Zedong was the same type as that of the Soviet Union. But from the end of the 1950s, when the conflict between China and the Soviet Union came to the surface, the viewpoint that they were different became dominant in the academic circles (Kokubu, aforementioned thesis, p. 60). That is, although it was called a totalitarian system, the Chinese political structure was recognized to have its own originality.

"Politics in China" (Japanese version "Comparison Analysis of Contemporary China") by J. Townsend (1974) takes into account this research trend. And it is one of the important studies of the political regime in the Mao Zedong era. This work started from a point of view of the political system and its development, and arrived at the conclusion that the political regime in Mao Zedong era started from a drastic totalitarian system and later deviated a little from the original (Kojima-J. Townsend, aforementioned, p. 177-179).

As for the Japanese research on China in this period, it has been pointed out that many remarkable works on limited issues and periods of Chinese politics appeared one after another, but so far they can hardly be said to have achieved some systematic and comprehensive study on the overall Chinese politics (Kojima - J. Townsend, aforementioned, translator's postscript, p. 389). Rather, the tendency to explicate and characterize the whole political regime in the Mao Zedong era was rather prompted by the 4th of June Tien Anmen occurrence in 1989. The work worthy of attention is Mohri's theory.[1]

Kazuko Mohri has characterized the political regime of China as having a system of 'vicarious authority of the Party', 'intensive centralization' and 'a political system of mobilization'. 'The vicarious authority of the Party' indicates the pursuit of exclusive and unitary leadership by the communist party. In the case of China, the tendency was much more eminent than that of the Soviet Union in the Stalin era. According to Mohri, 'intense centralization' centralizes power horizontally to the legislature and vertically to the party center. Thus, the checks and balances and the control of the power were strongly negated theoretically and practically. This tendency was entirely in common with trends in Eastern Europe and the Soviet Union in the era before reform and perestroika.

Lastly, 'the political system of mobilization' features "the great democracy" and enlightenment on the assumption of mobilization from above, charismatic power and the leader's moral qualities. This is a feature you can see only in China, not in Eastern Europe and the Soviet

Union of Stalin. In a work by Mohri in September, 1993, she points out 'there was a charismatically powerful leader, Mao Zedong, whose existence rose above a system (a party and state) as the fourth feature (p. 93).

Research on the Political Regime in Deng Xiaoping Era

The work by C. Johnson is one of the typical studies on the political regime in the Deng Xiaoping era from the viewpoint of a 'Totalitarian system'. He advocated analyzing the Soviet Union and China (including the Mao Zedong period) with the universal analysis of Leninism, the origin of comprehensively systematic and social contradiction, and he named such an approach the 'paradigm of Leninism government' (Johnson, 1982, p. 923). To our regret, however, his argument is not apparently to distinguish features of the political regime of the Soviet Union from those of China, but to apply the same type to both.

Also the aforementioned Mohri assertion is about the political regime of the Mao Zedong era, but she further insists China of Deng Xiaoping remained as it used to (Mohri 1990, p. 4-10). Contemporary China was actually under a loosely centralized system (Nakakane, Iwata version, 1981, p. 297-309) but the party leadership filled the gaps, and as a result, the vertical relationship between the center and the regions was maintained (Mohri, 1993, p. 130). Nevertheless, Mohri did not use the conception of totalitarian system in her argument. In her thesis of 1991 she stated her view that the Deng Xiaoping structure was authoritarian, or at least it was possibly in transition toward that state (Mohri, collaboration with Okabe, 1991, p. 24).

In 1977 "Relations on Party Politics in Cotemporary China," by Tang Liang, a Chinese scholar in Japan, was published. He did research on the system and in case studies in regard to the relation between the party (Communist Party) and legislation, grasping the political regime in China as 'a highly centralized regime', thus showing Mohri's opinion (Tang Liang 1997). Besides Mohri and Tang Liang, there is no comprehensive research on the Chinese political regime in Japan. However, there are some worthy works, though they are not more than presenting hypotheses. Two examples are "Unification of Party Politics, Politics & Economics, Politics & Law, and Politics & Society" by Shigeo Nishimura who revealed the horizontal links of the political actors (Nishimura, 1991, p. 306); and Watsuji Nakakane had demonstrated the vertical connection of each level in administration as the tight centralization of power in the Soviet Union, while that of China was a loose one.

In American scholastic circles the mainstream discussed the political system in the Dong Xiaopin era within the framework of the authoritarian structure from the beginning of the 1980s (Ishiri 1992, p. 112-116). For example, the collaborative work by M. Oksenberg & R. Bush, published in 1982, is based upon this viewpoint (Oksenberg & Bush, 1982, pp. 1-19). The thesis handles the mutation of Chinese political structures in the years from 1972 to 1982. It points out, as a result of the mutation, the totalitarian revolutionists controlled the state in 1972, but in 1982 the authoritarian revolutionists replaced them. M. Oksenberg continued to hold this viewpoint (collaborative work with K. Lieberthal). He proceeded with his research, focusing upon the highest figures of the Chinese Communist Party based upon his understanding that the power of policy making was held by an individual, the leader, and at that point he left the research work.

In addition to the above mentioned point, we can cite the insistences of Tsou who identifies 'China restored from revolutionary and feudalistic totalitarianism', and Barnett who says 'it evolves to the more plural forms of the authoritarianism' (Tsou 1983, pp. 53-58, 1986, pp. 144-188. Barnett 1986, p. 52). Although American scholars elucidated that authoritarian revolutionists came to control China, they did not affirm whether China had become an authoritarian state, only concluded that the country had plunged into the sequel of totalitarianism. It can be speculated that they were prudent in the use of the words 'authoritarian system'.

In China, too, 'neo-authoritarianism' was the focus of the discussion among political commentators from the latter half of 1988 to the beginning of the next year. The scholars of the time insisted that the authoritarian system was an inevitable step in the political development, arguing from a viewpoint that China must be a strong nation to enjoy economic growth. Their argument, however, was poor in content scientifically, for it was only utilized as a tool for a struggle within the Chinese Communist Party.[2] This author thinks that we should be cautious in applying the conception 'authoritarian system' to the Chinese political regime, because not only China acknowledges herself as 'a socialist regime', but also it is a scientific category, and also the socialist regime is different in quality from the authoritarian system.

The difference is in whether a society has an avant-garde political party or not. Even when the political system in China may be in the process of weakening, China still keeps the exclusive possession of power by the avant-garde political organization, the Communist Party, and the socialist system of thought control by a refined systematic idea of communism. Therefore, it must be appropriate to use the concept of 'the socialist regime'. If we easily call the Chinese state 'an authoritarian system,' we would commit the same mistake as J. Linz who called all the non-democratic societies authoritarian systems. As a result, we would delete the significance of categorizing the types of authoritarian regimes. As Kokubu says, 'beyond that there is a problem, that is, if we identify the Dong Xiaopin era as an authoritarian system or as a system including much of that tendency, we should point out concretely what type of authoritarian system it is, or in other words, what is the form of the Chinese authoritarian regime (Kokubu 1992, p. 26-27)."

The research up to this point showed a tendency of applying macro level (types of the totalitarianism and authoritarianism) to the political regime in contemporary China, and there had been little research calling for subdivided types. So they could not succeed in forming a type for the political regime good enough to include the features of China. At present, therefore, it is necessary to define the Chinese political type based upon reality, instead of applying the existing macro level classification pattern to the political regime in China. The author would like to do away with the research constraints existing to date, by setting forth the theory of the 'Multi-layered Centralized Regime'.

Research on Political Change in Contemporary China

It is said that in China the political, economic, and social crises have cycled. This cycle dates back to the Mao Zedong era. We can see it, for instance, in process from the Anti-Right Struggle in 1957, through the Great Leap Forward in 1958, which caused famine all across the country, to the Great Proletarian Cultural Revolution three years later.[3] When the cycle entered the Deng Xiaoping period, though stability was expected, economic stagnation happened in the years of 1981, 1986, and 1989. On top of that, in 1986 and 1989, Hu Yaobang and Zhao Ziyang, two secretaries general, lost their positions, and in June, 1989, the regular army fired live shells against people in the Tianan Men occurrence, which was unprecedented and indicated cyclic aspects of the social, economic and political crises.[4]

The cycle of changes and crises in China have, since some time past, attracted the attention of researchers who have been trying to delve into their causes. Yoshinari Kokubu says 'an aspect of researching Chinese politics is that models of political changes are more visible than models of the political regime itself (Kokubu, aforementioned, p. 21). The research on political changes has had various results, which, I believe, has been helpful to the study of the political regime.

The most dominant viewpoint in the study of political transition in the Mao Zedong era was to grasp the change pattern as the cycle of 'radical' and 'moderate'. It started from a process of trial and error around the policy, and behind it there was a Mao Zedong-ist conception that emphasized man's revolutionary consciousness and the importance of ideology, and there is a practical stance that stresses rationality and organization. It was said that the difference in the people's values and the prime object is the generative power of the political changes in China (Chang 1978). Also J. Townsend pointed out about the cycle of 'radical' and 'moderate' that it was a cyclic change of repeating the policy of 'mobilization' and 'in good order', and at the same time, the long term change toward one direction generated, that is, the society, economics, people's attitude toward the politics, guidance structure of the communist party evolved in the long run. (aforementioned translation, p. 161-176).

It is Yoshinari Kokubu, Satoshi Amako and Tomoyuki Kojima who made the research on the model of the political changes bring close to those of the political regimes, and tried to present an elaborate model of changes. The insistence of Yoshinari Kokubu is that there were consistently three standpoints behind the political processes and changes in the 1950s and 1960s during the Mao Zedong period; the first was Mao Zedon and his group who valued the continual revolution and their power based upon Mao individual; the second was Liu Shaoqi and Deng Xiaoping, the group esteeming the economic rationality and based their power on the bureaucratic organization; the third the group with Zhou Enlai as the central figure and they were eclectic of the former two groups, or ratified the status quo. They mainly based their power on the governmental organization of the cabinet.[5]

There was an insistence that is regarded as an application of the Kokubu's theory on the Deng Xiaoping era, that there were 'three socialistic visions through historical processes of economy and politics'

(Solinger 1984). These three visions are as follows; the first was the concept of mass mobilization of Mao-ism, the second a bureaucratic standpoint esteeming the centralized planned economy, the third taking decentralized market economy. The first faded away after the death of Mao Zedong, and in the 1980s there was a conflict between the second and the third. This is a conclusion of this theory. We can infer, however, that these three standpoints of Kokubu lasted till the Deng Xiaoping era. The reason is that we can perceive the survival of the group who lay stress on the continual revolution in the propositions of 'the four principles'[6], insistence of 'the objection to liberalization of the propertied classes'[7] and 'the revival of the objection to peaceful evolution.'[8]

If Yoshinari Kokubu's theory is taking the horizontal relationship of the political actors into account, Satoshi Amako's and Tomoyuki Kojima's theories can be said as trying to abstract the models of political changes extended over the Mao Zedong and Deng Xiaoping periods, taking notice of the vertical relationship of each administrative level. Satoshi Amako worked out 'the three layered structure model', consisting of leaders in the center, regional, and basic stratum, by 'the structure and correlation approach', and insisted we should pay much attention to the role of the regions and basic agencies. In his writings, "The Revolution in China and Basic Leaders" and "Introduction of Political Changes in Contemporary China" deal with the Chinese revolutionary period in the 1940s to the beginning of the 1950s as a research task; and "China, Mutating Socialist Large Country" and "Contemporary China - Transitional Political Society" are macroscopic analysis, stating the period after the time handled by the former two books, of Mao Zedon and Deng Xiaoping eras. Also Amako issued a review for the first time, used a conception of 'multi layer' and observing the political changes in contemporary China in the magazine 'Sekai (World)' in 1994, discussed that a possible transition to 'a cascade type of the authoritarian structure' that is forming a multi-layered authoritative hierarchy. Further in 1998, he pointed out that 'the style of unification of China is of the reign by the multi-layered centralized regime' and 'China seems to maintain firmly the dictatorship by the communist party and the centralized regime.'[9] Tomoyuki Kojima asserted that the relationship between the central, regions, and the basic strata is not only one way flow from commands to execution, but also it is reciprocal action, based upon a standpoint that 'mass movement' is 'a source of the political change in China', at the same time, it comes from 'the response of a guidance division of each level to the political movements. This standpoint comes mainly from his positivistic research on the history of the Communist Party of China from the time of the 1920s to the 1980s (Kojima 1985).

In America from the latter half of 1980s, the research on the relationship between the center and the regions in the period of the economic reform in China developed applying the approach of 'the model of nation versus society'. The researchers made an analysis that the central power in the relationship between the center and the regions weakened during the economic reform and the central committee could not carry on the policy as planned, therefore the Chinese society is not influenced, nor controlled thoroughly by the revolutionary communism of the party (the state) (Shue 1988, p. 19. Xie 1993, p. 314).

These theories on models of the political changes did not refer directly to the classification of the political regime, but inferred, as a theoretical tendency, that there is a standpoint to pay more attention to the fact that there is a relationship of dynamic conflict and cooperation. That differs from the aforementioned Mohri's argument that says the Chinese polity has a tense centralization of the power in the vertical and horizontal aspects. The more refined the fruit of the research on models of the political transformation is, the more the research on categorization of the political regime, which is regarded as fell behind, is demanded. Why should the avant-garde party, which is supposed to be highly unified by refined systematic ideology and monopolizing the decisive power of the politics concentrated into the center, be divided into three different forces with three different political aims in the central level? And why have they been repeating the cycle of crises of self-contradiction and collision through conflict and cooperation in the interaction of the three strata of the center, region, and basic? For solving this point, it is indispensable theme to investigate into the political system of the contemporary China that brought about the three powers and the interactive three strata.

Highlighted Research Subject

From the studies, hitherto, of the political structure of contemporary China, we know that there was a serious point of contention between the view of 'the centralized system' and others with the features to pose questions to the former view rather than the conflict between totalitarian or authoritarian regimes. In Japan, the former is

Mohri's argument grappling squarely by throwing light upon the political regime of the contemporary China, and the latter are the standpoints of Kokubu, Amako and Kojima indicated some features through the types of the political alteration. The following are the highlighted points of research; In the research, heretofore, on the political regime of the contemporary China, there is a tendency of adapting the existing macroscopic types such as totalitarian and authoritarian, rather than integrating extracted features into their own classified types. While those theories doubtful about the centralized regime did not seek after completing a systematic conviction of the political regime of contemporary China, because they narrowed their focus on the political change. Thus the categorization of the political system of contemporary China is left unsolved, and it is demanded to theorize structural analysis and distinguishing models based upon facts without being bound by the existing macroscopic type classification.

It has been common to research the political regime and political changes of contemporary China separately, their interrelationship and interaction were scarcely investigated. Therefore, the political, economic and social phenomena from the viewpoint of the political changes were not clarified, neither factors of the political structure in the political transition were analyzed much. We cannot see any comparison work of the politic systems of contemporary China with those of other countries, particularly with other socialist states, except Mohri's fragmentary indication. So we can say the categorization research distinguishing the types of political systems of socialist countries is an unexplored pursuits. The existing characterizing trials of the political regimes and changes of current China are short of the verifying work process by comparison study.

Most of the aforementioned controversial points are mainly due to an absence of theoretical framework of the study on political systems. It is needless to say that the structure analysis, making up of classification types, analysis of the interaction of the political system and changes, and comparison works about many countries call for the theoretical framework of a universal study of the political systems. There is a tendency, however, of thinking lightly of the study of the political structures, and the framework has not been yet established for the present. The development of a general theory is, undoubtedly, a major premise indispensable to the study of the political systems of present China.

Section 2: Theoretical Framework of Political Regime

Definition of Political Regime

It seems to be that there is no definition of the word 'political regime' well polished through logical and practical work processes. For the existing definition or prescription, there are opinions by Easton, Duverger, Hitoshi Abe, Mitsuru Uchida and Satoshi Yamaguchi. Easton regards the word, as well as 'political community and government' as one of the constituents of 'the political system', and accounts the word as 'pure structural conception' against the dynamic conception in the political processes, concluding 'structure supports the process' (Easton 1957, pp. 383-400). However, his interest, as he stated himself, was in 'the process of politics', not much in 'the structure supporting the process' (Easton - translated by Yamakawa 1976, p. 386, 394). So we should make clear what constitutes the structure supporting the processes. On the other hand, Duverger defined political regime as 'institutional framework where political struggles are carried out' (Duverger - translated by Hiroshi Yokotaji 1967, p.81). Also Hitoshi Abe and Mitsuru Uchida introduced the word 'political regime' into a dictionary of political science, defining it as 'the whole of political organization and institution whose power has secured extensive obedience, stable and successive control in a society' (Edited by Abe, Uchida 1978, pp. 156-157).

When Sadashi Yamaguchi defined 'political regime', he enumerated five constituents of the political regime (Yamaguchi 1989, pp. 9-10); (a) justifiability endorsing political regime, (b) makeup of the political elites and recruiting system, (c) institution and organization pertaining to policy making and declaration of intention of 'the nation', namely, 'the political community', (d) physical compelling power consisting of military forces and police, (e) a setup of social formation by political system or the state (particularly guarantee of the people's right, relationship between the center and locality, industrial/labor and educational policies); generally the setup of political socialization. Here, following the stipulations by Easton and based upon the above mentioned arguments, the author would like to propose that 'political regime is a structure of actors in charge of political processes including, though institutionalized, dynamic elements. The crucial points of this description are the following four, 'actors in the policy making process', 'makeup of actors', 'institutionalization', and 'dynamic element'.

On actors; Abe and Uchida used the conception of 'political power,' those who have the power are actors. Duverger stated the institutionalized framework where political struggles are held. The active strugglers are none other than the actors in the policymaking process. Yamaguchi brought up some concepts such as 'political elite', 'nation', 'military and police', and 'state'. The concept of 'actors' implies all of these words.

On makeup of actors: The 'actors in the policy making process' can be divided into inside and outside makeup. The inside makeup is a form of existence of the actors (inside being), and the outside makeup the relationships with other actors. The form of existence and the mutual relationships are featured by the distribution of the power among the actors, that is, the makeup of the actors is intrinsically the makeup of the power. This makeup of the actors cover all the notions advocated by Duverger 'institutional framework', Abe and Uchida 'a whole of the institution and political system', and by Yamaguchi 'system', 'institution and mechanism' and 'makeup'.

On institutionalization: This word means that the makeup of the actors, which is characterized as 'political regime' is not a transitory, but universal system, maintaining validity. Many arguments are endorsing this point. In short, those performers in the political processes are the actors, so political regime as a system supporting political processes, pointed out by Easton, must be an 'institutionalized makeup of the actors'.

On dynamic component: This phrase indicates that political regime has, on one hand, a static, institutionalized character, and on the other, it involves a kinetic phase. The structure of the actors involves a kinetic component by the behavior of the actors. Here this author applies a theory of 'new state' or 'new system' as a theoretical prop. According to the argument of this theory, the existing institution such as 'structure of a state and political legacy' will constrain the movement of a state and become one constituent to determine the capability of a state. Thus prescribed capability of a state influences the behavior and relationships of the actors. It also suggests, as a result, that the regime may vary. If the regime changed, it would be conceivable that the behavioral pattern of the actors, including that of a state, might undergo a change (Katzenstein 1978, p. 19, Skocpol 1985, pp. 9-11 & 21, Mabuchi 1987, p. 138, Tsunekawa 1996, p. 7-9). In a word, when a regime as a system of the actors is formed, an interaction among the actors of various policies comes into existence, which induces a change on the formula of the system = the political regime. The author thinks that we can seek after some theoretical ground on this theory of 'the new state' or (the new systems) to connect organically researches on the political systems and changes, which have been done sporadically. By infusing some dynamic tinge into the static, so far, theory of 'political regime', we may be able to develop more persuasive theory of 'political regimes'. Besides above-mentioned logical works, it is needless to say that we should do corroborative efforts to make the definition of political regimes more meaningful theory. The research on the political regime of contemporary China in this book will be one of the significant positive cases.

Structure of Actors

The makeup of the actors, an object of the study of political regime, has phases of the internal (existence form of each actor) and external (correlation of actors) setups; and each can be divided into horizontal and vertical make-ups. There are some actors existing horizontally, namely, political party actors, national policy actors taking their positions in the state organs such as legislation, administration and judicature institution, economic policy actors consisting of profit pursuing groups, and society policy actors composed of social groups, mass media and voters.

On the other hand, relationship of up and down is the one where the upper dictates and the lower executes it. So there is a big distinction in the power of policymaking processes between the upper and lower actors. Here, for the present, the author would like to show a hypothesis that, limiting to China, the leaders in the center, provinces, and localities are the political actors in correlation among them, based upon a theory of 'Three Layered Model' by Satoshi Amako that explains political leaders in (center-province-locality) relationship.

The internal mechanism of actors is, in the case of Chinese state policy actors, the horizontal relationship between state organizations such as legislation, administration, and judicature; and vertically up and down correlation in the respective machinery. Horizontal and external relationship of the actors is the correlation between the various actors of party, state, economic, and social policies. Also the actors can be divided into two groups, the one directly participated in the state policymaking processes, and the other taking in part bringing out the social profit.[10] Generally, administrative machinery of a state belongs to the former and makes up a social set-up. However, since the Chinese Communist Party controls the state organs absolutely, the political party constitutes the national mechanism as well as the state institution does. On the other hand, the economic and social actors make up the social set-up. Thus the relationship between the state and society can be said to be the relationship between the two types of actors in concrete terms. Also the political regime can be taken as an institutionalized mechanism of the state and society respectively and as mutual relations of the two.

External correlation of the actors in vertical perspective is the correlation between each guidance division of the center, province, and locality as the actors are connected up and down. The existing form and relationship of the actors at the respective levels are made up and characterized by distribution of the power to each level allocated by the political regime. Therefore the setup of the actors is essentially the makeup of the power, so it can be said that the political regime is an institutionalized correlation of the internal and external political powers. As for the power correlation, there are two basic forms, centralized (convergence of the political authority) or dispersed (divergence of supremacy) power. Since it can be recognized that non-democratic countries, particularly socialist states, are states of centralized regime, the concept of centralized power is essential for the comparison research on political regime of these countries.

There are two modes conceivable for the centralized power of the various actors, the horizontal and vertical centralization of the power, each corresponding to horizontal and vertical correlation. The horizontal centralization means that of the central, provincial, and local actors in respective administrative levels, generally the actors should stay in the social system, but here it has turned out to be members of the national organization by being integrated into the state makeup.

According to the research heretofore the concentration of power is apt to be considered the same as the centralized power, but this author thinks there are many types of concentration. As a matter of fact, depending upon the way of assorting the two types, horizontal and vertical concentration of the powers, there should be diversified centralization. So you should be able to classify centralized political regimes. Thus the setup of the actors under the centralized regime contains phases of the internal mechanism and external correlation, and moreover it has two modes of horizontal and vertical concentration of the power. So when you try to analyze setup of the actors, you should investigate a complicated assortment of the horizontal and vertical power structure of the actors in the external and internal makeup.

You can point out four variables in the classification of centralized regime; the first is the mode of centralized power, that is, in a certain type of centralized, which is more dominant, horizontal or vertical centralization? The second is the nucleus of centralization, that is, who will be the actor taking the nucleus position of centralized power. For example, shown in the chart 1-1, in the case of authoritarian regime, a limited number of people or groups approved by the state can be in the nucleus position, while in the case of totalitarian regime the sole avant-garde party will form the nucleus.

Chart 1-2: Relationships between Center and Actors in Political Regime

	Multilayered Centralized Regime(China)	Centralized Regime (Soviet Union)	Upper Centralized Regime (Authoritarian State)	Power Divided Regime (Democratic State)
Center	● → ◎	● → ◎	● → ◎	● ⇔ ◎
	↓	↓ ↓	↓ ↓	△ △
Locality	● → ◎	● → ◎	● ◎	● ⇔ ◎
	↓	↓ ↓	↓ ↓	△ △
Basic	● → ◎	● → ◎	● ◎	● ⇔ ◎

Note: ● Leadership, ◎ Other Actors, → ↓ Control, → ↓ Limited Control, ⇔ Govern & Participation, △ Autonomy, Source: Drawn by the author.

The third is the number of the actors integrated in the state structure. For example, Taisuke Murakami, Hisao Kumagai, and Shunpei Kumon pointed out that a combination of centralized power and private ownership is impossible logically, because the centralized power cannot instruct the owners with the true right of using in the manner of authoritarian regime (Murakami and others 1973, p. 186). The economic policy actors are included in the state structure under the totalitarian regime, but under the authoritarian regime they stay in the social mechanism, basically without being integrated into the state structure. The fourth is the degree of centralization of power. Watsuji Nakakane distinguished the economic policy of the Soviet Union and China as the tight centralization versus loose one. The degree of centralization is considered to be an indispensable variable to classify centralized policy structures.

In this writing, by measuring the structures of the authoritarian regime with these four variables, the author would like to show the effective discriminating types in the political regime of contemporary China, at the same trying to categorize the types of the political regime of social states, and also creating an index to distinguish authoritarian regimes. The types of the centralized political regime to be examined here are the multi-layered centralized regime, core centralized regime and top-echelon centralized regime; each applies to contemporary China, the Soviet Union before perestroika and Eastern European countries, and other political regime of the authoritarian states. The chart 1-1 is an image of comparing those political regimes. You can understand from the picture that, under the multi-layered political regime of contemporary China, the vertical correlation of leaders at each level from the center to the localities and the horizontal relationship between the leaders and the actors are the relationship of ruling.

Under the core-centralized regime of the Soviet Union, except the central leaders, relationship between leaders of local and basic levels and policy actors was limited ruling relations. Also in the top-echelon centralized regime of the authoritarian states, the ruling relations is close to that of the Soviet Union, but a feature is in weaker degree of ruling. Under the democratic regime, there is no ruling, but governing power and participation horizontally, and separation of the power vertically based upon the idea of autonomy. It is needless to say that the concern of this writing is mainly on the multi-layered centralized regime of contemporary China, but for unfolding the argument to describe the features more vividly, a comparison work with other types is requisite.

Lastly it may be necessary to add that not all structures of the actors are put in a statutory form. Particularly in China where it is said there are many things are ground on non-institutionalized causes, it is crucial to analyze things from two perspectives, mechanism based upon laws and ordinances and practical structures (Okabe 1986, p. 6). Furthermore, in China, besides the laws at large, the policy of the Chinese Communist Party is as effectual as laws and ordinances, so the mechanism based upon laws here has wider meaning than general.

Behaviors of the Actors

It is not too much to say that all the political phenomena are derived from the behaviors of the actors when all is said. Therefore, not a few political scientists made some results by approaching the political proceedings through the apparent movements of the actors (Ohtake 1990, p.144). Why did an actor take a certain behavior is a problem researchers should always pursue. After all, the political regime affects a society through the medium of the movements of the actors, and as a result a certain political, economical or social fact is generated.

The political processes, which combine the political regime with political, economical and social phenomena, are considered as stated in the following. To begin with, the power is distributed to the actors in a way depending upon the political regime, and the actor shows a certain type of behavioral pattern under the relationship with the power, and the results of that pattern come out as political, economical and social phenomena. The behavior of the actors is not passive to the political regime. The political, economical and social phenomena originated by the behaviors can trigger a change of the political regime, that is, the behavioral pattern of the actors functions as agency to connect casual sequences, in the political processes, between the political regime and the political, economical and social phenomena, and between political regime and its change.

Since the political processes can be divided into two types, the process of the policy making and the process of policy enforcement. This writing takes these two as subjects for the research. The reason is that the research on the policy making process has been the focus of the political science and vigorous after the war, however the study on the policy enforcement was not so enthusiastic (Morita, 1988, p. 5-12). This may be because that the study of politics was originated in modern Europe and America investigating mainly their policies. These countries are mostly law governed states and they usually enforce the law once legislated in the policy execution process, therefore, the policy making processes are regarded as a essential subject to study, while the policy execution processes have been considered to be self-explanatory. Most of developing countries, particularly China, are not sufficiently legislative states, and some policies enacted have not been often executed. Hence, so long as contemporary China is the subject of the study, we should research on the process of the policy making, but also the processes of the policy enforcement.

Analysis of the behavioral pattern of the actors as well as that of the makeup of the actors composes another field of the research of political regime. First, establish the parameter of the behavioral pattern of the actors, using it as a prop to proceed with the analysis work, then you can grasp a better picture of political, economic, and social phenomena from an angle of the political regime. Next, you can examine the process, mechanism and direction of a change of a certain type of the political regime through analysis of dynamic correlation between a type of regime and a behavioral pattern of the actors when the latter including the nation under the old regime has created a reform and brought about a new movement under the new regime.

The analysis of the actors' movement has two phases; an examination of the behavioral patterns of the actors and an analysis of the correlation of the behavioral patterns, and the latter is more significant. The reason is that their behavioral patterns evolve being correlated each other in the political processes, and this correlation itself can be considered to be the mechanism driving the political processes.

The question on governability of a political regime, which came out in the 1970s from the study of political regimes (Huntington, Crozier, Watanuki 1975. The Japanese version 1976), can be solved by clearing the sequence of cause and effect between political regimes through the medium of behavioral patterns of the actors and political, economic, and social phenomena. One of the research subjects of this writing is to value the governability of the political regime of contemporary China through the study of the policy making in the Deng Xiaoping era and behavioral patterns of the actors through the execution.

Furthermore, the study of the actor's behavioral patterns will also prove the significance of classifying political regimes. The reason is the type of the political regime defined through a study of the actor's structure can corroborate its significance only after its validity is proved through interpreting the behavioral patterns of the actors controlled under the political regime.

This author thinks that introducing some dynamic view point of the study of the actor's behavioral patterns into the static study of the political regime enlarges the domain of corroborative study of the political regimes, and combines organic researches on political regimes and political changes which were done, hitherto, separately, and heightens usefulness of the study of the political regime and helps to upgrade its status.

Approach to Research on Political Regime

The theoretical framework of studying political regime shown in this chapter is composed of the aforementioned new definition of political regime and the theory, derived from the definition, of the makeup and of the behavioral patterns of the actors. With this argument, this author would show and use an approach based upon the make-up and behavioral patterns of the actors as a tackling way to the study of the political regime grounded on the definition that the political regime is a structure of the actors, institutionalized with a part of dynamic elements, supporting the political processes. This approach, to put it concretely, is, through the analysis of makeup of the actors and its characterized behavioral patterns, to try classifying the political regime, to examine a sequence of cause and effect of the political, economic, and social phenomena, and furthermore to clear the processes, mechanism and direction of changes of the political regimes.

Conclusion

The following is the content of this writing. This chapter has insisted on the significance of a viewpoint of the theory of political regime for the research on China. In the second chapter you will find the historical processes, the origin, the formation and changes of contemporary China, explaining from the Monarchical age to the Mao Zedong and Deng Xiaoping eras. Here you will make observation of basic features of the political regime of contemporary China in the historical context, and inquire into how and why it has reached today's form of the state. In the third and fourth chapters you will see an analysis of the actors; how the features of the regime of contemporary China, shown in the second chapter, are substantiated by the correlation of the powers, and analyzing it from the inside and outside structures of the actors in both state and society. And then in the fifth chapter, you will compare the political regime of contemporary China with democratic, authoritarian political regimes and with the socialist regime of the Soviet Union type, applying the technique of the comparison political science in order to throw more light on the structural features. In the sixth and seventh chapter, you will see the analysis of the behavioral patterns of the actors, in the sixth a power of Provincial Party Secretaries as a sample of case study, in the seventh the as sample. Through these factors we try to clear the correlation between the political regime and the behavioral patterns of the actors in the policy making and execution processes, then we will see the relationship between the economical development and the political regime of contemporary China. At the last chapter we will analyze the mechanism and direction of the status quo and the changes of China in the post Deng Xiaoping era, bearing in mind casual nexus the Political regime of present China.

Notes

1. The quotation from Kazuko Mohri "Changes of Reform and System in China – Making Sense of 'Tiananmen Incident'' "The 64th Issue" Japan Contemporary China Society, 1990. p.4-10. Mohri's arguments are also stated in the following studies; "Features & Reforms of Political Regime", "Iwanami Lectures – Contemporary China 1 – Political World in Contemporary China 1" edited by Koichi Nomura, Iwanami Publisher, 1989, "China in Mao Zedong Era – On Contemporary China" edited by Kazuko Mohri "China in Reform-Opening Period – On Contemporary China 2" edited by Kazuko Mohri & Tatsumi Okabe, Japan International Issue Laboratory, article carried in 1990 and 1991. Kazuko Mohri "Politics in Contemporary China" Nagoya University Press 1993.

2. Zhao Hongwei "Discussing 'Neo-Authoritarianism' Dispute" Zhao Hongwei edit. "Dong Yin Qiu Sou" The 4th Issue, International Culture Hall 1991, p. 150-154. As for the bibliography on the dispute of 'Neo-Authoritarianism', Liu Jun, Li Lin edit. "Neo-Authoritarianism-The Dispute against the Platform of the Reform Theory" Beijing Economic Institute Press 1989.

3. There are many researches pointing out the cycles of political changes in the Chinese politics, here for your reference, the afore-named book by J. R. Townsend transferred into Japanese, p. 161-176.

4. A book observing these facts in details is, Susumu Yabuki "China Crises Major Bibliograhy" 3 vol. Soh-Soh Publisher, 1989. The same author "The Actual Facts of Tiananmen Incident" 2 vol. same pulisher 1990.

5. The afore-named book by Yoshinari Kokubu p. 23. His viewpoints are unfolded in the following papers "An Analysis of The Chinese Communist Party 8th General Assembly – Focusing on Circumstantial Cognition by the Central Leadership", "Collection of Theses Celebrating the 60th Anniversary of Prof. Tadao Ishiguro", "Contemporary China and the World and Its Development" Keio Press 1982, "Dispute in the Party about Great Leap Forward" 'Study of Laws' vol. 52, 7th issue, Law Research Society in Keio University, July 1979. "Socialism Education Movement and Dispute in the Party - History of the Great Cultural Revolution in the Preceding Time 1962-

1965" 'Research on Asia' vol.27, 3rd Issue, Asian Politics and Economics Society, Oct. 1980.

6. This is what was proposed by Deng Xiaoping first time, they are the following four principles; 'Hold fast to the way of socialism', 'Proletarian Dictatorship', 'Communist Party Leadership' and 'Hold on Marxism and Leninism. Deng Xiaoping "Let's stick to four basic principles" 'Deng Xiaoping Selection 1975-1982', Weiwen Publisher (Beijing), 1984, p.234.

7. The slogan brought forward by Deng Xiaoping first. Masao Murayama reported the result of this movement, 'Account of Spiritual Corruption Campaign' "This is Yomiuri" Yomiuri Press, April Issue 1984, p. 116-120.

8. 'Addresses of Jiang Zemin, Secretary-General of China Communist Party' "People's Newspaper" 1 Oct. 1990.

9. Satoshi Amako "Introduction to Political Changes in Contemporary China – Political processes around the Foundation of New China" 'Series of Asian Politics and Economics Society' 1984, "Pluralistic Make-ups of Political Changes" Tatsuo Yamada edit. "Contemporary China in History" Keiso Publisher 1996, p. 371-391. Same "Revolution in China and Local Leaders" Kenbun Publisher 1984 "China – Melting and Changing Socialist Large Country" Tokyo University Press 1992. Same "Possibility of Cascade Type Authoritarianism" 'World' Aug. Issue 1994, Iwanami Publisher p. 42. Same "Political Composition of Self-Reliance and Integration in China - Translation into Cascade Type Authoritarianism" Tatsumi Okabe edit. "Political Change in Greater China" Keiso Publisher 1995. Same "Social Transformation in the Contemporary China and Relationship between the Center and Provinces" Priority Area Research of the Ministry of Education, 113 Issue "Series – Chinese Area Study" 7th Issue, 1998, p. 30, 34. "Contemporary China – Political Society in Transition" Tokyo University Press 1998.

10. The way of dividing 'the actors taking part in policy making' and 'actors in profit making' is with reference to the argument of structure separation by G. A. Armond, translated by Hideo Uchiyama "Contemporary Politics and History Consciousness" Keiso Publisher 1982, p. 125-151.

Chapter 2

Establishment of Political Regime in China

Introduction

Since we handle problems of political regime in contemporary China, we should clarify the processes of changes from the origin through the founding period and to the present time. From its historical context of the passage, we have to find out basic features of political regime of contemporary China. That means we should deal with multifarious elements such as am few thousands years long historical passages, among them particularly the political, economic, and social factors which affected political regime and influences from foreign countries. That may be the reason why there have been no comprehensive and systematic research tackling these issues, except some arguments facing with limited ages or points. Hopefully we can challenge this task and propose one hypothesis in this chapter.

We can cite political regimes of monarchial and modern China, and that of the Soviet Union as original structures of the political regime of contemporary China. The reason we use the word, monarchial, here is that it will cover the formation period of ancient China, such as Chun-Qiu, Zhanguo, Qin and Han periods, and the last empire, Qing; also we can avoid disputes on division of the historical periods argued in the historical science society.

The word 'Modern China' indicates the period from the collapse of Qing dynasty to 1949, while 'Contemporary China' is after 1949. As for the formation and transition periods of the political regime of contemporary China, the former corresponds to the Mao Zedong era from 1949 to 1976, and the latter to the Deng Xiaoping era from 1977 to 1997. Here we would analyze these items one by one in hopes of setting up a hypothesis on the political regime of contemporary China being brought into existence. Further, the subject of the research is not Chinese history itself, but presenting a comprehensive and systematic hypothesis on the origin, formation and changes of the political regime of contemporary China, so we would not have no concern with the academic dispute about the Chinese history, but try to explain with the historical understandings widely accepted.

Section 1: History of Researches on the Origin

Roughly speaking there were two trends, hitherto, in researches on the origin of political regime of contemporary China, based upon viewpoints of 'impact and reaction' and 'tradition and modern ages'. One trend is to regard the occidental influence as important, the other takes notice of spontaneous mutation in the Chinese society. Metzger and Myers divided, in their thesis, American studies on China into three categories; 'Revolution Paradigm', 'Modernization Paradigm' and 'Developing Paradigm in the Chinese Way'. They insisted the 'Revolution Paradigm' and 'Modernization Paradigm' emphasizing backwardness of modern China before encountering the western modernism and the severance from the tradition, thus this standpoint took the outside influence seriously. Whereas they argued that Chinese traditional and systematic sources had succeeded to the time and played important roles. Also they said they were watching the Chinese spontaneous changes (Metzger and Myers 1983, p. 34).

However, the research making much account of the succession of 'the Chinese traditional and systematic sources' did not start from Metzger and Myers, there were many scholars insisting this point (Cohen, translated by Sato, 1988, p. 5-7). For example, in the classics, there is a masterpiece "Oriental Despotism" by Carl A. Wittfogel (Wittfogel, translated by Yuasa, 1991). When the first edition of this book was published in the 1950's, a stream of research had been in the making in Japan and the U.S.A to find out the features of the political regime or changes in the long political transitional processes tracing back to the Qing and Ming dynasties. After that, not a few researchers, who had been classified as the first group, participated in the Qing/Ming studies and succeeded in developing their own theories. The "Politics in China" by James R. Townsend, for example, points out 'the Chinese political tradition' as one of the origins, in the second chapter 'Origins of Communistic Political Systems' and developing his analysis utilizing the results of the Qing/Mings studies by U.S. political and historical scholars (Townsend, translated by Kojima, 1980, chapter 2).

John K. Fairbanks, a pioneer of the Chinese study in the U.S.A. and a representative of the first group, wrote a series of papers in 1989 and 1990 analyzing 'The 4th June Tiananmen incident' laying stress on the character of elitism of the Chinese political regime and historical analogy with despotic monarchy.[1] B. Moor who analyzed the Chinese history from a standpoint of comparative political science thought much of the roles of the local elite who were called gentry in the Ming and Qing dynasties, and traced the origin of the formation of the communistic regime to the social and economic relationship between the gentry and farmers, the bureaucracy of the agricultural society and an emperor in his representative work "Social Origin of Despotic and Democratic Politics" (Moor, translated by Miyazaki, 1986, p. 209-287).

Accepting that setting importance on the internal changes of the Chinese society is now an established theory in the academic society, we would like to rearrange the second trend blending the established theory with the theme of this chapter in order to highlight the controversial points. There is a classical theory of 'water power society and hydraulic power despotism' by K. Wittfogel, the keyword of which is 'Oriental Despotism'. It says ancient large-scale flood control and irrigation agriculture presupposed huge centralized power and monopolistic bureaucracy. When these institutions were once established, they parted from flood control and irrigation agriculture, and since the institutions were an effective way to organize people, emperors in the monarchic age used them as weighty tools to rule; in the 20th century Leninists utilized them.[2] Today the theory of Wittfogel is still accepted widely as a cogent argument to the formation of ancient empires in China. In Japan we can reckon the masterwork by Masao Kimura, which has delved into the formation of ancient empires in China from a standpoint of affirming the theory of Wittfogel (Kimura 1965).

As a matter of fact, Yuji Matsumura had pointed out the features of 'mixture of centralized regime as an institution and dispersed powers in reality' focusing on the Qing dynasty eight years before Wittfogel published his theory (Muramatsu 1949, p. 7-9). This led to the introduction of a key word, gentry, to the Japanese and American academic circles from the middle of the 1950s, and it was insisted we could see some peculiar points of the political regime and its changes in the economic, social and political dynamic activities by the gentry, or local elite. After the 1970s a research trend in search of the structural factors of political changes in China to the gentry or the local elite of the Ming, Qing and the Republic of China periods formed a stream of China study in the U.S.A.[3] In addition, a theory of regional system by W. Skinner and the study on the mode of the peasant behavioral pattern by Phillip Joan presented an economic and sociologic viewpoint to explain the structure of the local and populace level of the political regime of the Ming, Qing and the Republic of China periods.[4]

In Japan 'the theory of decentralized authority state of China' by Masataka Sakano attracted attention in 1973, and lately the books by Tatsumi Okabe, Yoshinari Kokubu and Satoshi Amako were published, whom this author calls scholars of 'Muramatsu School'.[5] A common point with these three is they started from re-reading the 'Social System of Chinese Economy' by Yuji Muramatsu and to connect 'the kaleidoscopic political changes' in China with 'the trend of stagnated social and economic system" in order to search for the origin of political regime and its changes in the traditional Chinese economic and social structure.

In the same period there were some researches belonging to the first trend. Kazuko Mohri stated that, although China traditionally had the reality of dispersion, the socialist regime and the control of the party filled those gaps. Her insistence seems to be taking the standpoint of discontinuity of history that was affected and brought forth by the West, Marx-Leninism, the Soviet Union and the communist party (Mohri, 1993, p. 130). Taking into account the aforesaid history of researches, we can think of the following issues; how can we construe the gap between 'the centralized regime led by the hydro power society in the forming period of ancient empires in China two thousand years ago' and 'the non-centralized regime of the Ming and Qing dynasties and the Nationalist China started at three or four hundred years ago'? In other words, if we can trace the origin of the political regime of contemporary China to the non-centralized regime in the Ming and Qing dynasties and the nationalist China, we might be able to seek their origin to the centralized regime in the formation period of the ancient Chinese empires two thousand years ago.

The theory of the water-power despotism, by Wittfogel, tried to explain the processes from organization of ancient empires in many oriental countries to formation of modern states of the centralized regime. When looking back the aforementioned history of researches, however, the researchers there insist the non-centralized regime in the study of the Ming and Qing dynasties opposite to the theory of water-power despotism. Also some researches on the ancient agricultural history of China stand against the theory of Wittfogel. Gennosuke Amano, for example, came to a conclusion through various verification that rain water farming and small scale irrigation were characteristics of agriculture in the Chunqiu and Zhangou eras.[6]

We cannot deny the possibility of applying the theory of the water-power despotism to many oriental countries. However, in the case of China it is skeptical to apply the theory not only to the Ming and Qing dynasties, but also to forming period of ancient empires. For explicating the origin of political regime in China, it is requisite to formulate a new theory replacing the idea of 'the water power society and despotism', and we need a new approach based upon the historical facts in the Chinese areas. We can regard that the centralized regime was not formed because political the structure of ancient China did not originate in water-power society. Therefore political regimes of the Ming and Qing dynasties, and of the Republic of China, on the extended line from the ancient China, did not come to be of centralized regime, but of non-centralized system. As for the Qing dynasty, Yuji Muramatsu has analyzed it was, in principle, of the centralized regime and in reality, the mixture with scattered powers. According to a later study of an American scholar, the local elite was the core of the mixture. Change of dynasties such as from Qin, Han, Ming and to Qing is a feature of the political changes in monarchic China, and the aforementioned researches give us a hint that the principal role of the dynasty alternation is not rebel peasants but local elite, that is, who overthrew the government was not the nucleus stratum of the society but the local powers.

Section 2: Features of Political Regime of Monarchic China

The features of monarchic China can be described by peculiar keywords such as 'landowners and tenant farmers', 'merchants', 'bureaucracy in agricultural society' 'home and Confucianism' and 'Dynasty Alternation'.

Landowners and Tenant Farmers

We can seek the origin of the political regime of the monarchic China in the society of landowners and tenant farmers, not in the water-power society. In comparison with the middle Europe, which is supposed to be of feudal lord system, a conspicuous feature of monarchic China is that landowners and tenant farmers were the central figure of the social structure. In China, there had been from old times a maxim saying 'there is no land that is not the imperial domain in all the corners of the earth. Noboru Niida pointed early, 'they did not think, because of the maxim of the royal domain, every piece of rice field was territory of the crown and private ownership was not allowed,' 'it is beyond doubt that private ownership of land prevailed in the Warring States period at latest,' and 'private ownership continued under the name of the royal rice fields'.[7]

In ancient China, as early as from 4000 to 3000 BC ago, incipient farming culture started, and the North China at that time had much rainfall, which with fertile yellow soil offered a good productive condition to agriculture. Later it has been gradually changing into the present climatic condition where precipitation is low (Tajima, Yamauchi edit, 1989, p. 154), however as early as the Chunqiu and Warring States periods iron agricultural instruments and cattle drawing cultivation appeared and diffused (Yamane edit. 1994, p. 74). It gave a boost to form, so called, dry farming. In the case of dry farming, irrigation activity was carried out on a small or middle scale, utilization of rainwater or local irrigation, employing a water mill, windmill or well at each farm house.[8] That is, the agricultural irrigation projects in the ancient China were not so large scale as stated by Wittfogel and the agriculture then did not rely upon national irrigation scheme. We can cite the ancient Egypt applicable to the theory of Wittfogel. The water control project in the ancient Egypt covered all agricultural area in the country, requiring national control. From this control, national slavery was induced with a Pharaoh at the apex.[9] Explaining the middle age Europe with the same logic, we can say that feudalism, where feudal lords dominated localities, prevailed rather than national slavery in ancient Egyptian style, because local water control was popular, not nationwide.

As for the case of China, the following is a summary of the theory of Masao Kimura who sympathizes with Wittfogel basically, that agriculture in China before Chunqiu period used lithic instruments for farming with only witchcraft water control, so the primary farm land was limited by geographical conditions and existed being scattered. This condition kept numerous village countries surviving for several thousand years long. As the spread of ironware in the periods from Chuqiu, Warring States to Qin, Han dynasties, manufacturing technique advanced and the relations of production such as the formation of private ownership in the primary farm land changed, at the same time, the secondary farm land featuring the large scale national irrigation built up. This inevitably required state power with centralized regime, as a result, ancient empire in China came into existence (Kimura, aforenamed, p. 818-825).

By comparison the explanation of Masao Kimura with the ancient Egypt and the middle Europe, the following two questions remain; First, a series of 'large scale water control project', that Kimura described, was regional when compared with the national scheme of ancient Egypt. The builder and administrator were only feudal domains in the Chunqiu and Warring States periods, not centralized power states reigned by a Pharaoh. Inferentially, Wittfogel argued that these regional water control projects might need feudalistic system, not a state of the centralized regime like one in ancient Egypt. In reality these regional water control works were done in the period of 500 years during feudal domains age in Chunqiu and Warring States. The bank construction projects at the downstream of the Huang River are called Qi, Zhao, and Wei banks, proving that they were each made by feudal domains with those names. Some argues that the embankment construction required a bigger centralized power (Kimura, aforenamed, p.824). Historically Qi, Zhao and Wei were the feudal domains founded by breakup of Jin in the Chunqiu period. And it was Qin who tried and succeeded in unifying China including the Huang river downstream area, but it was located in the Weisui basin apart from the Huang River.

In ancient Egypt the water-power despotism led by the water power society was equal to national slavery system. While in China the land private ownership system was formed at the same time when the secondary farmland was generated by the water control scheme after the Warring States age. And landowners and small farmers, whose life and production style was family operation, was the core of the social structure. This can be found only in China before the modern age. That means, even when you regard China as a water-power society, the outcome brought forth by the society was different. In comparison with national slavery in the ancient Egypt and feudal lord system in the middle Europe, the power concentration to the society in the monarchial China was much moderate. Therefore, it is not appropriate to explain the case of China with the theory of water-power society, nor water-power despotism. We can generally explain the formation of land private ownership and appearance of landowners and small farmers whose life and production style was family running by advancement of agricultural technique with the spread of iron tools after the Chunqiu period. That is, because of early spread of iron tools, the dry farming was developed fully, and it enabled the family running type farming, and evolved into the society of landowners and small farmers.

Merchant

The existence of merchants' integrated citified areas, a center of bureaucratic politics, and farm villages, a society like sands consisting of innumerable families of landowners and small farmers. The landowners and small farmers lived in dispersed condition, and bureaucrats in the city life demanded the development of commerce and the formation of merchant stratum, this is another feature of the monarchic Chinese society. Formerly the development of commerce and the formation of mighty merchant group were not recognized as a feature of dynastic Chinese societies, and contrarily it was a common opinion that Chinese merchants in the urban area could not break the shell of the traditional rural community (Moore, afore named, p. 219).

It seems that the researchers failed to notice the following fact; in the Chinese monarchic ages some big cities flourished, for instance, Changan in the Tang dynasty was an international city with the population of one million, and a record since the time some census was kept says that domiciled inhabitants of Beijing in the reign of Qing was around seven hundred thousand and five thousands (Yang Dongping, translated by Aoki and others, 1997, p. 64). To support such a big city the development of commerce was essential. So the real reason that Chinese merchants in the urban area could not break through the shell of the traditional rural community should be traced to somewhere else.

The study by W. Skinner in the 1970s on the merchants in the monarchical China opened up a new prospect. According to it the merchants then built up a vertically multi-layered market system from rural area to urban district, and a system consisting of eight almost consummated large market areas horizontally. One point we have to observe here is the market in the monarchical China was not a single national one, but they were large local markets, so the merchants were regional ones. In the 1980s we had more researches on regional merchants in the dynastic ages, delineating the realities of strong local merchants, dependence of local finance on local merchants, and advancement of local commercial elite into political segment.[10] Depending on this argument, you can look at the politics and merchants in the monarchic China in the following way; local governments relied upon the powerful local merchants for sustaining urban communities and the local finance, and the local merchants entered into local politics and controlled it with their financial power. As a result the local government turned to be a group seeking after local profits with a tendency of getting autonomy politically and economically from the central government.

Bureaucratic System of Agricultural Society

Bureaucracy of agricultural society in the monarchical China[11], as well as the society of landowners and small farmers, can be seen only in the monarchical China from the viewpoint of world history. The national scale water control and irrigation system of the ancient Egypt formed national slavery based upon slavery control. And the local water control and irrigation system in the middle Europe developed the feudal lord system, ruling serfs. Neither case conduced bureaucratic system of agricultural society like monarchical China did.

The bureaucratic system of agricultural society in the monarchic China appeared concurrently with the formation of landowners and small farmers, so it is conceivable that it had a structural relationship with the society of landowners and small farmers, not with water-power society. This bureaucratic system of agricultural society was crucial to unite, not the water-power society, but a sand like society consisting of innumerable and independent landowners and small farmers. In other words, the ancient Egypt and middle Europe needed not a colossal bureaucratic system, because they had not the society of landowners and small farmers as China had.

The bureaucratic system of agricultural society was in the making with the society of landowners and small farmers in the feudal dominions around the Warring States period. Once it was established the lords found it out to have high reigning power and to be very effective tools to expand their territories and to control e larger area. The founding of the Great Empire of China, Qin, unifying the nation in 221B.C. was an outcome of the bureaucratic system of the agricultural society.

The local water control and irrigation projects started by feudal domains in the Warring States were not a cause for bureaucracy of agricultural society, but we can interpret that it was rather means to rule the landowners and small farmers who were standing on their own legs and a project to enlarge and maintain the bureaucratic system of agricultural society. First the water control and irrigation projected by the nation let the autonomous landowners and small farmers rely upon the state owned irrigation system and had an effect to have them under the state control. The nation intensified the control over the farmlands, landowners and small farmers by establishing the water control machinery and water officials. That is, in other words, to mean enlarging bureaucratic system of the agricultural society. And for maintaining the magnified system, it is needless to say a great sum of funds was required. The development of water control and irrigation farming helped it through increase of agricultural production and, at the same time, improvement of tax collecting performance.

In the later period of monarchical China, there was a national scale project of utilization of water, that was the great canal, dug by the Sui dynasty, enlarged, dredged and managed by the successive regimes. The canal was great in scale starting from Hangzhou, the capital of the present Zhejiang Sheng to Beijing, crossing the Yangtze River and the Yellow River, the main object of it was not for irrigation, but for transporting food and military forces (Hoshi 1977). In fact, the canal, a national scale water control project, was not a cause of bureaucratic system of the agricultural society, but rather a result of the system, it was for maintaining and intensifying bureaucratic command from the ruling body with the emperor apex.

Once a massive bureaucracy system was formed, it became an autonomous state structure. That's why the effective management of the state structure and securing the loyalty of the bureaucrats were an essential requisite to the emperor's authority. For that, the system of appointing officials was implemented thoroughly, and hereditary system was limited to emperors and the royal family only. The system gave the imperial household secured position and power, which were supposed to be permanent. Also the appointment institution made the bureaucrats pledge their loyalty to the emperor by giving them a strain of instability.

Since it was bureaucracy, recruitment needed to be institutionalized, thus the classical examination system was originated and sustained, which is a test program for the public service personnel and seen only in the monarchic China from the viewpoint of the pre-modern world history. In such a manner, the bureaucratic system in the dynastic China became the core of centralized power and nearly to perfection.

Taking a look at the power of a county governor, he exercised administrative and judicial powers exclusively, but not conferred with proprietorship and management right of the economy (farm-land and labor) in a county, and not with control power over military forces. There was a regulation 'Guanwudingshou' (personnel transfer); county governors had to take a post out of their birth counties, and to be subject to regular personnel changes. A governor was just one of public servants. Furthermore for checking governors and other local officials, the government instituted the inspector for a province, the governor general for a few provinces, the superintendent (a minister extraordinary and plenipotentiary) and a supervisory organization, something like the Russian KGB, directly under the emperor's control.[13]

Home and Confucianism

The monarchic China was a society, the center of which, were landowners and small farmers with their families owning farmlands and operating them. The word 'home' was significant as a basic unit of the society. The nation built up a bureaucratic system of centralized regime style, as aforementioned, to rule innumerable individualistic farmers dispersed over vast area, but its control power reached only to the bound of a county, since the economic and technological strength was restricted.[14] It was the actual state that the bureaucratic control power did not reach to the farmer's level, the centralized regime then was just nominal, as Matsumura stated. Under this condition, the nation in the monarchic China executed the governmental administration by bureaucracy, and on top of that, in rural areas the people's administration was based upon families and clans, that were self-governing. It was a kind of dual controlling structure.[15] Such self-governing is not the resident self-governing of today. It meant granting compulsory administrative power, which should be originally a national function, to chiefs of families or clans, making them terminal controlling mechanism of the state.[16] In the rural level, dominant landowners grasped the power. Thus, the self-governing in the rural area was virtually self-governing of landowners.

The dynastic states established Confucianism, a state tool to control the people and to make them obedient. And the legislation institutionalized the ideology in order to secure the loyalty of the people.[17] Such control over the constituent members by the family and tribe chiefs was characteristic to edify their members in all political, economical, social and ideological phases. Therefore, Confucianism in the monarchic China was not just an ideology, but had a character of one constituent element of the regime. Lastly these families and tribes were the only life community giving a helping hand to guarantee the basic life to the constituent members. In returning being obedient the life was assured.

As we have seen, the four key words 'landowner and small farmer', 'merchants', 'bureaucratic agricultural society' and 'home and Confucianism' show the basic features of the political system of dynastic China. Advancement of the ancient Chinese agricultural techniques with diffusion of iron tools from the early time and establishment of dry land farming formed a society with landowners and small farmers as the central figure. Bureaucratic system of the agricultural society was made for ruling landowners and small farmers, and a strong merchant stratum for integrating economically and socially the rural area of landowners and small farmers and cities of bureaucrats. It seems that these are formed about after Warring States period. These political structures of the dynastic period characterized the concentration of the power with an emperor uppermost and the control by families and clans based upon Confucianism. The regime formed the dual power structure of the bureaucratic ruling down to the prefecture level with an emperor apex, and the self-administration by landowners in the rural area.

Change of Dynasty

The political structure in the monarchic China included dynamic components, the feature of the alteration was seen in the change of dynasties.[18] You can trace the structural factors of the change of dynasties to the features of the regimes in the monarchic periods aforementioned. The change of power relationship between the central and regional powers, resulted from the change between landowners and the bureaucratic government, from the change of control relationship between rural districts and cities, which had been resulted from the dynamic relationship between emperor, bureaucrats, landowners and small farmers, and among merchant themselves, caused the cyclic change of the dynasties in the monarchic China.

The change of dynasties evolved through the following procedures; in the early period, generally speaking, the central and regional governments were superior to landowners, small farmers and merchants; and cities to rural areas. In the middle period, however, with concentration of lands and development of commerce, landowners came to have more right to speak in the right of self-government of the village community, and landowners and merchant in the local politics. The superiority of cities and government turned into the equilibrium of forces between the government and landowners/merchants, and between city and village communities. This tendency developed into a situation in the end of the monarchic period that big landowners/merchants grasped the control over regional government and cities; in the local level, strong regional groups held their own ground with all powers. The power relationship went into reverse. This can be said to be a changing process and mechanism from that blended condition of the nominal centralized political power, as Muramatsu argued, to the decentralized state in the middle of the monarchic China as Sakano stated.

Yang Fengqiang pointed out the reality of the power relationship where the power shifting started from the middle of the Qing dynasty (1997). Many farmers lost their farmland due to centralization of land on a large scale as well as the change of power relationship, they raised disturbance triggered by natural or man-made disasters. Then some ambitious local forces organized a riot seizing an opportunity, started a war to change dynasties. For example, the collapse of the last dynasty, Qing, was not due to farmer's revolt. It was based on an uprising of the southern provinces with regional forces consisting of landowners, merchants and military clique, and by treachery of northern provinces. It was, as a matter of fact, a district rebellion.[19]

As a result of the war for the change of dynasties, the old collapsed and the new came out. The new emperor took full advantage of the old wrecked proprietary system of farmland, and effectuated a neo-land policy, dissolving to some degree the great land proprietary system which was a source of regionally grounded forces, and built up a new centralized power system with the emperor uppermost. This is the cycle of the change of dynasties from the foundation through the collapse and to establishment of the new authority. For instance, till Sui and the first half of Tang, an equality field law was in force. That let farmers owned land in order to limit the vast land-holding.[20] In the middle of the dynasty, however, the policy stagnated, and in the late period it disintegrated with the development of centralization of land, and soon after that the dynasty itself.

Section 3: Features of Political Regime of the Modern China

Features of Political System of the Republic of China

If the cycle of the changes of dynasties had been still valid, the regime of the Republic of China founded in 1911 should have been considered to be in the early stage of the new power to reconstruct the system with the central power dominant. Hiroaki Yokoyama analyzed comprehensively and systematically various types of regimes appeared in the Republic of China by 1949 (including ones holding the controlling position really or those desired theoretically). He analyzed nine regimes from admonition system by the Nationalist Party to the dictatorship of coalition governments by the Communist Party; and concluded the Republic of China had diverse choices of regimes competed their own legitimacy, the attractive period of that all sorts of flowers are blooming as if rivaling each other in beauty. However, it was believed that for ruling China, a decentralized country and coming to difficulty in defending outside pressure, a ruling system with centralized power was needed, and so really made its appearance (Yokoyama 1996, p. 220-226).

Now let's take a look at main measures to make a new system taken by the Republic of China. Following one party dictatorship of Stalinism in the Soviet Union, they formed the Nationalist Party, a quasi Leninism party, and tried to make a central leadership with power and charisma by means of the party state (Yamada, Nakajima edit. 1981, p. 95). Jiang Jieshi, president of the party, was given power as much as an emperor, and commanding the Nationalist Party, government, military forces and secret police all together. Organized the central army and strengthened it so as to weaken the regionally based forces and to ruin them. Organized secret and mighty police systems, called the central and military control, with the exclusive powers of control, personnel and operation to check any movement against the central leadership. Tried to dissipate, with a slogan 'Only who tills has fields', the vast land proprietary system, the social, economic and political foundation of regional powers. Tried to unify people's ideology with a slogan, 'the three principles of the people'.

What was the result? In 1928 the nationalist government succeeded in national unification and having the local elites pledge loyalty, but could not implement farmland reform as scheduled, so the vast land proprietary system survived. As a result, the union of big landowners and the local military cliques still controlled the localities.[21] This shows that the government of the Republic of China, the Nationalist Party, the central army and the secret police system could not rule the provincial as they desired.

During the reign of the Republic of China, the Nationalist Party instituted a party state, so called 'quasi Stalinism', which tried hard to reform the strong central power and succeeded to some degree, but could not abolish the local control by the combined local elites consisting of big landowners, merchants, local bureaucrats as desired. In the end the regime of the Republic of China did not get out the political situation of the middle and end of dynastic ages characterizing strong centralization in the central area, and in the region local powers held all powers strongly. Incidentally some research says even in the central area there was competition between some political groups, and the leader's despotism by Zhan Jieshi himself first emerged after the government moved to Taiwan in the reformation of the Nationalist Party early in 1950s (Matsuda 1994).

Features of Regime in the Liberated Areas of Communist Party

There is a research by Masao Fukushima on the regime in the liberated area of the Communist Party, a great work 'People's Democratic Political Power in China – the Theory and Processes of Formation' (Fukushima 1965). Here this author would like to indicate the following points based upon his work and adding some other data and researches:

> First the liberated areas of the Communist Party was the same as other local bases in terms that each held his own sphere of military influence. Its economic foundation to sustain itself was same as other military cliques, the self-sufficient local economy. Mao Zedong, the base leader then pointed out this point clearly.[22]

The political and social foundation were different in the rural area, however, the military cliques relied upon landowners, while the Communist Party obtained the support from farmers who were seeking after lands, poor farmers.

Next, each base was built at a basic unit of the leadership (Party local committee), and in the base a horizontally centralized structure with the party leadership centered was organized. Military affairs, administration, judicature, economy and society, all are controlled in a lump by the party leaders, but the different features from the time, after the foundation of the People's Republic of China, were that the judicature was legally part of the administrative machinery. The economic system was not of public ownership, but privately owned though limited (Fukushima before named, p. 94, 106, 192, 249, 384). Also making a military company and a farmer's village a unit, a Party branch was organized with three Party members or more. And the Party branch controlled all tasks. This was said to be done under the Mao Zedong's instruction. And later in the communist China it was called a unit, a terminal Party work organization (See the chapter IV, Section II).[23]

Lastly, two features of the vertical relationship between the central and provincial leadership, that is, the relationship between the leadership of the center of the Communist Party and that of the provincial branches in the Chinese Workers' and Peasants' Red Army period till 1935 can be cited; one was the fact that special envoys from the center were dispatched to all bases to give instructions forming a vertical centralized power structure (Fukumoto 1992, p.57-108). The other was, under the guerilla warfare the communism ideology unified the party organizations, even when dispersed, politically and ideologically secured their loyalty. The Party center and its special envoys got hold of obedience from the local leadership of each base, the terminal Red Army companies and village leaders not coercively, but with legitimacy as the embodiment of the Party ideology. That is, the ideology was not only a thought, but also one of the elements in the vertical structure of the regime since the period of local strongholds. Besides the forcible pressure of the outside enemy also worked as accelerator to unify the center of the Party and the local strongholds.

The Party relied upon this vertically centralized power structure to lead the revolutionary bases, also dispersed military strongholds under horizontally centralized structure. Nevertheless, the way of dispatching the special envoys resulted in a negative outcome, 'great purge' by enlarged spy hunting under the situation of strong pressure from the foreign enemy (Hashimoto, afore-named work). Both Mao Zedong and Deng Xiaoping were limited in their powers by this system, and purged. From this experience, they were afraid of being regarded as enemy and purged or losing their positions.[24] Mao Zedong, therefore, abolished the central special envoy institution after he got control over the Party in 1935, and after that he kept the principle that the Party committee operated the inspection institute and not to make an independent vertical inspection network taking a ground that no party was established outside of the Party.

As stated above, the regime in the revolutionary base was the first one the Communism Party made, where you can see the prototype of the regime of the present China. The Party was engaged in guerilla warfare and built up many military strongholds in vast village communities. These strongholds had their own army, administrative institution and judicial section (a part of administration) independent of the Party center having strong autonomy. To keep these highly autonomous bases loyal to the center, the Party set up the party committee at each base and a party branch at each terminal organization, so that all power centered to the Party leadership. Through this measure at the foundation level and the provincial levels all the powers were gathered to the Party leadership at each level, and from the foundation level to the provinces, from which to the center being converged through the vertical channels. Mao Zedong called it the unitary leadership of the Party. The Party leaders had mastered the behavioral patterns respecting the Party leadership and mobilization ability from the experience of the bases over twenty years, rather than importance of legal organization.

Section 4: Influence of Political Regime of the Soviet Union

The first thing we can cite as the influence of the Soviet Union is that, from the beginning of the Chinese Communist Party, it was established as a Leninist party. And the time when the regime of the present China was influenced most by that of the Soviet Union was the period from the foundation of the People's Republic of China in 1949 to 1957. At this time when the Chinese Communist Party inaugurated a socialist state, the Party converted from 'the unitary guidance system by the Party' into the centralized regime of the Soviet Union type.

Structure of State Institution

During the time from 1949 to 1957, the state institutions of the present China were built up copying after the Soviet type structure of the centralized regime. This is shown in the Chinese constitution (1954) and in the relative laws (Takeuchi edit, translated 1991, pp. 29-56). It is reflected clearly in the centralized regime structure of the administrative and judicial institutions. In the case of the administrative institution and according to an interpretation of the state council law by a person concerned to the Chinese government, the local administrative offices could be divided into two in the way of their activities (Fukushima, afore-named, pp. 515-516).

The first type, local administrative offices (the offices for various industries, railroad and foreign trade and so on) were directly under the command of the center, since their activities were not related too much to the provincial institution. Even when they accepted some guidance from local offices, that is secondary important. Mainly they took orders from the center. The second type local offices (the interior, public security, finance, agriculture, food agency and so forth) were closely related to local institution and they accepted the double guidance from both the center and local offices.

At that time, however, the local autonomy was blamed as an independent kingdom. Judging from that it was emphasized the planned economy should be under the central control, the administrative and inspective organizations such as the interior and public security should obey to the center, we can recognize that even in the case of the double guidance of the second type of local offices, the locality was secondary and the center was primary (Song Xinwei, Wan Zhongtian edit, 1988, p. 236. Nobuyuki Tanaka, Mohri edit. 1990, pp. 70-75).

In the case of the judicial offices, the tradition since the period of the revolutionary bases was that they were under the same level of the administrative offices. It was checked again and the people's court got independence from the administrative offices. Also about the prosecutorial office, the Chinese constitution (1954) stipulated, following the Soviet Union, the institution was under the command of only the supreme prosecutor, and the People's Prosecutors office is independent with centralized power (Takeuchi, afore-named, p. 51-52).

Structure of Command of the Party

Here I would like to point out two features of command authority to the state institutions then. First as mentioned before, since the state institutions adopted the Soviet type administrative structure with powers centralized and the judicial system, local and lower level party committee lost most of the commanding power to local administration and jurisdiction. Thus local and lower level party committees were no longer the ruler to their own territorial jurisdiction. Second it was stressed the command of the Party should be lawful (Dong Biwu 1956, pp. 109-119). Under this kind of situation, at all center, local and terminal levels the party committees lost their commanding power, their authority was no longer absolute.

Structure of Economic Policy Actors

The economic system was basically of centralized power, since most of non-agricultural enterprises were under the direct command of the central leadership. For example, the number of big enterprises under the direct command of the center increased from 2,800 in 1953 to 9,300 in 1957, and their product output was half of the whole industrial output. The center controlled 90% of the investment for fixed assets, and only 10% the locality had charge of (Ishihara, Mohri edit. 1990, pp. 148-149).

In agriculture, large area land proprietorship institution dissolved by land reform, and villages of small farmers appeared. However since 1954 the collectivization in agriculture proceeded, and in 1957 in all national farm villages the Agricultural Producers Cooperative were organized, the small farmers basically vanished, but this Cooperative was not a combined organization of the Party and administrative constituents, such as hamlets, districts, village, unlike People's Commune in future. In this way, in the case of non-agriculture, main parts of the economic entities were unified by the central leadership. Whereas in the case of agriculture, it was under the control of leadership of hamlets, districts, villages; but neither case it was not so framed to be commanded directly by local leadership.

Structure of Social Policy Actors

Here let's look at the traits of the early Mao Zedong period from three aspects; election, labor union and social terminal organization. First, at the end level of enterprises a system called 'one chief', a Soviet type management system, was adopted. The system designated head of enterprises as the person in charge, not someone from the Party committee. This was a control system with an enterprise chief controlling it with full power and responsibility (Shinichi Kawai 1990). Second, 'the people's representative assembly' election was established (same as the congress, hereinafter called the Assembly). The direct election was held only for selecting delegates to the Assembly at the terminal level. From prefectual assembly representatives and managing director committee up to the city, province and central level assembly representatives and managing director committee were elected by indirect election from one level lower (Fukushima, afore-named, p. 505). Lastly labor unions took the Soviet style industrial vertical union with centralized power, in parallel with the proprietorship and managing right converging to the central leadership, different from the form of area horizontal distinction in the later time. Besides other eight democratic parties announced that they would take the direction from the Chinese Communist Party, but kept appealing some objections (Fukushima, afore-named, pp. 548-549).

From the statement above, we can conclude that, from the early Mao Zedong period, from 1949 to 1957, the Chinese Communist Party was greatly affected by the regime of the Soviet Union. At the regional level the administrative and prosecutorial institutions, economic and social substance were under the direct command of the central government, not to provincial or local Party committee, forming vertical centralized regime. By this reform, unitary leadership system since the time of revolutionary strongholds was revised into the situation where not only the power of provincial and local Party committee, but also vertical power system of the Party was remarkably weakened.

Section 5: Formation of Multi-layered Centralized Political Regime of Present China

The regional Party committee at all levels felt a sense of incompatibility with the Soviet type centralized regime from early stage, and tried to regain the power they once lost. It was Mao Zedong who absorbed the discontent of the Party principal members. As the leader of the Party he spoke for their demand and accomplished a series of policy changes. The period of Mao Zedong can be divided into three, the early period till 1957, the middle till 1966 and the late till 1976. It is considered as the centralized regime, being built up then, was changed into the multilayered centralized regime in and around 1957.

Unitary leadership by the Party committee, which had been carried out widely in the period of the revolutionary strongholds, was reestablished more firmly (Kotake, Mohri edit. 1990, pp. 44-47). In August, 1953, Mao Zedong said, in his speech of objecting to the belief of propertied class, "there has been an increasing trend of dispersion idea, for overcoming this issue, we have decided that the Party committee will examine all crucial and important issues and make a decision on them, then the government will carry the decision out" (Mao Zedong 1977). Since about this time they pushed on with various projects in line with the unitary Party guidance. This movement made itself definite by the anti-rightist campaign that was incited by Mao Zedon in 1957. In 1958 Mao Zedong wrote 'Way of Policy Activity 60 Articles' (draft), and directed that the crucial powers had to be concentrated on the central and local Party committee (Liu Zhenwei 1987, p. 67).

With reestablishment of the unitary leadership by the Party committee of the provincial and local levels, the state organizations in the local level lost their independence from the Party committee, which had been stipulated in the Constitution of China (1954). For example, it had been stipulated that the local prosecutorial offices were under the command of only the supreme prosecutor, now the local judicial organization was made to obey to the Party committee of the same level by the Central Party decision in July 1957. Also in September 1960 the Chinese Communist Party decided that the people's courts and procuratorates at all levels came to be under the direct command of the Party committee at the same level. Again in September, 1960 the Party center determined that the people's courts and procuratorates at each level were under the command of the public security organs which were part of the administrative offices at respective level (Han Gang 1988, p. 89, 139, 140).

At the basic levels, one chief system was abolished at the 8th Party Assembly, instead the Party committee leadership system was adopted [25]. In rural area the people's commune institution was organized in 1958, and all of the village community was incorporated under the command of the Party committee of the people's commune. Whereas the mobilization system based on the communism ideology was strengthened through the anti-rightist struggle in 1957. The anti-rightist struggle forced all of the nation to accept the ideology of the communism, rejecting all other ideologies. Through this struggle of the society, other democratic factions were unified, to be controlled by the Party committee of all levels. Also, the struggle was carried on by the local and basic Party committee. Because people who were sentenced as rightists were expelled, the populace were made to believe that the local and basic Party committees were the primary power.

In the phase of economy control, the controlling right of the enterprises changed from the central leadership to provincial leadership at all levels. The controlling right over around eight thousands, 87% of the enterprises under the direct command of the center was transferred to the local leadership at all levels. According to a case study the radical economic developing policy, the Great Forward Leap in 1958, was motivated by Mao Zedong, with the local authorities by politicizing a conflict between the center and the locality around economic profits (Asanuma, Okabe edit. 1995). Later because of the failure of the Great Forward Leap, the controlling right over the enterprises was converged into the center again in the early 1960s. From 1970, however, it was transferred down to the local leadership at all levels once more with Mao's initiative (Wang Haibo 1986, p. 143, 221, 282). In this way the enterprise control system built up after the Soviet sample came to be altered.

Thus around 1957, the Party unitary leadership originated at the revolutionary stronghold was being reestablished, so it included all social and economic substance.

Then, what does the reestablishment of the unitary leadership by the Party mean to the formation of the multi-layered centralized regime in China? Unlike the Soviet Union style centralized regime where various powers were converged from basic level and locality to central government offices, the Party unitary leadership system proposed by Mao Zedong gathered first each power to the Party committee at the basic and local levels, then unitarily to the Party central through the Party power channels. It is just because this feature that the power meet to the center through the multi-layered strata at the local levels, entirely different from the Soviet Union type of centralized regime, the type of the multi-layered centralized system is adopted for classification. Reestablishment of the unitary guidance system by the Party constructed the basic power system of the multi-layered centralized regime.

While in this period, the direct domination by a charismatic leader, Mao Zedong, formed. It revealed evidently in Mao's direction to collectivization of agriculture during the period from 1955 to 1958. Mao Zedong, indifferent to not only the laws and existing resolutions of the Party, but also the central and local Party organizations, and in the cause of the public route or great democracy, mobilized and guided the people and basic leadership with his own speeches, theses and quotation and proceeded with the collectivization of agriculture in the form of people's movement. He criticized and purged some of the central and local leaders who adhered to the existing laws, party decisions, system structures and expressed some doubts on the radical collectivization of agriculture (Tokuda 1977, Chapter 9).

When looking at the anti rightist movement in 1957 from the viewpoint of instituting the direct guidance by Mao Zedong, he abolished the law abiding tendency held till that time, organized the unitary leadership by the Party committee and strengthened unification of the society by the communist ideology. He tried to eradicate the framework of all laws and regulations that was binding his direct control. However, his effort worked only to establish the concentration of the powers by the Party committee of each level, but failed to formulate his own direct guidance system with collapse of the movements of people's commune and the great leap forward that he took the lead.[26]

While, it was so organized that the provincial Party committee under the multi-layered centralized regime would control all state units in the provinces, that the center came not to be able to control or inspect the provincial Party committee through these provincial organization. It brought about an unexpected result of the control power decrease of the center and enhancement of local autonomy. Under these circumstances, Mao Zedong started to prepare the Cultural Great Revolution in 1964 and ignited it in 1966. One of the targets of the Revolution was no longer the Soviet type centralized regime carried on in the 1950s, but the provincial leadership which Mao Zedong called the independent kingdom.[27]

He once dissolved all local leadership by the power of the Revolution and reorganized it later. However he succeeded in having the local leaders pledged loyalty to himself, still he did not reform the institution to overcome the multi-layered centralized regime. His success was only temporary and partial. His individual despotism depended on the communist ideology and his own charismatic character; and as these points declined, his power weakened inevitably. The first criticism from the people against him appeared in the 5th April Tiananmen incident in 1976 (Nakakuni 1979). Considering why the control was so strong in the Mao Zedong era, it was not because the organization of the centralized power was solid and firm, but because the direct command by the charismatic leader worked strongly.

As mentioned hitherto, it is clear that the political system of the Soviet Union and that of China were the same in the point of socialistic states, but different in the form of centralized power. The Soviet system was that the vertically divided powers concentrated to the center, while the Chinese was multi-layered where all powers gathered into different levels, the center, and local Party committees. This is the reason to name the political system of present China as the socialist multi-layered centralized regime in comparison with the Soviet type centralized regime.

Section 6: Transfiguration of Political Regime in the Deng Xiaoping Era

Political System Reform in Deng Xiaoping Era

In the Deng Xiaoping era they advocated to reform economic and political systems. Deng Xiaoping indicated a different idea about the regime. He once appealed the 'cat theory' which goes 'regardless white or black, any cat who catches a rat is a good cat.' He said that in early 1960s when the nation suffered from a severe famine and he made a speech insisting to improve the people's commune institution, which brought agricultural crisis, and let the farmers undertake farmlands (Deng Xiaoping 1992, pp. 455-457). This cat theory resulted in a severe criticism, in the cultural great revolution started in 1966, from Mao Zedong as a process overthrowing the socialist flag and heading for the capitalism, being counted as one of the charges throwing Deng Xiaoping out. However, during the Deng Xiaoping era started about 1978, the first thing he tackled was to spread the contract system of farmland, at the same time, to dissolve the People's commune.

Speaking of these points, we can see the difference between the two leaders, Mao Zedong sticking to the socialist ideology, and Deng Xiaoping making much of practical benefits. The following is the speech Deng Xiaoping made in 1987:

> 'When we evaluate the political system, structure, and policy of a country, we must look at three points; first if the political situation is stable, second if the nation is well united and their life is improving, and third if their production is successively developing' (Deng Xiaoping 1993, p. 213).

Deng Xiaoping entertained an idea that China was in the early stage of socialism, that is, still in an undeveloped phase. Therefore, the economic development should be the focus for all activities of the whole Party throughout the nation, and all action should be centripetal to this point. The basic route of the socialist primary stage of the Party consisted of one center of economic development, two basic points of reform and opening policy and four principles (the way of socialism, people's democratic dictatorship, guidance of the Chinese Communist Party, and adherence to Marxism and Leninism and Mao's ideology (Jiang Zeming, China Press 25 Sep. 1997). Reform and opening were for economic development, four principles summed up to adherence to the control by the Party, also to preservation of political and social stability that were requisite to development (Deng Xiaoping 1983, p. 341-342).

Also Deng Xiaoping preached, adducing high efficiency of the decision and execution of reform and opening, the necessity of the adherence to the Party guidance. At the speech site he rejected clearly the political proceedings of the democratic systems such as conflicts among various parties, the separation of three powers, bicameral system, criticizing there were too many checks, taking excessive time in discussion, delay in decision making and execution; although he did turn down the unlimited election and said about the national direct election, the condition was still immature and the national cultural level still low (Deng Xiaoping 1993, pp. 240-242).

Judging from the above mentioned remarks, we can say that, in his political idea, Deng's standard of value judgment was whether it was useful for social productivity. He did not accept the communism ideology as a scale, appealed the control of the Communist Party but refused the separation of the three powers as the necessary condition for political and economic stability and kept effective political decision and execution for economic development. According to Deng, if the conditions are met, unlimited election is acceptable. Among these, he did not advocate positively thought control and public mobilization, so we can understand that he would justify the current social structure not forever.

Although Mao Zedong set up the unitary guidance establishment, he relied more on his own communism ideology and his own charismatic standpoint as a representative of the righteous Party route than the organized system itself, and through his speeches and writings he controlled the Party members and the public. But the disasters brought by the Cultural Revolution made the Communist ideology and the Party route collapsed. Deng Xiaoping took over this situation, so could not rely upon the mobilization power of the Communist ideology, and had to prove the correctness of his own Party route with actual result of economic development. Then he came to esteem the unitary control system of the Party more than his own charismatic character. He advocated the reform of the regime and tried to normalize and make the Party organization and the system of the people's congress sound.

What was the result of the reform of the regime Deng Xiaoping proceeded? Kazuko Mohri examined in details what was reformed and what was systematized during the Deng Xiaoping era (Mohri, co-edit. with Okabe, 1991 pp.18-22). The following are Mohri's six views; First, it is about election system of the nation and of the Party, including enlargement of the direct election and partial adoption of competitive election, raising the direct election for the deputy to the National People's Congress from the village level to the county level. Changes from non-competitive to competitive election for ordinary standing committees, representatives of the people's congress, vice directors general, members of the central Communist Party, members of regulation examination committee, except chairmen and vice chairmen and secretary general of the local and national people's congresses, and ban for three times being elected. Second, the separation of the party and politics (separation of the functions) was discussed, and its first step was that the Party was put in relative position by the constitution for the first time; that is, a line 'any organization or any individual cannot enjoy any privilege beyond the constitution and/or laws' was added in the constitution of China. Third, the course of the political deliberations and decision-making at the Party or National People's Congress were open to the public, though limited. Furthermore, the person in charge or spokesmen came to do press conferences. Fourth, an experimental system of government officials had been attempted, but it is not clear if the system was adopted widely, or systemized, or it will be fixed or not. Fifth, the separation of the Party and political functions advanced a step since 1988, however it was suspended after the Tiananmen incident, 6th April 1989, condemned as a failure of Zhao Ziyang to dispute the Party guidance. Sixth, there was some relaxation to the news censorship, but it was never systemized. Instead, it relapsed by clampdown on thought after the Tiananmen incident. Kazuko Mohri stated below the results of the regime reform; the actual results of the reform of the political system over 10 years was not significant. The most of the items that were discussed, decided and carried out were hardly ratified by laws and institutions. They went down the drain, except a handful of improving measures.

In 1994, a long later from Mohri's summary, when Deng Xiaoping transferred the power to the Jiang Zemin there was not much progress. Those policies above stated were only normalization or making better the existing Party policy or the system of the people's congress. After all the degree of changes of the political system was little.

Actual Change of Regime

In the Deng Xiaoping era there was in reality some changes of the regime, though it was not direct reform of it. The economic reform, aiming at the market economy, made the political system changed structurally. Deng Xiaoping repeatedly advocated transferring powers to lower levels. His aim was that, since the right of economic control was excessively concentrated, it should be handed over widely to the lower levels, so the locality and enterprises had more autonomy (Deng Xiaoping 1983, pp. 145-146).

First by the economic reform the family management of agriculture was revived at the terminal level. Also autonomy for the public owned enterprises and foundation of the private businesses were recognized. That means the society had a certain distance away from the state. Although the market economy progressed during the Deng Xiaoping era, the state itself was on its way to develop, though still in an immature condition. So most of the right to manage the businesses transferred to the lower level did not come down to the enterprises. It is still held at the some levels of the local leadership. The local leaders had stronger powers to possess and manage the public owned enterprises and to control the local economy and finances than ever before.

Even in the Mao Zedong era, the various leveled local leaders had the right of controlling enterprises, but the control over investment, production, sales and distribution from the center was so strong that they could not really execute the managing right. On top of that, since there was no market economy, no profit produced. Therefore, the motivation for the local leadership to run business for profit was scarce, they were loyal to the upper leadership in economic activity.

When it came to the Deng Xiaoping era, the local leaders of various levels, who had come to control more of the local power organization under the multi-layered centralized regime, happened to grasp more rights to run the businesses. It was not so much serious transition in terms of the power structure. Still the impact was significant. Under the environment where the market economy went forward, the impetus for profit drove the local leadership into economic profit seeking groups at the respective area. They were not necessarily loyal to the upper leaders in their economic activities, sometimes they opposed or appealed something; they became to act autonomously and diversely on the axis of economic profit.

As for the power and behavioral patterns of the local leaders in the Deng Xiaoping era, Xu Jiatun (in exile in the U.S.A.) held the posts of the first secretary of the Jiangsu Province, Hong Kong, Macao Secretary of the Party and Head of Xinhua Press in Hong Kong Branch. He provided, in his memoir, some evidence as a person concerned. GDP of the Jiangsu Province made remarkable advance and took the top across the country, Xu Jiatun told Deng Xiaoping that our province advanced a different way than other provinces, the way Shanghai going was the national policy itself and not characteristic, along that way it is hard to show its ability. Zhejiang and Shandong Provinces who did a field trip through Jiangsu Province started already to go along the same way. Also Li Peng drove the economic reform adversely after the Tiananmen incident, and Hebei Province followed the directions from Beijing and fell into economic doldrums, while Shandong Province pretended to follow the command, really did not carry it out. As a result the province pushed the GDP to the top in the country. Ironically

Jiang Chunyun, the Provincial Party secretary was promoted to a committee of the Party Central Political Bureau and Vice Premier for the achievement accomplished by not obeying the Party Central (Xu Jiatun, translated by Aoki and others, 1996, vol. 1 pp.1-7, vol. 2 p. 253).

Deng Xiaoping, the highest influential person and one of the reform group, with other central leaders like Hu Yaobang and Zhao Ziyang proceeded with the reform to transfer the economic rights and profits to the locality and enterprises supported by the local leaders. On the contrary, Chen Yun, Li Xiannian and Li Peng, those regarded as the conservatives and ex-central bureaucrats, showed the trend of regaining the economic rights and profits back to the central authorities seeking for stronger controlling power over economics, and they conflicted with the localities. However, the transfer of the economic rights and profits to the local leaders activated the local economy by stirring up the motivation of the local leaders for profits and livened up the local economy; on the other hand, they stood on the government side after all, having nothing to do with bankruptcy. They tried to invest more fund into their territorial jurisdiction and caused an investment competition, as a result, the economy was overheated to provoke cyclic inflation.

These cyclic economic crises and the accompanied wave of seeking after a reform of the regime gave an impetus to the conservatives to attack the reformists. Consequently Deng Xiaoping dared to sacrificed Hu Yaobang and Zhao Ziyang one after the other. Because the structural change of the multi-layered centralized regime by the reform of political system was very little, so an efficient party system and the state administrative machinery were not prepared, the result of Deng's leadership was limited.

Under such a situation, Deng Xiaoping came to insist the importance of the role of the supreme Party leader. After the Tiananmen incident in 1989, when Deng singled out Jiang Zeming from a Shanghai Party Committee Secretary to the Party central secretary general, Deng emphasized to the members of the central instructors that they should safeguard Jiang Zeming consciously as the nucleus of direction with the power to fix the final decision (Deng Xiaoping 1993, pp. 296-301). Deng tried to stipulate protecting the nucleus of the Party guidance by institutionalizing the role of the Party highest leader.

Summing up the statement hitherto, the features of Deng Xiaoping are the following three points; first, institutionalization of the unitary guidance system by the Party, including establishment of the nucleus of the direction that is the highest leader. Second, intensification of the power of the local leadership by acquiring more rights of managing enterprises for developing market economy. Third, weakening the role of the communist ideology in the regime and some separation of the society from the state.

These features of Deng Xiaoping, in comparison with the situation of Mao Zedong era, can be said to have deepened the multi-layered centralized regime characterizing horizontal power concentration by the provincial and local leveled Party committees. The regime in the Mao Zedong era was basically that of multi-layered and centralized, and its establishment necessarily augmented the autonomy and absoluteness of the power of the provincial and local leveled leadership. Since the charismatic character of Mao Zedong was so intense, however, and the economic profit motivation for the provincial and local leveled leadership was so feeble, that centrifugal trend of provincial and local leadership was restrained and the regime seemed to be centralized. When it turned to be Deng Xiaoping period, the decline of the charismatic character of the highest leader and a partial procurement of the managing right over enterprises by the provincial and local leadership took place. By these trends, there were some political changes going such as the multi-layered centralized regime was more intensified and the centrifugal trend of the local leadership became more obvious.

Conclusion

Here this author would like to present a hypothesis on the formation of the regime of contemporary China by pigeonholing the results of the analysis heretofore. First, as the structural feature common through the monarchic age, the Republic of China, the Communist Revolutionary Strongholds and the Soviet Union, we can cite two things, the absolute being such as the emperor or the charismatic highest leader of a despotic political party and social unification by the national ideology like Confucianism, the Three Principles of the People, and Communism. These two still remain in the regime of contemporary China.

Next, there are three points of the sameness in the regimes through the monarchic age, the Republic of China and the Communist

Revolutionary Strongholds; at the terminal level of the regime, in the monarchic age and the Republic of China, families and tribes were the nucleus of control. And in the period of the Communist Revolutionary Strongholds the Party branches were. The three groups had something in common, that is, they controlled the whole man politically, economically and socially, making the constituent people as the terminal element of the national organization. In contemporary China there are some units having the same character.

In the monarchic age and the Republic of China period, there were strong local powers and the relationship between the center and locality. They were a main cause of the political changes. As it was pointed out before, the revolutionary strongholds as well as local military clique had a character of the local power to the nation of the Republic of China. Even to the regime of contemporary China, the relationship between the center and the locality is still an essential element.

During the periods of the monarchic age, the Republic of China and the Communist Revolutionary strongholds, the unification of the administration and judicature, and the control of administration over judicature were the common features. In contemporary China for some duration till 1957, the administrative and judiciary organs were independent each other, coping after the Soviet Union. But later, internal regulations stipulated to put the judiciary organs under administration. In the Deng Xiaoping era, these organs were separated again, however, they were the same as before controlled by the Party committee of all levels.

Subsequently this author will try to pick up some features that were found in the regimes of China of monarchic age and the Soviet Union, but not in the regime of contemporary China. The regime of the early neo-dynasty had something in common with that of the Soviet Union, both had a strong vertically centralized regime. In contemporary China for some period till 1957 they tried to build up the centralized regime after the model of the Soviet Union. This was something, from the viewpoint of the cycle of dynastic alternation, like a phenomenon happened in the founding stage of a new dynasty, corresponding to rebuilding a strong horizontally centralized power structure with the emperor atop. As a matter of fact, the centralized regime was revised into the multi-layered centralized regime later. After all the tradition in the founding period of a dynasty and experience of the Soviet Union were not selected.

Besides, in the monarchic period, there was the consummately prepared bureaucratic tradition, as the public servant examination, like the imperial examinations, furthered family operated agriculture. None of them remained in contemporary China. In the Deng Xiaoping era, family farming was approved and the reconstruction of the public servant system was proposed, but farmer's land ownership was not recognized, either reorganization of the public servant system did not progress.

From the studies above, we can come to some concluding remarks; the features of the regime in common with the monarchic age, the Republic of China and the Soviet Union, also seen in the Communist Revolutionary Strongholds, can been found in contemporary China. However, the features of the monarchic age, the Republic of China and the Soviet Union, but not of the Communist Revolutionary Strongholds cannot be found in contemporary China. In other words, all of the prototypes of basic power structure in multi-layered centralized regime of contemporary China can be searched for in the political system of Revolutionary Strongholds. Some of these prototypes came from monarchic China, and some from the Soviet Union. Mao Zedong called these features the unitary control system by the Party.

Therefore, we can describe the foundation of the regime of contemporary China as in the following; the regime that the Communist Party built at the Revolutionary Strongholds inherited from the tradition of monarchic China, taking in some experience of the Soviet Union that China found adaptable. That evolved into the multi-layered centralized regime of contemporary China around 1957 in the Mao Zedong era, and in the Deng Xiaoping era it deepened more. The reason why the tradition that the revolutionary strongholds succeeded to and the influence from the Soviet Union were so strong can be considered as follows; when the communist leaders including Mao Zedong tried to erect a regime for the first time during the revolution strongholds period, they rejected the modern democratic politics ideologically, the only alternative must have been the tradition of their own country and the experience of the Soviet Union after all.

The history of the communist revolutionary strongholds was quite long, and Mao Zedong and others passed the time of forming their thoughts, from around twenty years old to their forties. So it can be said that their fixed idea was fostered at revolutionary strongholds. For example Mao Zedong, Deng Xiaoping and others had an idea from the experience of the strongholds that they more respected the Party organization and the charismatic character of the highest leader than legal institution. That is because that the strongholds were dispersed and what unified them was the Party organization and victory or defeat at the guerilla warfare relied greatly upon commander's wisdom.

Also the reason why they did not make an independent inspection organization with the centralized power was said that Mao Zedong and Deng Xiaoping had a bitter experience of being furiously purged in the period of the Chinese Worker' and Peasants' Red Army. In 1978 Deng Xiaoping denied the proposition of making a system independent from the local Party committee in regard to reconstruction of the party discipline check up committee, and insisted to put the discipline check up committee under the control of the Party committee of the same level, he gave his opinion then, from his experience of the stronghold, there should not be two different systems of power.[28] In this way, although both Mao Zedong and Deng Xiaoping regarded much the centripetal force of the nation and the Party, as a result they made and maintained the multi-layered centralized regime which gave a centrifugal trend to the local leaders.

Lastly in the founding process of contemporary China as stated by now, the relationship between the center and locality has been brought into relief. The chapter I points out that the regime, generally so called, is an institutionalized power structure of the makeup of a state and society, and their interrelation. As explained before, however, to the regime of China the power relationship between the center and the locality is a nub of the question, rather than between the state and the society. The motive power for the regime alternation came mainly from the relationship between the center and provinces.

You can understand this difference by observing the substance of the relationship between the center and the locality. First, it is common to socialist states, including China, that the society is integrated by the state. Next, it is a remarkable feature in China that the societies are integrated by local leaders at various levels, under the multi-layered centralized regime illustrated until now. Therefore, relationship between the center and locality in China connotes two phases, the national power relations and interrelation between the state and the society. That is, the local leaders at various levels can be societies to the central leadership that is at the same time, the state. In that sense they are responsible to produce the social profits.

Notes

1. John K. Fairbank, "Why China's Rulers Fear Democracy," New York Review of Books, September 28, 1989, pp. 32-33. "From the Ming to Deng Xiaoping," New York Review Books, May 31, 1989, p. 18. "'Preface,' Children of the Dragon, dy Human Rights in China," New York: Collier Books, Macmillan Publishing Company 1990, p. 9.
This is the summary by the author based upon a work by Carl A. Wittfogel.

2. Chang Chunli, The Chinese Gentry: Studies on Their Role in Nineteenth Century Chinese Society. Univ. of Washington Press, 1955. Chuzo Furuichi "Politics and Society in the Modern China," Tokyo Univ. Press, 1977. Keith Schoppa, Chinese Elites and Political Change: Zhejian Province in the Early Twentieth Century. Harvard Univ. Press, 1982. William Rowe, Han Rowe: Commerce and Society in a Chinese City, 1976-1889. Standford Univ. Press, 1984. James Cole, Shohsing: Competition and Cooperation in Nineteenth Century China. Univ. of Arizona, 1986. Mary Rankin, Elite Activism and Political Transformation in China; Zhejiang Province, 1865-1911. Stanford Univ. Press, 1986. Joseph Esherick and Mary Rankin, eds., Chinese Local Elites and Patterns of Dominance. Univ. of California Press, 1990.

3. W. Skinner/Translated by Seiichi Imai and others "Market & Social Structure of Chinese Farm Villages," Horitsu Bunka Publisher, 1979. William Skinner, eds., The Chinese City between Two World. Stanford Univ. Press, 1974. The City in the Late Imperial China, Stanford Univ. Press, 1977. Philip, Huang. The Peasant Economy and Social Change in North China, Stanford Univ. Press, 1985. (Chinese Version) "North China Peasant Economy and Social Changes" Oxford Univ. Press, 1994. The Peasant Family and Rural Development in the Yangzi Delta, 1350-1988.

4. W. Skinner, translated by Seiichi Imai and others "Market & Social Structure of Chinese Farm Villages" Horitsu Bunka Publisher, 1979. William Skinner, eds., The Chinese City between Tow World. Stanford Univ. Press 1974. The City in the Late Imperial China, Stanford Univ. Press, 1977. Phip Huang, The Peasant Economy and Social Change in North China. Stanford Univ. Press, 1985. (Chinese Version) "North China Peasant Economy and Social Changes" Oxford Univ. Press, 1944. The Peasant Family and Rural Development in the Yangzi Delta, 1350-1988. Standford Univ. Press, 1990. (Chinese Version) "Standard Recognition Crisis in China Study" Oxford Univ. Press, 1994.

5. Masataka Sakano "History of Politics and Diplomacy in China Study" Tokyo Univ. Press, 1973. Tatsumi Okabe "Political Economics of Chinese Modernization" PHP Laboratory, 1989, pp. 2-10. Satoshi Amako "China – Transforming Great Socialist State" Tokyo Univ. Press, 1992, pp. 55-56.

6. Motonosuke Amano "History of Agriculture in China" Agricultural

General Laboratory, 1962 is a reference book based upon these viewpoints.

7. Noboru Niida "Chinese History of Laws" Iwanami Publisher, 1963, pp. 282, 285. This viewpoint is the general trend of the Chinese Law History Institute. For example, Zhang Jinfan "Treaties on Law History of China" (Beijing) Law Publisher, 1982, p. 21. Zhang Hongsheng and other edit. "Brief History of Laws in Chin" (Beijing) Law Publisher, 1983, p. 44.

8. Yukio Noshiro "Comparison Farming" is known as a specialized study on the dry farming in North China, Ochanomizu Publisher, 1969. Toshio Tajima "Unfolded Structure of Agricultural Productive Power" Kazuo Yamaguchi and others edit.

9. "Iwanami Lectures, Contemporary China 2, Economic Turing Point in China" Iwanami Publisher, 1989, pp. 154-155. "Iwanami Lectures, World History 1, Ancient 1, Ancient Orient and Mediterranean Worlds 1" Iwanami Publisher, 1969, pp. 45-54.

10. William Rowe, Han Rowe : Commerce and Society in a Chinese City, 1796-1889. Stannford Univ. Press, 1984. This is known as a masterwork analyzing the development and advance of commercial elite into urban administration of the commercial elites. Lloyd E. Eatman, translated by Shin Ueda and Yoko Fukao "Society of China" Heibonsha Publisher, 1994, Chapter 6 "Commerce in Late Period of Imperial Age – Trading Structure and Geography" pp. 137-182.

11. 'Bureaucratism in Agricultural Society' is a conception employed by B. Moore. (Translated by Takaji Miyazaki and others) "Dictatorship & Social Origin of Democratic Politics" Iwanami Publisher, 1986, pp. 209-287. Incidentally M. Weber used a conception of 'Bureaucratism in Family Property Fashion'. Translated by Koichiro Sera "Sociology of Control" Sobansha Publisher, 1960, Section 4.

12. Ichisada Miyazaki "Kuju (Imperial Examination)" Chuokoron Publisher, 1963 is a widely read book. He Bingdi, translated by Takanobu Terada and Shinichi Chiba "Imperial Examination and Modern Chinese Society – Stepping Stone to Success in Life" Heibonsha Publisher, 1993.

13. Zhang Jinfan, aforenamed book, pp. 16-17, 21. Qiu Yongming "History of Supervisory System in China" (Shanghai) Huadong Terchers Univ. Press, 1992.

14. The latest research in Japan is yujiro Ueda "Cultural Symbol and Power in the 20th Century China – Empire, Nation, Ethnicity" "Series – Study of Chinese Area" Issue 5. ' Preponderant Area Research, Ministry of Education' Issue 113K, 1997, p. 55

15. Wu Yue, Wu Weisheng "Duplexity of Village Relationship – Developing Historical Revelation in Villages of Our Country" Dao Tianding edit. "Research on Local State Organization in China" (Wuhan) Qunzhong Publisher, 1991, Reference.

16. Isamu Ogata "Household and Country in Ancient China – Discipline System under the Emperor Control" Iwanami Publisher, 1991, pp. 187-197 gives a full account of relationship between household and state in medieval

China.

17. Refer to Yoshio Togawa "History of Confusianism" Yamakawa Publisher on Confucianism, also refer to Noboru Niida "History of Laws in China" Iwanami Publisher, 1963, Chapter 12 & 13 on history of laws of Confucianism.

18. Jin Guantao, Liu Qingfeng, translated by Masataka Wakabayashi and Yujiro Murata "Ultra Stable System of Chinese Society" Kenbunsha Publisher attracts public attention as a reference book on changes of dynasties.

19. Chuzo Ichiko regards the revolution of 1911 as a revolution of conservative squires' self-protection. Chuzo Ichiko "Politics and Society of Modern China" Tokyo Univ. Press, 1977, pp. 331-360.

20. Refer to Keiichi Hori "Research on Equal Farmland System" Iwanami Publisher, 1975 for studying the system.

21. There are many researches on the local military cliques. Refer to the following books Donald Sutton, Provincial Militarism and the Chinese Republic: The Yunnan Army, 1905-1925. Univ. of Michigan Press, 1980. Gen Tsukamoto "Research on Military Clique in U.S.A." "Being Close By" Issue 13, 1988. The same author"Present State of Research and Problems on the Chinese Modern Military Clique" "China – Society and Culture" Issue 4, 1989.

22. Refer to Mao Zedong "How Long Can We Wave the Red Flag?" Mao Zedong Sellection, Vol. 1 (Beijing) People's Press, 1977.

24. Refer to Padouk Savetier, under the supervision of Mineo Nakajima, translated by Katsuji Hanagami "Life of Deng Xiaoping" Jiji Press, 1995, pp. 75-77. Guo Hualing, supervised and translated by Kinji Yajima "Historical Essay on Chinese Communist Party" Vol. 2, Shunjusha Publisher, 1998, Chapter 19.

25. "Documentary Records of the 8th Chinese Communist Party National People's Congress" Vol. 2, Waiwen Pubisher, 1956, pp. 378-381.

26. Refer to Yasugo Tsuji edit. "Famine and Poverty in Today's China – Witnesses to 20 mil Death of Hunger" Kobundo Publisher, 1991.

27. Masashi Ando "Various Issues on Cultural Revolution" Shinji Kojima edit. "Iwanami Lectures – Present China 4, History and Modernization" Iwanami Publisher, 1989, pp. 232-233. And as a historical record, "Decision by Communist Party Central on Development of Cultural Revolution (16 May 1966)" "Important Documentary Records on Chinese Communism Cultural Revolution" (Taiwan) Communist Research Magazine Publisher, 1973. There are many books on cultural revolution, and the first book to recommend, Shoko Ota and others edit. "Cultural Revolution and Today's China" Iwanami Pulisher, 1986.

28. This is regarded as an inside classified document.

Chapter 3

Political Regime and Structure of the State

Introduction

As pointed out in the first chapter, in the research on the political regime in contemporary China in Japan, there are two theoretical trends. One is the theory of the centralized regime, and the other is with the features negating the first. The typical scholar representing the first group is Kazuko Mohri who wrote many books and theses on the Party, the state, the military power structure, and the power relationship between the center and locality.

Among the second group, we can quote works by Yoshinari Kokubu, Satoshi Amako, Tomoyuki Kojima. They rather focused on the political changes of contemporary China, rather than the political regime, and through constructing models of the political changes, pointed out the dynamics in the horizontal relationships among the Party, state and militaries, and in the vertical relationship between the center and the locality. Although they rounded off many corroborative researches on the political changes in modern China sustaining their argument, they did not come to grips with the structural analysis of the today's Chinese regime. So they could not set forth a systematic theory of the contemporary Chinese regime.

From this viewpoint, this author has presented the multi-layered centralized regime as a counter concept of the centralized regime. For proving the validity of this classification, structural analysis of the contemporary Chinese regime is needed. In China, the state and the Party are the actors holding the positions in the state structure to realize profits and to make policy, and it is needless to say how they have characterized the Political regime itself. This chapter is divided into two paragraphs, each handling the state and the party respectively, and both of them constitute the state structure.

Section 1: Structure of Actors of the State

The state actors are generally embodied in the national institutions such as the military, and the three powers of the legislature, administration and Judicature. In the case of China, where there is such an avant-garde group as the communist party, the state actors are closely related to the party actors. So it is primarily necessary to inquire into both. But here, in order to avoid excessively complicated description, we wait to analyze the points related to the communist party to Section 2.

Inside Structure of the Legislature

The Chinese legislature is called the people's congress. Accordingly, the people's congress is a legislature and the standing committee of the national people's congress is a permanent organization. These legislative organs are established at each administrative division from the center to localities (Takeuchi edit. and translated 1991, "The Chinese Constitution" 1982 article 2, hereinafter it is called the constitution). It is characteristic that there are dual structures of control and obedience, from the center to the localities, of legislative systems established over the administrative divisions, and in parallel are the double legislative organs of the leadership in the people's congress and the standing committee respectively.

The Chinese demarcation divides the whole country into provinces, autonomous districts, and municipalities directly under the central government, taking factors such as area, population and historic facts into account. Under the province and autonomous district there are cities, counties, autonomous prefectures and autonomous counties; under the city, country and autonomous prefecture are townships, ethnic townships and towns; under the township, ethnic-township and towns are villages. Under the municipality directly under the central government and the big city, there are districts and counties; under the autonomous prefecture are cities and counties (Table 3-1). The autonomous district, autonomous prefecture and autonomous county are provided as areas for minority races (the constitution, articles 1, 30, 57, 58). The legislature in the center is the national people's congress, in the locality the local people's congress established from the provinces, autonomous districts, municipalities directly under the central government. The people's congress is the supreme power, and the local people's congress at all levels is provided as the local authority, and each is posted with the people's elected representatives (the constitution, articles 3, 59, 60, 97, 98).

Chart 3-1: Administrative Districts in China

Center Level	Whole Country		
Provincial Level	Province	Autonomous District	Municipality Directly under the Central Government
City Level	City	Autonomous Prefecture	District
County Level	County	Autonomous County	District
Township Level	Township	Ethnic Township	Town

Source: Drawn by the author.

The state and the local people's congresses at all levels have a dual legislative system with the people's congress and the standing committee (Table 3-2). All the local people's congresses above the county levels elect the standing committees as a permanent organization. The standing committee is made up of chairman, vice chairmen (called a manager and assistant managers at the local people's congress), chief secretary and a few members of the committee (the constitution, articles 57, 58, 65, 96, China Research Institute edit. 1988, "Law of the Local People's Congress and Government Organization" articles 35 and 36). The legislative power is allotted to the people's congress and the standing committee in the following way.

Taking the case of the national people's congress for example, opening a meeting once a year, the main authorized limit of powers are; (a) formulating and revision of the constitution, (b) formulating and revision of laws that are characteristic of the fundamental laws, (c) examination and approval of national and social developing projects, and examination and approval of the budget and settlement, (d) revision or revocation of improper decisions by the people's standing committee, (e) supervising execution of the aforementioned laws. Under the congress, there are specialized committees of legislation, finance and economy, education and science, races, foreign affairs organized respectively as the permanent machinery (the constitution, articles 61, 62, 70).

Chart 3-2: Inside Structure of the People's Congress of China

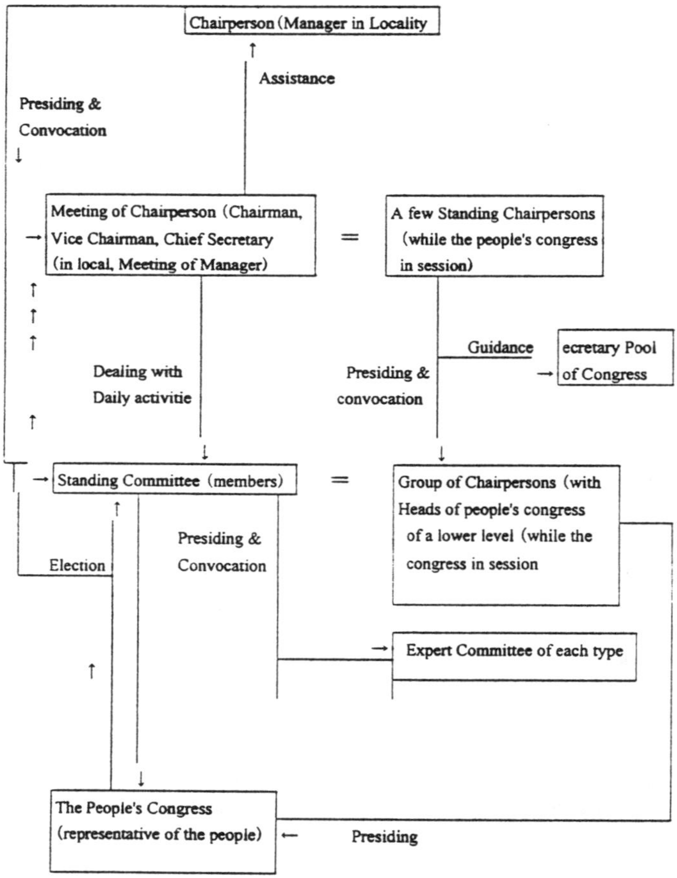

Source: Drawn by the author with reference "The Chinese Constitution" Chapter 3. Para. 1.
Note: Arrows signify election, guidance, and presiding.

In the case of the standing committee of the people's congress, meetings are held once in two months. Their main authorities are; (a) convocation of the people's congress, and proposition of principal deliberative agenda, (b) enactment and revision of laws, except fundamental laws, (c) interpretation of the constitution and the laws enacted by the people's congress and the standing committee, (d) supervision and inquiry into the execution of the constitution and the laws, (e) examination and approval of projects for the national economy and social development and revision of the budget, and (f) guidance to the specialized committees, which are the permanent organs of the people's congress (the constitution, articles 67 and 70, China Research Institute edit. 1988, 'The people's congress organization law' articles 2 and 29).

From the facts above stated, we can understand that the right to legislate belongs to the standing committee rather than to the people's congress; that is, (a) a meeting of the people's congress is just once a year and only for two weeks, so it is the standing committee which takes actual and real legislative action, (b) the people's congress legislates the constitution and the fundamental laws legally. In reality, however, the standing committee executes proposition of bills, drafting bills for the people's congress and the specialized committees, deliberation on drafts at the standing committee, and controls and decides the opening date and duration of the people's congress, (c) the people's congress has veto power over the enactment of the standing committee, however, because the standing committee has the rights for interpretation of the constitution, and for proposing deliberative bills of the people's congress and for convocation of a meeting of the people's congress, the veto power over the people's congress is in fact useless. That is, the standing committee exercises the tasks of the people's congress vicariously.

The power relationship between the local people's congresses of all levels and the standing committees is almost the same as that of the center as stated before (the constitution, articles 96-104). Also there is a leadership section in the Chinese legislature (Table 3-2). For example, the chairman of the standing committee is positioned atop of the people's congress, and under him are a few of vice chairmen and the chief secretary. They jointly compose the council of the chairman, dealing with the daily activities, the details of which are:

(A) Deciding the duration of the meeting and the agenda for the

> standing committee, (B) deciding to transfer bills to the specialized committee for deliberation, or to be discussed in a council of the standing committee, (C) leading the daily activities of the variously specialized committees of the people's congress (the constitution, article 68; the law of the people's congress, article 25).

As you see it here, the power of the people's congress is further concentrated in the chairman's council. It controls all processes from drafting bills to bringing them up for deliberation. The Chinese chairman and the group of chairpersons are not just a neutral legislative director, as in a democratic regime, but they are legislative leaders with power over legislative activities.

The election of the standing committee is exercised at the first people's congress each term. To make it fair, the existing standing committee is not allowed to function, and at the outset of the congress a big group of chairmen is elected to superintend the congress. However, the existing standing committee presides over the election of the people's representatives before the assembly, the nomination of the group of chairperson of the congress, and deciding the agenda of the congress (the constitution, article 60 and 61). And it comes to be that the members of the newly elected chairperson' group are generally the members of the existing standing committee, the group of the people's representatives from different provinces, the chairperson of the military representatives, and candidates of the new standing committee. Also some of the standing chairpersons are the member of the existing standing committee and its new candidates. The authorities of the chairpersons' group are; (a) decisive power of proposing bills and voting, (b) nomination of the candidates for the next term of the council of the standing committee, the state president, the vice president, president of the state military commission, the chief justice of the supreme court, the chief prosecutor, and confirmation of these candidates based upon the majority opinion of the people's representatives, (c) decision of open voting or secret voting, (d) decision of a closed or open meeting.

Since no one but the head of the representatives is allowed to speak at the congressional meetings, the right of speaking by the people's representative is considerably restricted (the law of people's congress, fifth, articles 5-10, 13, 15, 18, 20). Thus the people's congress is operated under the control of the council of the standing committee or the he chairperson's group of the congress. The inside structure of the Chinese legislature is does not produce equal relationships among the deputies. It is so designed that a small number of the leaders, the chairperson (in the center the chairman, in the locality the manager) and a few members of the committee control the deputies (members of the standing committee) and the people's representatives. Here we call this kind of feature a change of legislative organs into administrative ones. In this transformed legislature, the legislative leaders command the obedience of the members of the standing committee and the people's representatives by the way of the administration, and deal with bills in their own way. While the inside structure of the legislature, which has changed into a sort of administrative organ and they can handle bills in their own way, contains an unexpected mechanism.

Lastly, I would like to point out two phases of this process. First, the representatives of the people are not organized according to the difference of parties or political groups, but organized as the representatives of different areas. This is the way to put the representatives of the people under the control of the Party committee. Next, the legislative leadership has a bureaucratic mechanism to deal with the legislature in the way of administration. In the case of the people's congress, there are sections called chambers under the permanent institutes of specialized committees of law and finance/economy. The chamber is a bureaucratic mechanism. According to Wang Shengming, chief of the civil law chamber of the law work committee:

> A chamber is a government office, equivalent to a bureau, one level lower than a ministry. The civil law chamber takes charge of enactment and revision of such fundamental civil laws as civil affairs, administration and economy (Interview by the author, 17 and 18th August 1997).

This is a strong authority that an office like parliamentary legislative bureau in countries of democratic countries does not have. Chambers of this type have the expertise and information in their own field and this authority can be a target of the petition. They must have a powerful voice in the legislative leadership.

Inside Structure of Legislative Organ

The present constitution of the People's Republic of China (1982) says that the state council of the People's Republic of China, namely, the central people's government, is the supreme executive organ of national power and the highest administrative institution. The local people's governments at all levels are the executive offices of the local authorities and the local administrative institutes (the constitution, articles 85, 105). These authorities of the central and local administrative organs can be divided into three sections; the general administration, management of enterprises, administrative supervision (public security, national safety, inspection, and audit).

General Administration

Legally, the state council has the right to control the execution of all national administrative organs collectively, to decide proper distribution of the administrative powers among the center, provinces, autonomous districts, and municipalities directly under the central government, and correcting (or revoking) improper decisions by the local administrative organs of all levels. Also, the local people's governments above the county level have the right to control all lower governmental offices and the lower people's governments and to correct (or revoke) their improper decisions (the constitution, articles 89, 108). Here we can discern their aim at a vertical centralization.

Yet there is a provision stipulating that the local people's governments of all levels are responsible to the people's congress of the same level and the immediately upper national administrative organs. Here they are asked to be obedient horizontally to the same level of the legislative institutes, besides to the national administrative organs one level higher. Then what are the real horizontal and vertical power relationships? This author hopes to clear up this point in the following analyses.

Right of Management of Enterprises

The right of managing enterprises is the right to operate all the processes from investment, production, sales, and to distribution. In China the production of the national and collective enterprises, which are called officially the public enterprise, account for 70.6% of the industrial output (Jiang Liu and others edit. 1997, p. 29). These public enterprises are classified as the central national enterprise belonging to the central administration, the local national enterprise to the local administrative institutes of all levels, and the collective enterprises to the city public organizations or to the village and township leadership (in the rural area called the village and township enterprises). The managing right, in part, is held by the central, local and basic administrative institutions respectively.

Concretely, in regard to investment, the center, local, and basic administrative organs control enterprises through examination, approval and economic planning. There are three resources for investment; treasury fund, bank loan, and entrepreneur's own fund. Let alone in the case of treasury fund, the cases of bank loans and their own funds require the examination and ratification by the government. In other words, enterprises have no right to invest even their own money without undergoing examination and ratification by the government. In the production processes, the center, local, and basic administrative organs have the right of appointment and dismissal of the executives of enterprises. The production planning itself requires their examination and ratification.

Regarding sales, it is reported that market price is fundamentally established, in fact, however, it is not to be overlooked that the administrative organizations of all levels control and deal with funds and merchandise of the enterprises under the control (Tajima, Yamauchi and Kikuchi edit, 1991, p. 121-124). In the phase of distribution, the center, local, and basic administrative organs fix the amount of government subsidies for wages, welfare, and even for deficit. The taxes related to enterprises are levied by all levels of the governments mainly according to the ownership relations of the enterprises under the names of tax, surcharge and other pretexts.[1] Here, we have to explain more, that is, the Chinese government does not collect taxes from salaried employees directly, so the taxes from the resources related to enterprises are the biggest income source for the government. Lastly in the case of bankruptcy, they need the examination and ratification by the government.[2]

In January, 1998, the Japan Overseas Economic Cooperation Fund and the Chinese Academy Social Sciences Economy Research Institute compiled a joint survey report on autonomy of management in Chinese state-owned enterprises. According to it, 70% of the business have no autonomy concerning investment, purchase and disposal of assets, close to 50% have no power to decide hiring and personnel affairs, and almost all enterprises replied the government appoints the management personnel (The Yomiuri Press, 11 January 1998). Thus, the Chinese administrative organs of all levels take part directly in the management of enterprises, and their own income is mainly from the proceeds of the enterprises, which excites the administrative institutes' desire for profit from the enterprises. In this way the profit pursuing groups have been formed at each administrative division.[3] That the local and basic level administrative organs have the right to manage enterprises, which has made them local groups pursuing the economic profits, clearly contradicts the aim of the strong centralized regime, which was shown in the right of the administration.

When the central policy becomes inimical to the profits of the local and basic administrative machinery, friction or conflict will inevitably occur between them. In such a case, since the local and basic governments have administrative right as well as economic power from their activity of managing the enterprises, they have a tough bargaining position against the center. The local governments do not necessarily always obey the State Council as one of the national administrative organs under the strong control of the State Council as stipulated in the contitution.[4]

Administrative Right

The administrative right is the authority held by the central and local and basic administrative offices covering policy, administration, and economy, and the rights of public security, national security, inspection and auditing. Taking the case of the State Council, for example, the Ministry of National Security takes charge of political items, the Ministry of Public Security of security and criminal items, from that fact, any matters related to administrative organs or bureaucrats are taken care of by the Ministry of Inspection. In the economic field, the Board of Audit and the Statistic Bureau have been established, the former collects information and the latter is responsible for auditing.

In any country the administrative structure has a department in charge of administrative supervision. Here we take a look into the auditing system, which has been studied specifically, in the hope of finding out of some features of Chinese administration (Fujita, Kyushu univ. the Chinese Economy Research Group edit. 1991). In 1983 the State Council set up the Board of Audit, and the local administrative offices of all levels had the Auditing Bureaus. By the year of 1988, a series of laws and regulations regarding the auditing mechanism were established, by which the responsible person in a local auditing office is commissioned by the administrative organ of the same level with the consent of one level upper auditing office and controlled by both offices. This is called a dual leading system.

This dual leading system found it more and more difficult to function as the workload of auditing tasks increased. First the board of audit and the auditing bureau are part of the administrative office of the same level and operate under their command, so it is difficult to do effective auditing of the public enterprises under its command of the administrative and finance/economic offices of the same level. Also because the local administrative organs of all levels, as profit pursuing groups, are vying with the offices of other areas and the center economically, and while the auditing machinery should originally carry on equitable auditing, they are apt to be involved in common interests with the administrative organs as part of them. As a matter of fact, a lot of cases of negligence in auditing and false reports to the upper agencies are often revealed.

Regarding the malfunction of the auditing, a notification from the State Council emphasizing the independency of the auditing organization was issued in 1985, but as it lacked a revision of the points of control and appointment by the administrative office of the same level, the emphasis of independency did not materialize in the end. Under this type of dual leadership, the local administrative organization of each level has the authority for guidance and personnel affairs. So for the administrative supervisory systems, the administrative organ of the same level is the first object to pledge loyalty.

From the above analysis, the inside structure of the Chinese administrative organs are supposed legally to have an aim at the centralized regime, but in reality the local and basic administrative mechanism of all levels hold part of managing power of the enterprises, becoming local profit pursuing groups. On top of this, they control the administrative supervisory mechanism, and monopolize information. In contrast with the fact that their laws and regulations are pointing at the centralized regime, the present situation is that the local and basic administrative systems hold horizontally most of authority.

Inside Structure of Judicature Institution

As for the Judicature, the constitution stipulates that The People's Court of the People's Republic of China is a state judicial institution, and that the People's Procuratorate of the People's Republic of China is a state prosecutorial institution (the constitution, articles 123, 129). In

China, the supreme people's court is established in the center and the local people's courts of all levels in the locality, according to the administrative division (China Research Institute edit. 1988, the law of organization of the people's court, articles 2, 18, 23, 26, 30). We can observe some features here that the Chinese judicial mechanism has been transforming into the administrative organization as the people's congress has. This transformation is due to the supervisory system of the people's court from high level to low, and due to the instruction system from the chief prosecutor in the institution.

According to the constitution (1982), the supreme people's court is the highest judicial mechanism, supervising the Judicature activities of all the people's courts. In the locality the upper courts should control the lower people's court (the constitution, articles 124 and 127). This supervising characteristic of the people's courts has given the following features to Chinese trials; Since the lower courts do not have autonomous jurisdiction, they frequently would rather rule based upon the decisions or intentions of the upper courts than upon their own judgment. Since the trials in lower courts are carried on under the supervision of the upper courts, there is almost no possibility of having a different decision at an appeal court from the lower court. We see quite often the same ruling as at the first trial. The court should be an organ to reject any intervention from outside, but in the case of the people's court, there is a lawful route to intervene from an upper court under the stipulation of 'supervision from the upper people's court'. Through that route a court is subject to intervention from other organizations.

Inside of the people's court there are triple layered power systems including judge (higher-class judge), judicial committees, and president of the courts. The president applies for appointment or dismissal of judges or member of the judicial committee to the standing committee of the same level. Also he presides at a judicial committee to summarize trial cases, to discuss important items and doubtful problems or any other trial issues, and to make decisions (Law of the people's court, article 11). The president of the people's court has a bureaucratic structure under his command to perform duties and to manage the court administratively. Thus each judge should in essence have individual jurisdiction, but in fact the autonomy of the Judicature is not assured, as the president holds the right to implement personnel management and to preside over the judicial committee. The judges are virtually staff controlled by the president, and the people's courts are changed into administrative organs.

Inside of Prosecution

In China, the supreme people's Procuratorate is established in the center and the local people's Procuratorate of all levels in the locality, at each administrative division (China Research Institute edit. 1988, the law of organization of the people's, chapter 3). The constitution stipulates that the people's Procuratorate of all levels are responsible for the upper people's Procuratorate, for the people's congress of the same level, and for the standing committee of the same level. That is, the inside structure of the prosecutorial organization is of the same dual leadership as that of the administrative supervisory organization in the administration. In the organizing law of the people's Procuratorate, which was enacted later, the word 'the upper Procuratorate was deleted and stipulated that it should be responsible for only the people's congress and the standing committee of the sale level. It should be a serious problem that any single law contradicts the constitution, but there has been no explanation so far from China about it. In any case, the responsibility assumed by the Procutorial machinery toward the upper organs is of secondary importance in comparison with that toward the people's congress and the standing committee of the same level.

The dual leadership of the prosecutorial institute is that the central or upper Procuratorates do not hold the rights to control personnel management. Instead, the people's congresses and the standing committee of the administratively same level hold them horizontally. And as far as daily work concerned, they are subject to the control by the upper prosecutorial organs (the constitution, articles 10, 21, 22, 23, 24, 26). Thus the local people's congress and the standing committee of each level make their existence more solid. They make themselves the target of respect. We will further examine later the relationships between the prosecutorial organs and the people's congresses. Here we would like to emphasize the inside structure of the prosecutorial mechanism in China is far from the centralized power system.

Tripartite Relationships among the Legislation, the Administration and the Judicature Relationship of the Three Powers as seen by the Legislation

According to the Constitution, Chinese Legislation at each level from the Central to the local is a centralized entity in each jurisdiction with the administrative and Judicature offices functioning under the direction of the Legislation.(chart 3-3) We shall take the National People's Congress here for example:

> (A) the National People's Congress elects the members of the Standing Committee of the NPC, the President of the People's Republic of China, the Vice President, the Chairman of the Central Military Commission, the President of the Supreme_People's Court and the Procurator General of the Supreme People's Procuratorate. It also elects the Premier of the State Council upon nomination by the President of the People's Republic of China. (B) NPC and the Standing Committee elects the ministers of the State Council upon nomination by the President of the PRC and elects the members of the Central Military Commission upon the nomination of the Chairman of the Commission. (C) The Standing Committee decides on the Vice Presidents and the Judges of the Supreme People's Court, members of its Judicial Committee at the recommendation of the President of the Supreme People's Court and the Deputy Procurators-General, members of the Procuratorial Committee and the higher ranking Procurators. at the recommendation of the Procurator General of the Supreme People's Procuratorate. (D) The Standing Committee supervises the work of the State Council, the Central Military Commission, the Supreme People's Court and the Supreme People's Procuratorate (The Constitution Article 62,63,65-67).

According to the laws referred above, the relationships as observed by the Legislation are as follows: (a) At each administrative level ranging from the Central to the local, the major positions are solely appointed or removed by the People's Congress, leaving no room for the appointment by other organizations, not to speak of the free competitive elections (Article 13, NPC Law). (b) The right to supervise the daily work of state organs is concentrated horizontally on the Legislation at each level. (c) Although NPC is the highest organ of state power, powers do not lie in the hands of rank-and-file members of the Standing Committee, but in the Presidium and the Council of Chairmen, which constitute the mainstay of the Legislative organ. These people monopolize important personnel affairs, day-to-day lawmaking and supervision of the work of governmental offices.

Aside from the relationships brought about by these laws, we have to see the outward influence caused by the inside structure of the Legislation that has come to function almost like administrative institutions. In March 1996, it was reported that the fourth National People's Congress vested Shantou City and Zhuhai City of Guang Dong with the legislative authority on the ground that the same authority had been granted to Shen Zhen City and Amoy before. However, in the course of discussion, voices of opposition rose from many of the Provincial deputies. Under such circumstances Liang Guangda Party Secretary of the Zhuhai City and concerned members of the both cities went strenuously around the deputies of the other provinces to ensure their support (Hon Kong: *MING BAO YUE KAN*, 1996,3). By this example we see that provincially organized team of deputies showed a way to the locality's participation in the policy-making. Another example of this is the fact that the bureaucrats in the Legislation with abundant authorities, expertise and information are constantly lobbied by the bureaucrats from other organs of power. All these contribute towards up-grading the status of Legislative leadership from the other power organs.

Tripartite Relationships as Seen by the Administration

The relationship between the Administrative and Legislative organs are prescribed as "dual responsibility" by law. The Constitution stipulates "Local people's governments at various levels are responsible, and report on their work to the equally ranked Standing Committee of the people's congress and the state administrative organs at the next higher level"(Article 110, Constitution). However, through the inside analysis of the administrative organs, it became clear that each level of the local Legislative organs does not show much interest to the Central. But they are more autonomous and more interested in the local economic benefits. As is shown above, for the_administrative organs at various levels, the equally ranked local legislative organs are superior by law to the Central Government since the local Legislation has the power over the personnel and supervisory affairs of the corresponding local Administration.

In regard to the relationship between the Administration and the Legislation, we have to understand that it is not that of the Administrative organs versus "the Congress" in general, but rather it is the relationship between the Administrative organs versus the leaders of the Legislation who run the congress in an administrative way. In other words, it has actually turned into the relationship of the leaders of the two "administrative" organs. Such kind of relationships are liable to lead to the formation of tacit alliance, where the supervision by the Standing Committee of the NPC becomes a dead letter. Thus, the Chinese administrative government possesses not only strong administrative power and extensive economic interest in the locality, but it can even make the supervision by the deputies of the congress ineffective. The supremacy of the Legislation stipulated in the Constitution has become nominal and in fact the administrative organ is taking the lead.

Let us next proceed to the relationships between the supervisory organs of the administration and the Judicature. Chinese legal procedures begin when the administrative supervisory organ decides to indict. They then move from the approval of the arrest by the people's Procuratorate to the deliberation of the indictment, prosecution, and to the trial. (Article 1,13,15, Constitution) The procedure presupposes that the administration has the initiating power of indictment, which means that without the initiative on the side of the administration, the legal procedure does not get into gear. All this shows that the administration is in a position superior to the Judicature. There is also a marked difference in the legal process for the common citizens and for the administrative organs (including people in charge).

In the case of the common citizens, the legal process begins with the investigation either by the state security institution or the police for public peace. But in the case of the administrative organs, the process starts with the instruction by the chief of the administrative organ. The inspection or statistics/auditing office, then, begins to inspect or audit. After this, the chief of the administrative organ determines either on the administrative disposition or criminal prosecution. By creating such discriminatory legal process between "government" and "common people", "government" can often get away with simple administrative disposition instead of being indicted by criminal law.

Let us now have a look at how the inspection was carried out in 1989 to one of "The Five Big Enterprises" which were directly under the State Council (People's Daily, March 15, 1989). "The Five Enterprises" had been the talk of the town that they are making easy money through underground dealings. The denunciation against this was taken up in one of the demands of the people in the 6 Beijing Tiananmen .in 1989. After this denunciation the Auditing Office of the State Council started audit on "the five Enterprises" "at the instruction of the State Council". On August 15 of the same year the chief of the Audit Office held a press interview "about the Audit they have made at the instruction of the State Council." He admitted there to the illegal act on the side of the five Enterprises. However the punishment for the violation of the law was the mere dissolution of the three of the five Enterprises by the order of the State Council. None of the executives in the five Enterprises were indicted by the Criminal law. Looking at the outcome of this incident, it is evident that without the instruction by the administrative chief the invocation of the inspection and the inquiry into the criminal circumstance will not be realized.

On top of all these, the Administration has the right to the interpretation of the administrative laws (Resolution of the Interpretation of the law, Article 3, 1988 China Institute). Thus in the face of trials concerning administrative laws, the Judicature is obliged to obey the interpretation of the Administration which represents the other side of the interested party. For example, when the Higher People's Court in Zhejiang Province examined the case of the accuser's objection to the punishment against the violation of public order, the court gave a judgment against the accuser for the reason that the legal ground for the punishment lies in "the Regulations for Punishment for Public Order". Since the right to the interpretation of the regulations is given to the executive organ of the law by the "Resolution of the legal interpretation by the Standing Committee of NPC ", the People's Court made the decision based on the interpretation of the Public Peace Institution, or the accused in this case. To conclude, we may say that Chinese administrative government at each level stands superior to the equally ranked Legislation, and moreover, it is superior to the Judicature since it has in its hands the right whether or not to initiate legal process and the right to interpret administrative laws.

Tripartite Relationships as seen by the Judicature

Following are the articles that define the relationship between the People's Court and National People's Congress:

> (A) Each level of People's Court is responsible to the equally ranked People's Congress and its Standing Committee. (B) Each level of the Standing Committee supervises the work of equally ranked People's Court. (C) The President of People's Court at each level is appointed or annulled by the corresponding People's Congress at the nomination of its Standing Committee. (D) Each level of the

> Standing Committee appoints or annuls the Vice Presidents, members of its Judicial Committee and judges at its corresponding level at the recommendation of the equally ranked President of the People's Court. (E) The Standing Committee of the National People's Congress interpret the Constitution and supervise its enforcement (Article 62,63,67,104,128, Constitution, Article 13, NPC Law, Article 20,39, Law for Local People's Congress and Government).

To summarize the above, we can assume the following is the characteristics of the relationship between People's Court and the People's Congress. (1) People's Congress has two powers towards People's Court: one over the Court's personnel affairs and the other the power to supervise the Court's daily work. These show the lawful legitimacy of the People's Congress in regard to its interference into the personnel affairs and the judicial work of the People's Court. (2) While the Chinese Judicature does not possess the right to judicial review of the constitution, the Standing Committee of the National People's Congress has the power to interpret and supervise the enforcement of the constitution. In fact, the right to judicial review is in the hands of the Standing Committee of the NPC. Thus, the enactment, interpretation, supervising the other actors from the constitutional viewpoint, and the right to judicial review are all exercised by the Standing Committee or the lawmaking organ. In this way, arbitrary interpretation, supervision, and willful judgment become possible. There is no authority to prohibit them.

The laws regulating the relationship between the People's Procuratorate and the People's Congress are given hereunder:

> (A) Under the law of the organization of the People's Procuratorate, each level of People's Procuratorate is responsible only to the corresponding People's Congress and its Standing Committee. (B) People's Procurator-General at each level is either appointed or annulled by the corresponding People's Congress. The Deputy Procurators-General and members of the Procuratorial Committee and Procurators are appointed or annulled by the corresponding Standing Committee at the recommendation of the Procurator-General. The appointment or removal of each level of local People's Procurators must be reported to the People's Procurator General at a step higher level and must be approved by the People's Congress at a step higher level. (C) The Procurator General at each level presides over the People's Procuratorial Committee, which discusses and determines matters of importance. When the Procurator General does

> not agree with the majority opinion of the Committee, he may report about it to the equally ranked Standing Committee and ask for its decision (Article 3, 10, 21, 22, 23 Law of People's Procuratorate).

The relationship between the People's Procuratrorate and the People's Congress may be summarized as follows. (1) As is the case with the People's Court, the People's Congress exercise power over the People's Procuratorate in personnel affairs and the supervision of its work. In other words, the People's Congress in the capacity of the legislative office has legitimate right to interfere with the personnel and daily work. (2) People's Procuratorate at each level is responsible only to the People's Congress and its Standing Committee at the corresponding level. The Procuratorial power is attributed horizontally to the equally ranked Legislation. The People's Procuratorate does not have the nation-wide independent vertical command system concerning personnel affairs or instructions.

Let us finally observe the relationships between the court-Procuratorate and the supervisory organs in the administration. As we have seen above, the administrative supervisory organ has the initiating right to start legal process and the right to interpret administrative laws. However, we could go much further to point out that the administration is lawfully guaranteed to interfere with the Procuratorial and Court process itself.

Regarding the relationships among court-procuratorate and administration, Chinese Constitution (1982) defines them in the Article 135 as:

> "The people's courts, the people's Procuratorates and the public security organs shall, in handling criminal cases, divide their functions, each taking responsibility for its own work, and they shall coordinate their efforts and check each other to ensure the correct and effective enforcement of the law." Here, we must pay attention to the word "coordinate"

The Court, Procuratorate and the Administration are, in essence, three separate state organs, each engaged in the legal functions and each restricting the others so that errors might be avoided in the judicial process. If the three should "coordinate", it might naturally lead to unfair backdoor alliance, weakening the restrictive effect.

The tripartite relationships are defined in the "Law for the Organization of the People's Court" in the following way. "The

Committee of Judges of each level of The People's Court is presided over by the President of the People's Court. The People's Procurator General may attend the Committee"(Article 11, Law of The People's Court). In other words, the court organ invites the head of the prosecution, opens meetings behind the closed doors and makes decisions. The coordination of the prosecutors and the judges will weaken the position of the accused seriously.

Let us point out at the end, that the tendency of the People's Court turning into pseudo administrative organs, together with the same tendency of People's Congress, comprises unexpected side-effect. According to Mr. LI Xiangdong , the head of the public relations to the Supreme People's Court, the judicial precedents are not recognized valid as law in China but the fact is that the precedents published by the Supreme People's Court are considered as the basis for the court judgments. Moreover, since the Supreme People's Court most abundantly accumulates the knowledge and information about the Judicature matters, they make proposals to the Legislation and they themselves draft bills (Interview by this author, Aug.18, 1997). In democratic regimes, the Legislation and the Administration make bills. But the Judicature does not join in. In China the Supreme People's Court is given the authority and power as "an administrative institution", yielding certain impact on other power institutions.

The Legislation, the Administration and the Judicature are the actors exercising state policy. Through the analysis in this chapter the tripartite state organs may be characterized in the following way. First, the Legislation has become like administrative organs under the leadership consisting of handful deputies. The Administration possesses the authority of administration in general, management of enterprises and the administrative supervision. The Judicature has also become like administrative organ under court leadership, while the Procuratorial organ lacks independent leadership and authority over personnel affairs.

Although by law, power among state organs should show tendency to concentrate horizontally on to each level of the Legislation with the simultaneous tendency of power ascending vertically from the local to the central, in reality the Administration stands superior over the other organs, armed with versatile authorities, economic profit motivations and strong bargaining power. This structure results in the backdoor alliance of the three power leaderships at the same administrative level. The Standing Committee and the People's Court are influential to a certain point on the other organs as administratively oriented institutions. But the impact is secondary. The structural singularity lies in that it is not so much a vertical centralization as a horizontal centralization. Since such horizontal concentration of power in the state organs are seen at each level of the Central, provinces, cities, counties in multi-layers, we call this "Multi-layered Centralization Structure."

Section 2: Structures of the Parties

There are eight political parties in China. In addition to the Chinese Communist Party, there is 'Democratic Alliance' which includes 'Democratic Party Group', 'Chinese Nationalist Party Revolution Committee', 'China Agriculture and Manufacturing Democratic Party', 'China Democratic Founding Party', 'China Democratic Promotion Party', 'China Public Party', 'Jiu San Xue She', and 'Taiwan Autonomous Alliance' (Kima [Oguchi *ed*] page 79, 1991). However, since the 'China Constitution (1982)' prescribes the Communist Party as the only leading party (Constitution '*Introductory Remarks*'), the Communist Party is in fact the only significant party as actual actors. This section will review the power structures of the Communist Party from two aspects, the internal structures and external relationships.

Internal Structures of the Chinese Communist Party

The following is an examination of the Communist Party from four aspects: (1) The organizational structures of the Communist Party, (2) The 'charismatic Leader' in the organizational structure, (3) Ideology in the context of a political regime, and (4) Internal inspection structures.

(1) Organizational Structures of the Communist Party

In China, Communist Party Committees are located in line with each Administrative Region from the Central to local and basis layers. ' The highest leading organization of the Party is the Central Council, which is an elected organization by the Party's national representatives. The Party's local administrative leaders' organization is an elected Committee by the party's local representatives.' In addition, in any basis organizations, corporations, schools, towns, villages or army troops where there are more than three official Party members, basis organizations such as 'Basis organization Party Committee' or 'Branch' would be established. ('China Communications' September 29, 1997, 'Chinese Communist Party Regulations ' Article 3, 4, 5, later 'Party Regulations') In state organizations, e.g. various administrative level government organizations, the legislative body, the judicial body and their various departments, and in other public organizations such as women's groups and labor unions, 'Party Groups' are established as the Party's leadership organizations (Tang Liang, 1997, pages 7-34).

The Communist Party is a multiplex organization. The following Central organization of the Party is one example of such organization ('Party Regulations' Article 3). The 'National Congress of the Chinese Communist Party' (later 'Party Congress') is held every five years. The representatives consist of provincial delegates and army delegates. These delegates are organized under control of the Party Committee, but is also a desirable structure for the Local Committee as well, in order to protect their interests. The National Congress is called by the Central Committee. The Central Committee decides the agenda and schedule of the National Congress, and also the number of seats assigned and how-to-elect of the Congress participating representatives. We can see from the above that the Central Committee has more leading power in the Communist Party than the National Congress.

Next, the Politburo of the Central Committee (later abbr. 'Politburo') holds a general meeting at least once a year. The Politburo consists of over twenty persons; and above this, five to seven members are elected for the Politburo Standing Committee. Both the Politburo and Politburo Standing Committee exercise their authorities while the Central Committee is closed. Therefore, the Communist Party power is centralized from the Central Committee to the Politburo, from the Politburo to the Politburo Standing Committee. The Communist Party is thus a four-fold structure organization and the power is in the hands of a small number of core persons in the Politburo Standing Committee.

'The Central Work Conference' plays an even more important role in the Party's policy-making process, and is held in prior to the Party Central Committee. For example, China's 'Reform and Liberation Policy' is known for being decided at the Party Central Committee Meeting held for four days from December 18, 1978; however it was actually decided earlier at the 'Central Work Conference' held from November 10 through December 15 (Amako Mouri *ed.* Pages 18-22). The characteristic of the Central Work Conference is that it invites the government and party leaders of local provinces to attend. Unlike other democratic countries, we can see that China's local leaders are players in the Central policy making process.

'The Central Secretary Office' is a secretariat organization of the Politburo and the Politburo Standing Committee. Between years 1982 and 1992, there was also the Central Advisory Committee where senior status members of the Communist Party belonged. The Standing Committee member of the Central Advisory Committee was able to attend the Central Committee (Yabuki, 1990, pages 82-85, '*People's Daily*' June 22, 1989).

(2) The 'charismatic Leader' in the organizational structure

Following is a quotation from Deng Xiaoping's statements:

> It is necessary for any mass group to have a core. Without leadership of the core, there will be nothing to rely on. The core of the first generation leaders group was President Mao Tse-tung. Because we had Mao Tse-tung as a leading core, the Communist Party was not defeated during the Great Cultural Revolution. In the second generation, I am the acting core. By having this core, even though we had changes in our two leaders (Hu Yaobang, Zhao Ziyang), there was little influence on the leadership and stability of our Party. We will still need a core when we enter the third generation. Any fellow member who becomes the core needs to have highly motivated concentration in all processes. In deliberate need to support one core, everyone agrees that the core should be Jiang Zeming (The Communist Party Central Document Papers).

This quotation is cited from 'The Communist Party Central Communication' distributed to the local leaders in June 1989, which is said to be a summary from Deng Xiaoping's remarks made to Yang Shangku, Wan Li, Jiang Zemin, Li Peng, Qiao Shi, Yao Yilin, Song Ping, Li Ruihuan, according to 'WEN HUI BAO' (June 28, 1989), a Communist Party press in Hong Kong.

According to Deng Xiaoping's remarks, the 'charismatic' feature and the role of a leader in the Communist Party organization can be clarified as follows. The highest 'charismatic' leader of the Communist Party Central should concentrate all central power in a horizontal organizational relationship as the 'leading core'; and in the vertical context, display an intra-party supra-organizational leadership and demand obedience from all parties as stated in Chapter 10 of 'Party

Regulation' where 'All parties follow the Party Central'.

The existence of a 'charismatic' leader is institutionalized. The Communist Party's basis organization principle is 'Democratic Concentrated System', which requires 'highly concentrated' discussions in the Committee meetings. However, the term 'concentration' describes integration of the Party's policies and actions. The Party Committee Secretary (later 'Secretary') has the authorization to make final decisions on such policies and the right of command to pursue actions, both to materialize 'concentration'. During normal times in the Party Central, role of the 'charismatic' leader is played by the Communist Party Central General Secretary (later 'General Secretary'), and the 'Communist Party Regulations' states that the leader holds the authorization to 'call Politburo Meetings, Politburo Standing Committee Meetings, and takes lead in the activities of the Central Secretary Office' (Party Regulation Chapter 21).

Deng Xiaoping was a non-managerial-level party member, however, as seen from his own remarks, he was in the position of the 'leading core'. This was not normal for the Communist Party. The procedures to institutionalize such irregular situations were among the 'internal confidential decisions' made by the Party Central Committee. Start of such decision-making procedures goes back to the Mao Zedong era.

The Central Committee Meeting in prior to the 7th National Congress in 1945, upon proposal from Liu Shao-chi, officially decided that Mao Zedong should have the final authorization to all policy decisions.6) 'Confidential decisions' such as the ones made to decide Deng Xiaoping's level of authority, became known to public from statements made by the Party General Secretary Zhao Ziyang, during a conversation with Soviet Union Communist Party Chief Secretary Gorbachev in May 1989.

One official decision was made at the first plenary session of the 13th Party Central Committee. We courteously decided that in driving our most crucial issues, his (Deng Xiaoping's) steering would become necessary. Since the 13th Party Central Meeting, we always report and consult with Deng Xiaoping for his advice in order to deal with important issues. We have never disclosed this decision and I am telling this fact to you for the first time' (Yabuki Shin 1989 Chapter 1 page 268). (c) The Communist Party has always created a 'charismatic' leader from its organizational necessities. From the earlier statements by Deng Xiaoping we can suppose that it was necessary to create and support a 'charismatic' leader figure in order to maintain the Party's autocracy whether right or wrong, during the Great Cultural Revolution and the 6.4 Tiananmen Square Incident.

An autocracy does not accept plural parties. In the case of China, furthermore, does not accept factions within the Party ('Party Regulation' Article 3). Not accepting factions means that the Party is the only body to include and enjoy benefit from various social profits. Conflicts over benefits and policy arguments are all 'Internal Party Disputes'. [7] In order to maintain a firm party autocracy holding such internal inconsistency within, a 'high level concentration', a organization principle of 'democratic concentration' ('Party Regulation' Article 19) becomes necessary. Also inevitable is an individual in the position to enforce integrated command for 'concentrated' policy decisions, and his 'charismatic' features with absolute rightness.

The 'charismatic' leader of the Communist Party is created for this end. As Deng Xiaoping stated that it is 'necessary to intentionally support one leading core' as referred earlier, this reflects that the charismatic leader of the Communist Party is not always found in the normal party practices. Mao Zedong created a charismatic character, however, that was not the case for Deng Xiaoping. Even in situations where people were forced for strong obedience, they would not consider Deng Xiaoping as an authority of absolute rightness. His power and influence level was quite limited compared to that of Mao Zedong. When it comes to Jiang Zemin; he had no charismatic features at all. The term 'charismatic' was put in parenthesis for the above reasons that the charisma of the Chinese Communist Party is merely a creation.

A 'charismatic' leader is required at the local level as well. The local Party Committee Secretary usually plays the role of a leader. The reasons why they also needed a 'charismatic' leader is that it was inevitable to have an authority to symbolize absolute rightness in party internal disputes as referred in above (c). It was also important to materialize 'the Party's absolute leadership rules' at the local level. According to Xu Jiatun, former Jiangsu Province Party Committee First Secretary and also former Hong Kong Macao Work Committee Secretary, policy making at local Party Committees is not by vote, but is rather a consensus of the Party Committee Secretary (from the author's interview to Xu Jiatun, May 22, 1996, ZHAO Hongwei, 1997, pages 16).

It must be pointed out here that the Communist Party's leadership structure with a 'charismatic' leader as a core, was not a structure that would assure 'sustainability of the Party's leadership' as Deng Xiaoping had hoped. It often caused political crisis. Maintaining 'sustainability of the party's leadership' with a 'charismatic' leader as a leading core is based on the assumption that there is no inconsistency among the leaders and that the 'charismatic' leader is absolutely infallible: which is clearly an assumption that cannot be achieved.

In the Communist Party history, when the 'charismatic' leader's policy decision turned out to be misdirection, or when an argument over a policy should occur, situations would always result in power struggles. To reveal or correct an error of the 'charismatic' leader would cause to question the charismatic abilities and legitimacy of the leader's power itself. Therefore, party leaders who oppose to the views of the 'charismatic' leader is likely to be accused for 'opposing to the Party' or 'disunited the Party' and made situations difficult to seek common grounds.

Political crisis of the Communist Party has actually occurred on a periodic basis. Mao Zedong himself had mentioned that internal struggles within the Communist Party had occurred 'once every seven to eight years'.[8] During the years of Deng Xiaoping, in eleven years until 1989, three major internal struggles occurred involving the downfall of Secretary Zhao Ziyang, Party President Hua Guofeng and Secretary Hu Yaobang. As described above, the 'charismatic' highest leader of the Communist Party Central is one of the prime actors in China's modern political regimes. In the central-level, he is the core of power concentration; he also performs direct leadership to the local level on a supra-organization basis.

(3) Communism Ideology as an element of the Political Regime

The role of communism ideology has always been an important research subject among scholars. There were two ways of viewing this: either to view ideology as an element of the political regime, or to consider it as an element of the political movements. Kazuko Mouri's definitions in '*Mobility Type of Political Regime*' (Mouri 1990, page 5) is an example of the preceding view, and Shrum's 'China's Ideology and Policies in the Reforms' (Shrum, Yabuki *transl.* 1987) is the latter. A research which includes both views is F. Schurmann's *Ideology and Organization in Communist China* (Schurmann 1968) and J.R.

Townsend's analysis in Chapter 4 '*Communist System – Change and Ideology*' of '*Modern China: Comparative Analysis of Political System*' (Townsend 1974). Based on these research results, and in particular from the definition made by J. Townsend, 'Ideology as a source of integration and confrontation' (Townsend, pages 183-200), I would like to assess communism ideology in a political regime.

First of all, communism ideology is 'the source of integration' within the Communist Party. As Rowenthal indicated, communism ideology is 'a thought and faith that supports the political regime'. Whether or not 'refined systematic ideology possessed by the avant-garde party' is an index to distinguish a communists' political regime from others, in particular, the political regimes of a 'revolutionary ethnicism state' which also flags socialism. (*ibid*)

Communism ideology provides legitimacy to the Communist Party's organization structure. The authority of the Party Central to lead local Party Committees, and the authority of the higher Party Committees to lead lower Party Committees considers communism ideology as its primary source. (p184) Since the Party Central and the higher Party Committees 'follow Marx-Leninism, Maoism, Deng Xiaoping theory as their discipline' (Party Regulation Introduction) and interpret their ideology to the local level, their leadership is supposed to be in absolute rightness.

In regards to the relationship between a 'charismatic leader' who is at the top of the Communist Party organization structure and communism ideology, the following two findings can be emphasized. The first is that communism ideology provides legitimacy to 'charismatic' leader's leadership. And the second point is that existence of the 'charismatic' leader enables communism ideology to exist. Further to the second point, while communism ideology is determined as the only legitimate ideology in the world, 'it only provides a broad systematic framework for long-term goal setting, and does not provide all solutions to important policy issues that a leader must deal with. Moreover, the basic doctrines demand that all such decisions must be made in order to maintain legitimacy and integration of the system' (Townsend *ibid* page 185).

Therefore a 'charismatic' leader who has the ability to materialize the ideology and at the same time make absolutely right decisions is required. Therefore a 'refined systematic ideology possessed by the avant-garde party ' is the source of 'charismatic' communist party leader, and at the same time its existence is secured by the 'charismatic' leader. The communism ideology is also 'the source of conflicts' inside the Communist Party. Since communism ideology which 'cannot force everycne to agree with all issues' and 'political conflicts could always give rise to disputes and changes at the ideology level', could result in intra-party conflicts and political changes *(ibid)*. Therefore, communism ideology is the 'source for both integration and confrontation' of the Communist Party, which could be elements of both political regime and political change.

Communism Ideology during Deng Xiaoping's era was proposed by Deng Xiaoping himself. (Deng Xiaoping1983, page 234) It is summarized in the so-called 'Four Principles' also included in the 'Chinese Constitution' (1982); 'Maintenance of the Communist Party leadership, maintenance of Marx-Leninism and Maoism, maintenance of proletariat autocracy, and maintenance of socialism principles'. Judging from the 'Four principles', ideology has not changed in Deng Xiaoping's period compared to the previous period. However, its position in the political regime saw changes.

Deng Xiaoping set the Communist Party's 'standards' to be 'one Center and two fundamental points': 'economy construction' as the Center, 'four principles' and 'reform and open-up' as the two fundamental points. (Communist China Central Research Institute 1986, II pages 1450-1451) 'Economy Building' has become the 'principal issue', replacing communism ideology that 'is supposed to be situated in the Center of the political regime' (Townsend *ibid*, *transl.* page 185). It suggests a decline in the position of communism ideology within the political regime.

These changes have occurred in line with drop in functions of communism ideology that is supposed to provide legitimacy to the political regime. The Communist Party had to bring 'economy construction' as the source of legitimacy because communism ideology could no longer provide enough legitimacy to the political regime. With the decline in functions of communism ideology's 'role to provide legitimacy', the 'charismatic' features of the Communist Party leader weakened. It meant a decline in effectiveness of direct leadership performed by the highest leader whose grounds were on legitimacy of the communism ideology, a decline in the highest authority of the party Secretary to various levels of the Party Committee, and the political mobilization power where 'enlightenment' to the party members and citizens were compulsory.

(4) Internal Party Monitoring Structures

There is a rule in the 'Communist Party Regulation' which refers to the election structures of the Communist Party that 'The Party's various level leader positions are decided by elections'. However, there are no specific 'Party Rules on Election' but only few related statements in the 'Communist Party Regulation'. They are summarized as follows. The quorum and election methods to elect representatives for the National Congress of the Communist Party is decided by the Central Committee, and the quorum and election methods to elect representatives for local level congress is decided by the equivalent level Party Committee with authorization from a one higher-level Party Committee.

Each local level congress elects a representative who attends one higher-level congress. The party organization and electorates should discuss and prepare sufficiently before making the list of candidates for the election. Each local level Committee elects their Standing Committee members, their secretaries and Deputy secretaries, all whom require authorization from one higher-level Party Committee. One higher-level party leaders are able to, if necessary, and if their own congress is closed, appoint leaders of a lower-level party. These rules on party elections reveal the following characteristics of the Communist Intra-Party election structures.

Representatives of township-village enterprises and end-organizations of the Communist Party are directly elected by party members. Representatives of any party organizations above this are elected by the party congress from a lower level. This system indicates that representatives for the National Congress are elected through seven indirect elections in total, four indirect elections in the township, prefecture, city, and province. Then five elections through the Central Committee, then the Politburo of the Central Committee, finally Politburo Standing Committee makes the highest leader of the Communist Party finally elected. These multiplex-indirect elections have made the party leaders distant from end-members, and have made the elections appear as opportunities for the lower-level organizations' to show their loyalties to the superior organizations. It has thus weakened the check-and-balance function that an election system is supposed to have.

There is only one phrase in the 'Communist Party Regulation' that prescribes the nomination of candidates for intra-party elections. It is only referred as 'The party organization and electorates should discuss and prepare sufficiently before making the list of candidates.' According to the regulation, a list of candidates is presented from the party leaders, then 'sufficient discussions and preparations' are to be made on the list, and finally the party leaders are supposed to finalize the candidates. Major candidates, however, are leaders of the party themselves; which means that discussions and preparations by 'the party organization (party leaders) and electorates' are actually done by 'candidates and electorates'. Since the 'preparation and discussion' is the actual election maneuver process, those who have managed to pass through this process have a good chance of being elected. The voting process was merely formalization to a great extent. However, the majority of representatives who attend these party congresses are regionally organized delegations. Leaders of these delegations are key players of the election maneuver process, and therefore are influential positions.

As the candidate requires approval from one higher-level after the election, the candidate needs to receive consent from the higher-level leaders before running for the election. Furthermore, one higher-level party leaders have the authority to appoint lower-level party leaders at any time, without any election process. This means that while leaders of each party levels are supposed to be elected by votes according to the regulation, they are in reality, appointed from superiors. Because of the Communist Party's multiplex indirect election structure, one higher-level party congress representatives are elected from one lower-level congress representatives. This also means that leaders of one lower-level attend one higher-level congress meetings that elect leaders of one higher-level. Consequently, the Communist Party's election has a 'mutual election' structure, where one higher-level leaders appoint one lower-level leaders who in return votes for them at elections.

From the analysis above, the election structures of the Communist Party is not democratic as emphasized in the 'Communist Party Regulation'. It is merely a ''top-to-bottom hierarchic centralization of power in personnel matters, and does not have the least function to monitor the highest leaders. The organization to supervise the Party's orders is the 'Committee of Discipline'. Its organization structure is as follows: ('Party Regulation' Articles 43, 44,45) Each Committees of Discipline is elected at Party Congress meetings of various levels, and the Standing Committee, Secretary and Deputy Secretary is elected at the Committee of Discipline General Meetings respectively. The elected Standing Committee members, Secretary and Deputy Secretary requires approval from the same-level Party Committee, then approval from one higher-level Party Committee, and finally the election is confirmed. The position of the Secretary is usually occupied by a Standing Committee member of the same-level.

The Communist Party Central Committee of Discipline pursues its activities under leadership of the Party Central Committee. The local level Committee of Discipline functions under dual leadership of the same-level Party Committee and one higher-level Committee of Discipline. Their duties are to inspect that the Party Regulations are in effect. The Party Regulation does not have a prescription on the independency of the Committee of Discipline's inspection authorities.

As stated above, organization structures of the Committee of Discipline suggests that the Committee did not have any independent authority in personnel matters nor inspections. Also, while 'dual leadership' is supposed to be applied to the Committee of Discipline, both leadership and personnel authorities lie in the hands of the same-level Party Committee. This means that the Committee of Discipline primarily shows its loyalty is the Party Committee, and such structure makes it impossible for the Committee of Discipline to inspect their subject of loyalty. I can conclude that inspection capacities of the Committee of Discipline are very limited.

External Relationships of the Communist Party

What is referred to by external relationship here is the relationship between the Communist Party and other actors. In this section I would like to review the relationship between the Communist Party and 'national' actors (referring to the analysis in Chapter 1). The 'Chinese Constitution (1982)' defined to 'maintain leadership of the Communist Party covering all race groups and citizens of China'. On the other hand, it defined 'legitimacy' of the law that 'all national institutions, armed forces, political parties, social institutions and corporations must observe the Constitution and the law. Any institution or individual should not be privileged over the Constitution and the Law' (Constitution Article 5). There is also an article in the 'Party Regulation' that 'the Party's activities must be within the range of the Constitution and the Law'. These articles explain that the relationship between the Communist Party and the 'national' political actors is that the Party leads the state within the range of the Constitution and the

Chart 3-3: Structure of State of Multilayered Centralized Regime in China

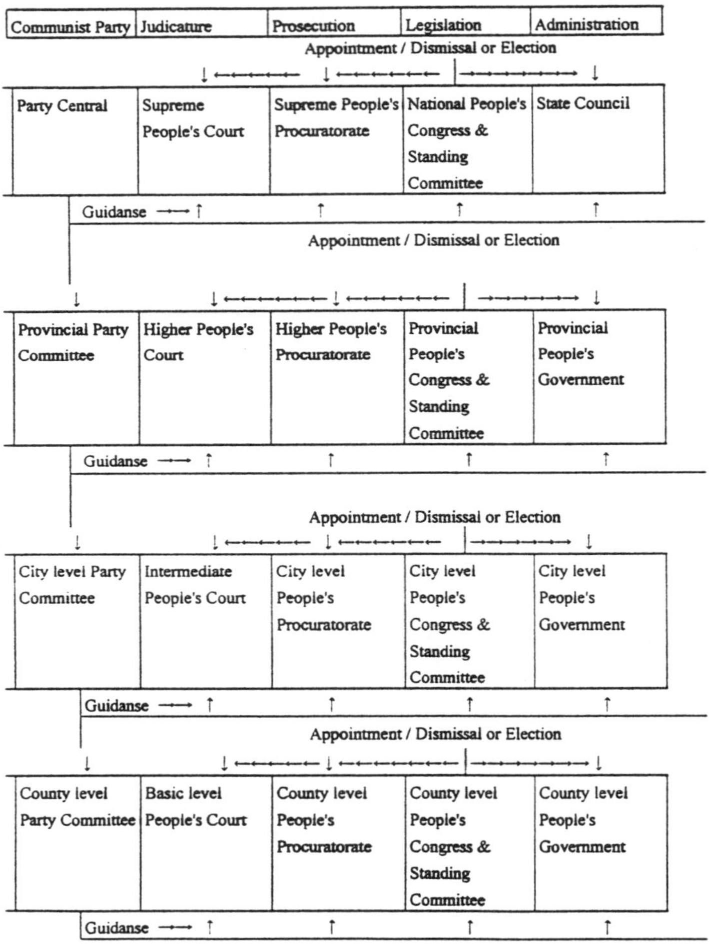

Source: Drawn by the Author.

What is, then, the relationship between the Communist Party and the state's 'Those who lead' and 'Those who are lead'? According to the 'Communist Party Regulation', it is a relationship of 'those who lead' and 'those who are lead' 'mainly in the areas of politics, organizations, and thoughts' (Party Regulation Introduction). The followings will examine the contents of political leadership, organizational leadership and thought directions by the Communist Party and the State.

Political Leadership

Actual structures of the Party's leadership toward the State could be seen in the 'Responsibility Sharing Institutions' of various level leaders. The 'Responsibility Sharing Institution' is what enables authority in state institutions such as legislature, administration and justice among the Communist Party leaders.[9] Since 'Responsibility Sharing' is usually distributed in accordance with the seniority of the party leaders, it reveals the order of importance of these national institutions within the Communist Party. Therefore, by analyzing the 'Responsibility Sharing Institution' in the Communist Party leadership, it becomes possible to find clues for recognizing the relationship between the Communist Party and the 'National' actors. First of all, I would like to focus on the relationship between the Party and Legislative body. Usually in a parliament system, political leadership is displayed by ruling party parliament members; a system not adopted by the Communist Party.

In other countries, parliament members of the legislative body are politicians of the country as well as Actors of the party who are in positions to control the party. And since the party is under control of elected parliament members, they are responsible for and controlled by the voters through elections. The People's Representatives Standing Committee members (parliament members) of the Communist Party, on the other hand, are in a much lower position within the party. Most of them are not Committee members of the Party Central or the local committees who have policy-making authorities to control the Party. Therefore, a majority of various-level legislative body parliament members cannot take part in the policy-making process of each party leadership. They are only liable to executing policy decisions made by the party leaders.

In regards to the relationship between the Party and the administrative body, according to the 'Responsibility Sharing Institution' of the Communist Party leadership, most of the Standing Committee members of various-level Committees have administrative duties besides party duties. And the head of an administrative body is in a number two position within various-level party leadership. This explains that administrative body members hold a higher position within the Party compared to legislative and judicial body members. The power relationship between the Communist Party and the administrative body is not just execution of policy decisions. Since major administrative body leaders are at the same time important party leaders, they are able to participate in the policy-making process and the two are always in one in the policy-making and execution process. For example, their close relationship could often be seen in an official document called 'Party Central/State Council Decisions'. In order to characterize the relationships between the Communist Party and the administrative body, I would like to adopt the concept of 'integration'. I believe this 'integrated organization' is equivalent to the various-class Standing Committees of the Communist Party.

Furthermore, while reviewing 'Responsibility Sharing Institution' of the Communist Party leadership, it became clear that there is always one Standing Committee member in the Communist Party various-level Committee who leads judicial administration. For example, Politburo Standing Committee member Qiao Shi, used to be a specialized leader in judicial matters. His jurisdiction range covered all areas of the judicial and inspection; Supreme Court, Criminal Investigation Authority, administrative inspection organizations such as Public Safety Ministry, National Defense Ministry, Inspection Ministry, and intra-party inspection organization such as Committee of Discipline. ('Chinese Who's Who' 1994, pages 502-504) Currently as of 1998, Communist Party Politburo Standing Committee member Wei Jianxing is in this position.

Since each-level Party Committee takes control of all same-level power organizations relating to judiciary and discipline, the Party Committee itself is not inspected in its own jurisdiction. This is a structure that breeds corruption. Only when a corruption case is revealed for some reason, the local-level leader may be inspected by a higher-level Party Committee member. Even in such case, the leader will first be examined by the 'intra-party examination' of the Committee of Discipline, and then the Party Committee will decide whether the disposal should be an intra-party disposal or an administrative disposal, or otherwise sent further to a judicial process. The 'Five Major Corporation' inspection case, referred to in Chapter One, was ordered for inspection by the Sate Council after decision by the Party Central. A more typical example is the corruption case of

Chen Xitong, Secretary of Beijing City Communist Party. (Sasaki, 1996, 1997, page 38) His corruption became public in May 1995, was put under an intra-party 'isolated investigation (restrained investigation)' until September 1997, and finally the Party Central decided to pursue his 'criminal liability' (Nakai 1998, page 8, 'People's Daily' September 10, 1997). These facts reveal another nature of the 'political leadership' by the Communist Party. 'Political leadership' is exercised not only in the area of politics, but rather in all reigns of national power, through 'responsibility sharing institution' in legislature, judiciary and administrative bodies. Scholars regarded this as a characteristic of politics in China, namely 'vicarism by the Party'.

In order to pursue such 'political leadership', a 'national business operation organization' was established under the Party Central and various-level Party Committees (chart 3-4). Politburo Standing Committee member Qiao Shi was at the time 'Chinese Communist Party Central Political and Judicial Committee' Secretary, and managers of various departments such as the Committee of Discipline were members of the Political and Judicial Committee. Qiao Shi acted as leader in all areas of the judiciary and discipline through the Political and Judicial Committee.

Xu Jiatun, is currently a political refugee in the U.S. and ex-Chinese Communist Party Hong Kong and Macao Work Committee Secretary. In his memoir, by presenting numerous evidences, he refers to the works of 'Chinese Communist Party Central Foreign Affairs Leading Group', a superior leadership organization in Hong Kong works. (Xu Jiatun, [*transl.* Aoki] 1996, Volume I, pages 19-21, 53-69, 248, Volume II page 290) During most of the years of his office in Hong Kong, (1983-1990), the head of the Foreign Affairs Leading Group was President Li Xiannian, and the Deputy head was the State Council Premier Zhao Ziyang.

The functions of the Foreign Affairs Leading Group are to demonstrate unitary leadership to Foreign Affairs related departments of the Party and the State. The State Council established the 'Foreign Affairs Office' as the Group's operational organization. The duties of the Foreign Affairs Leading Group are to lead and coordinate all foreign affairs related organizations and businesses, such as the Party's Foreign Correspondence Group, Foreign Ministry, State Economy and Trade Commission, Foreign Culture, Hong Kong and Macao Works, Foreign Affairs of the Military Forces. The Foreign Affairs Leading Group and the State Council Foreign Affairs Office is usually called the

'Foreign Room' (Management of Foreign Matters).[11]

Chart 3-4: Chinese Communist Party Central Committee Organization Chart (1998)

The Politburo of the Chinese Communist Party
The Secretariat of the Chinese Communist Party

↓ → → → ↓

National Business Operation Organizations
Central Finance Works Leading Group Central System Organization Committee Central Monetary Works Committee Central National Enterprise Works Committee Central Advertising and Thought Works Leading Group Central External Advertising Group Central Works Leading Group for Taiwan Central Hong Kong and Macao Works Leading Group Central Foreign Affairs Works Leading Group Central Farming Works Leading Group Central State Organization Works Committee Central Political and Judicial Committee Central Social Security General Committee Central Public Health Committee Central Tibet Works Cooperative Group

↓ → → → → → → → → → → → ↓

Party Leading Organization	Party Business Organization
Central Administration Office Central Organization Department Central Advertising Department Central Tong Zhan Department Central External Communication Department Central Policy Research Office	Central Party School Central Archive Research Office Central Party History Research Office Central Edit and Translation Bureau Central Dang An Guan People' Daily News Qiu Shi Publishing Etc.

Source: Compiled by Author based on China Research Institute *ed. 'China Almanac 1997 Edition'* 1997 page 232. 'Asahi Shimbun' December 12, 1997
Note: Besides the 'National Business Operations Organization' as written above, other organizations inclusive in the category of 'Party Affairs Organizations' are 'Central Confidential Committee', 'Central Party Construction Works Leading Group', 'Central Party History Works Leading Group', and 'Central Direct Organization Works Committee'.

The appointment of Xu Jiatun to the Hong Kong Works position was confirmed when Li Xiannian passed approval to the Politburo Standing Committee. Upon such policy decisions and executions, Xu Jiatun always reported first to the Foreign Affairs Leading Group to ask for its leadership, but waited for official approval from the Politburo before executing the new policy. While the Foreign Affairs Leading

Group did not possess authority on personnel and the policy making process, it was key in the policy planning process and therefore demonstrated great influence.

Not only have the Responsibility Sharing Institutions materialized the horizontal Centralization of power to various-level Party Committees, it also connotes following mechanisms. In Chapter 1 I indicated that the National People's Congress and People's Council have become to function more like an administrative body, and such functions connotes a mechanism that has impact to other power organizations. The Responsibility Sharing Institutions allocates the Party Committee Standing Committee to become heads of the three bodies. However, since they are on top of both the administrative body and the institutionalized National People's Congress and People's Council, they tend to possess more knowledge and information in the respective areas, and as a result became most influential.

State organizations in China have been the power base of these Party Committee Standing Committee members, and they have displayed their impacts through these organizations. These impacts, however, are not results of independence-of-power structures, but more secondary; as a result of horizontal power structures made by various-level Party Committees. We have seen from above that the Communists Party is centralizing its power to various state organizations through Responsibility Sharing Institutions, the party's 'State Business Operations Organization' and other party organizations.

Organizational Leadership

In China, the political term 'organizational leadership' means 'personnel management'. The Communist Party has its internal regulations aside from the state law, based on which personnel matters of state organizations are controlled. In 1979, the National People's Congress adopted 'Law on Local People's Congress and State Organizations', 'Law on Elections', and 'Law on Organizations' of the People's Law/Inspection Council. These Laws regulated appointments and dismissals of personnel related to these organizations. By 1980, however, the Communist Party Central Organization had already released a 'Notice to address several issues upon executing "Organization Chart of Senior Positions managed by Communist Party Central" (Tanaka 'China Research Institute' *ed.*, 1988, pages 461-462).

This 'Notice' specified the requirement to seek judgment and approval from various-level party leaders in appointment and dismissal of a state organization executive. Procedures to address and dismiss state organization executives were determined by the party leadership, aside from the Law on Elections and Law on Organizations. 'Organization Chart of Senior Positions managed by Communist Party Central' was revised twice, in 1984 and 1990, and it was determined that the Communist Party Central will appoint one lower-level leaders, of both the party and state. The 'Notice' was revised as 'Notice of 1982', and again in 1995 and was proclaimed from the Party Central as 'Provisional Regulation on Appointment Works of The Party Leaders'.[12]

On the following is a case of an appointment and dismissal procedure of provincial state organization senior personnel. A provincial level party leader is either a provincial Party Committee Standing Committee member, a Deputy Secretary or a Secretary. A provincial level state leader is either a state level People's Congress Standing Committee chief or the Deputy chief, Premier or Deputy Premier of Political and Commercial Cooperation Conference, Province Chief or Deputy Chief, Premier of Province Supreme People's Judiciary Council, Premier of Province People's Inspection Council, or others of related levels. According to the Law, appointment and dismissal of provincial-level state leaders is under authority of the same-level Representatives of the People's Conference or its Standing Committee. However, according to 'Provisional Regulation' mentioned above, these personnel matters should be a joint effort of the Communist Party Central Committee and the Provincial level Party Committee, in the order of recommendation, evaluation, hearing, votes by the Party Central, and then election or appointment at provincial level Representatives of the People's Conference or it Standing Committee. Appointments and dismissals of lower-level provincial and state leaders will proceed accordingly with same-level administration.

As seen from the above, the Communist Party Committees of all levels held control over personnel related authorities of all state organizations including the three bodies through its internal party regulation that surpass the Constitution and the Law. The Communist Party called this structure 'Party controlled leaders' (the party is in control of the leaders) and defined this as 'Organization Principle of the Party' (Chukyo Chuo 1995). Needless to say, it is centralization of power that appointment and dismissal of a state leader is under control of the Communist Party. This is a very strong basis for supporting the theory of 'Centralization in China'. Before jumping to conclusion, however, we should review an actual process of personnel appointment and dismissal.

If you would like to promote a leader to provincial-level, monopolizing information on the concerned leader becomes the key basis of making decisions. Since the Party Central does not have its own inspection organization at local levels, 'information' is usually controlled at the same-level Party Committee at which the candidate leader belongs. As proceedings show, the province level Party Committee is involved in most of the processes, recommendation, evaluation, and opinion hearing, besides 'votes by the Party Central'. It is clear that those who control information; the province level Party Committee, have a very strong influence on personnel appointment and dismissal process.

Xu Jiatun's memoir has, for the first time, revealed a live case of a leader's enigmatic appointment process in the Communist Party. (Xu Jiatun, *ibid*, Volume I pages 3-16, 74-87, 240-263) For example, in 1983, when at the time Xu Jiatun was First Secretary in Jiangsu's Province Party, his treatment was being discussed within the Party Central that he was already over retirement age for a province level leader. During spring of the same year, Deng Xiaoping and his family visited Jiangsu Province on vacation. Xu Jiatun tour-guided them throughout their stay, and explained to Deng Xiaoping in details about his accomplishments in Jiangsu. After his return to Beijing, Deng Xiaoping highly praised Xu Jiantun in an 'A Talk in Beijing After Seeing Jiangsu' (Deng Xiaoping1993), and proposed that Xu Jiatun should remain in office. However, a few 'Old Leaders' of Jiangsu Province who were political opponents of Xu Jiatun deliberately circulated rumors unfavorable to him and maneuvered opposing activities. As a result, Xu Jiatun could not remain in the post, but not for retirement. It resulted in a compromising solution to appoint him in the same-level, highest level leader of the Communist Party resident in Hong Kong. We can assume here that province level leaders such as Xu Jiatun and opposing 'Old Leaders' both demonstrated great influence on personnel appointment and dismissal matters by possessing important information.

As former Secretary of Jiangsu Province, Xu Jiatun utilized his full knowledge about Jiangsu Province leaders. He took part in the Party Central group who were discussing personnel matters to decide successors of Jiangsu Province, and his opinions swayed the appointment of new leaders to a great extent. Also, during Xu Jiatun's assignment in Hong Kong, he chose to reform the Hong Kong and Macao Work Committee on two occasions. These processes explain that Party Secretaries had the discretion to decide personnel matters of his Party Committee members to a great extent.

We can also see from China's Central-locality political relationship that behavior of province level leaders are influenced by the Province's interests, despite 'personnel decisions' on appointment. For example, Beijing Mayor Lin Hujia was dismissed from his position when he opposed to the Party Central's directions to draw back from investing in Beijing. Lin Hujia was formerly a State Planning Committee Deputy Chief, then landed to the position of Shanghai Municipality Party Secretary, and in October 1978 he was appointed to Tianjin Municipality First Party Secretary; four months later he was then appointed Mayor of Beijing (Kokubun 1992, pages 80-90). Furthermore, Beijing Municipality Party Secretary Chen Xitong who was overthrown for corruption as mentioned earlier, was assigned as successor to Lin Hujia and became Deputy Mayor, then Mayor, and afterwards became Party Secretary.

The other reason why Lin Hujia was dismissed, was because he intensely opposed against the Party Central in order to protect the interests of Beijing City (Sasaki 1997). In Chapter I, I have indicated the tendency of local leaderships appearing more like interest groups; which can be described as one basic axis of what influences the activities of local leaderships. While authorities to appoint and dismiss province level leaders are in the hands of the Party Central, these appointments are not influential enough to change the current political, economic, and social structures in the local leadership who are becoming more interest-oriented. The newly appointed leaders too, have been absorbed into the interest groups.

Thought Directions

Thought directions of the Communist Party, namely control over thoughts, have been conducted through control over communication means. More specifically, two attempts have been made; one was the Communist Party's control over mass media, and the second was control over communication means by party organizations. Among numerous political science studies on modern Chinese communication we have seen, the following two; Alan P.L. Liu's studies of the Mao

Zedong era, and Masaharu Hishida's studies, which cover up to Deng Xiaoping's era, are a broad collection of research results. Based on these studies, I would like to focus on two characteristics; 'rank structures' in the Communist Party's control over mass media, and 'Small Group Drive in the party organization's control over communication (Chart 3-5).

Chart 3-5: Structures of the Chinese Mass Communication Business

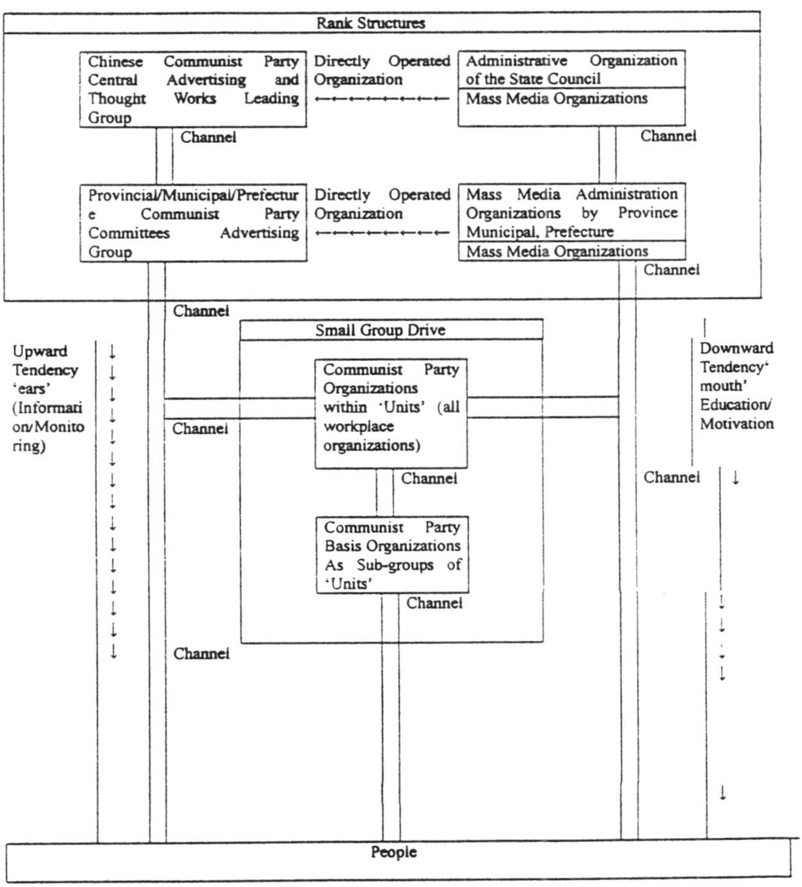

Source: Written by Author based on Masaharu Hishida '*Mass Media Institutions in China*' Chart 2, Kazuko Mouri, '*Modern China I China in Mao Zedong's Era*' Japan International Research Institute, 1990, p.303

First, we will examine 'rank structures' in mass media. 'Responsibility Sharing Institutions' established Standing Committees at each-level Party Committees to be in charge of advertising. Their duties were to lead mass media in general. From 1989 to 1992, for instance, Politburo Standing Committee member Li Ruihuan was in charge for Communist Party Central. Li established two organizations to control mass media: a state operation organization 'Party Central Advertising and Thought Works Leading Group' and Party Central Advertising Group which is a 'party leading organization' (Chart 3-4). There were also State mass media administrative organizations such as Ministry of Culture, Ministry of Radio/Television/Movies, and Bureau of News Publishing. These organizations are separate administrations, however, in fact, and his two organizations, Party Central Advertising and Thought Works Leading Group, and Party Central Advertising Group lead these ministries and displayed integrated control over mass media policy decisions, monitoring authorities and personnel matters.

As Masaharu Hishida indicated, 'A mass communication function group organization established for the purpose of sending information to the unspecified majority is combined into the ranking structure of the power system.' (Hishida [*ed.* Mouri] 1990, page 304), the characteristics I believe to be even more important. The mass media control structure adopted by the Party's Advertisement Standing Committee is 'not only in Central organizations, but is the same in local organizations.' Liu refers to this as 'ranking structure' in mass media control. By using the concept defined in this paper, these 'ranking structures' are called multi-layered control structures over mass media, with party leaders of each administrative level placed in the Center. Such multi-layered control structures of the Communist Party were influential to the functions of mass media in the following sense. The Communist Party prescribes that mass media has two roles: 'The Party's mouth and ears' which means 'propaganda education and opinion hearing'(Chart 3-5). However the actual functions of mass media show a 'downward tendency' as the Party's 'mouth'.

As for the role of 'ears', there are private newspapers[14] in China called 'internal references', in addition to public newspapers. Private newspapers bear the role of delivering to the leaders 'truth in society' and revealing 'injustice by state officials', news that will be unfavorable to the image of the Communist Party. They should play the role of 'ears' to listen to public opinions and deliver information.

However, because of the Party's multi-layered control over mass media, various mass media organizations are not able to deliver the truth, and watch over regional party leaders who are their superiors, and the officials who work for them.

'Small Group Drive' in communication control should be examined next. According to Masaharu Hishida's statements, a 'small group drive' is a role that the Communist Party's 'basis organizations' (Small groups) should play, as mediators of mass communication in China (Hishida *ibid*, page 323). Roles of the Party's basis organizations characterize control in modern China that 'it does not seem to be the same as dictatorships by Hitler or Stalin. It relies much more heavily on mental pressures such as enlightenment and persuasion, or close personal supervision by leaders, rather than police terrorism. (Townsend, *ibid*, page 16) ' 'Communist Party Regulations' prescribe that 'the Party's basis organizations are the Party's battle fort against basis organizations in society.'

As seen above, unlike the Centralized secret police system and mass arrests by secret police in former Soviet Union, in China control forms and supervision over party members and citizens are up to respective basis party organizations. These forms, consequently, resulted in increasing power of the party organization leadership. While arrest conducted by police is at least a universal standard conduct by Law, criteria of supervision by the party organization leaders vary by individuals. Therefore, those who are supervised are obliged to subordinate to the leader personally, rather than to the Law.

The 'ranking structures' in mass media control, and 'Small Group Drive' in communication control both encouraged regionalism and 'small group orientation'; they were clearly negative factors for mass communication organizations who tried to service its purpose of integrating the society at state citizen levels.

Vertical Power Systems

From preceding analysis, it has become clear that horizontal power Centralization structure between the state and the Communist Party is one characteristic of China. What are, then, the vertical power systems between various administrative bodies in China? How should the relationships between vertical power system and horizontal power system be interpreted?

Vertical Monolithic Leading Structures Built by the Party

When we speak of hierarchic power relationship between Central, local, and basis, we are usually referring to the leader-executor relationship and vertical information flow process. When we look at the 'hierarchic relationship between the leader and executor' in the political institutions of modern China, we could see that the Communist Party Centralized its local power in all legislative, administrative, judicial bodies to various local level Party Committees, and developed a horizontal monolithic leading structure. They have also Centralized its power in the vertical sense, from the basis to local and then to Central along the vertical structures of various level Party Committees, and developed a vertical monolithic leading structure. The Communist Party's objective was to establish a political institution that was 'a strong Centralization of power in both vertical and horizontal structures'. I indicated earlier in Chapter Two that in referring to political terms, they call such leadership structures 'monolithic leading institution by the Party'.

The 'monolithic leading institution by the Party', however, made the state organizations' Central, local, and fundamental hierarchic relationships rather secondary. In the actual policy process, when lower-level state organizations receive assignments from a higher-level state organization, they would first report and execute the assignment upon approval from the same level Party Committee. Or otherwise, assignments would likely come directly from higher-level Party Committee, or a joint assignment (as referred earlier as 'party Central and State Council') from both higher-level Party Committee and state organization in the form of an official document, would be passed down to the lower-level Party Committee and then would be put into practice. The hierarchy relationships among various level state organizations are not so direct as a leader and an executor relationship, but rather 'organizations connected in daily business processes in order to execute policies' under leadership of various-level Party Committees. The purpose of the vertical monolithic leading structures is to integrate all hierarchy relationships of the state organizations into the hierarchy relationships of various-level Party Committees. Therefore, the hierarchy relationship between the leader and the executor exists only within various-level Party Committees.

Next, we shall examine hierarchy relationships of power in the context of information communication. In many countries, providing information from lower-level organizations to higher-level is processed in line with hierarchy relationships and by business of the state organization. Therefore it becomes important for the local government and its various departments to provide accurate information to the Central government and various ministries. In addition, Central power organizations use various inspection and audit organizations that are independent from local power organizations, pluralize information sources and audit the credibility of information. The system is legally the same in China. In reality, however, various-level local Party Committees monolithically control all same-level state organizations including inspection and audit organizations under the party's vertical monolithic leading structures.

The Communist Party Central and various Central state organizations do not have independent inspection and audit organizations on a local basis, and do not have the measures to collect information through their own source. Therefore, the Communist Party Central and various Central state organizations must rely on information provided from the local organizations. In addition, as various state organizations at the local level are placed under leadership of the local Party Committees, they must first provide important local information to the local Party Committee, and only upon approval they can send the information to various Central state organizations. Similar to the hierarchy relationship of the leader and executor, hierarchy relationship in information communication is also monolithically integrated into the hierarchy relationships of various level Party Committees.

How are these vertical monolithic leading structures of the party meaningful to the political regime of China? First of all, in the context of leader-and-executer hierarchy relationship, orders from the Communist Party Central and various Central state organizations must first be approved by local various-level Party Committees, then goes to process under their leadership. This system secures and strengthens Centralization of power on a horizontal basis for various-level Party Committees.

Secondly, in a usual context, a political system begins with entering information, and therefore those who control information gives great influence to the functions of the political system. In China, important local information is delivered to the Communist Party Central and various Central state organizations after it has passed through and approved by the local Party Committees. This means that in passing information from the lower-level to the higher, the lower-level Party Committee has the authority to inspect the information. Information control clearly contributes to the Centralization of power, not in a vertical context, but in horizontal Centralization of power to local Party Committees. In the case of various-level 'Party Committee of Discipline' in preceding studies, for example, conducts discipline inspection under leadership and cooperation from the Party Committee. It is very unlikely that the various-level 'Party Committee of Discipline' should report information to higher-level Party Committees that are unfavorable to the same-level Party Committee. Furthermore, since the local Party Committees possess most of the information, the party Central leadership is obliged to respect their opinions as well in the policy-making process; and thus they have increased their presence.

The Communist Party aimed to establish a political regime called 'monolithic leading institutions by the Party' that is a 'strong vertical and horizontal Centralization of power by the Party'. Vertical monolithic leading structures built by the party, however, gave the local various-level Party Committees the authority to conduct independent policy executions and the authority to control information. As a result of strengthening Centralization of power to local various-level Party Committees on a horizontal basis,
vertical Centralization of power to the Party Central was weakened.

Direct Leading Structures by a 'Charismatic' Highest Leader

In the history of the Chinese Communist Party, there were two 'charismatic' highest leaders, Mao Zedong, and Deng Xiaoping. The two leaders held significant authority to process policies throughout the state at their own discretion. Such policy phenomenon is often considered to be the basis for 'Centralization of Power in China Theory'. However, rather than a power Centralized organization structure, I believe we should consider this as more of a supra-organizational direct leading structure with a 'charismatic' highest leader.

The characteristics of a direct leading structure with a 'charismatic' highest leader are that the leader demonstrates direct leadership beyond the power of existing organizations. Mao Zedong delivered a series of policies in the 1950s such as the 'Socialistic Reform of the Economy', 'Struggle against the Rightist Movement' and 'Grand Leap Forward', by speaking directly with the people through his lectures and papers, and generated a political movement. His strategies were the same during 'The Great Cultural Revolution' in years 1966 through 1976. Mao Zedong generated and lead the public into the direction of 'Critic Movement' and 'Anti-establishment Movement', and used these movements to dismantle existing party organizations and state organizations from the Central to local. Various-level party organizations and state organizations were later rebuilt, however, Mao Zedong rarely utilized these organizations, and relying on his own charismatic attraction instead, he demonstrated direct leadership toward all party and state with his 'analects' and 'highest orders'. The lower-level Party Committees and state organizations subordinating to Mao Zedong during these years, were not reflections of their loyalty toward superior organizations. It was rather loyalty to the charismatic highest leader Mao Zedong himself, with 'all-party follow the Center' ('Party Regulation' Article 10) nature. Even to rebel against high-level Party Committees and state organizations as a proof of loyalty to Mao Zedong was justified.[15]

As seen from above, Mao Zedong did not build a strong power Centralizing organization and apply to use in order to demonstrate his strong leadership. Since Mao Zedong never took any importance in the roles of organization systems, a strong organization system was never built. The reason why the Communist Party Central still maintained its authority, and why de-Centralization did not occur in the localities under such circumstances was because direct leadership by 'charismatic' highest leader was significantly strong. In other words, Mao Zedong's direct leadership supplemented the area where the Central authority institution was not sufficiently secure, and was able to maintain loyalties of the basis and localities toward the Central.

There were no noteworthy reforms in the organization systems in the Deng Xiaoping era after Mao Zedong's; which means 'Centralization of power' was not yet assured. There were, however, changes in the direct leadership structures by the 'charismatic' highest leader. Compared to Mao Zedong, charismatic nature in Deng Xiaoping was not as strong, and therefore loyalties from party organizations, party members and general people diminished. It became difficult for the highest leader to demonstrate direct leadership without going through existing organizations. Deng Xiaoping tended to rely more on organization systems compared to Mao Zedong's direct leadership method, and the above is one of its reasons.

The Deng Xiaoping period could not overcome its weakness at Centralizing power within the organization system. Moreover, direct leadership structures by the 'charismatic' highest leader diminished as well. Therefore, the Center gravity of power within the political regime of modern China further shifted in horizontal directions, to local various-level Party Committees. Incidents were often seen during Deng Xiaoping's era, that local various-level party leaders would not execute assignments sent from Deng Xiaoping, the highest leader. The following is a typical example:

> A direction sent from Deng Xiaoping in 1983, the 'Campaign against Spiritual Pollution' was never put into practice due to strong opposition from the great majority of local province-level leaders (Yang Zhongmei 1989, page 210).

Nonetheless, the highest leader has the authority to take 'forcible measures' to the local leaders and the people. For example, when the '6.4 Tiananmen Square Incident' occurred in 1989, Deng Xiaoping took forcible measures; dismissed Party Secretary Zhao Ziyang and enforced the use of armed forces to repress the public.[16] Such forcible measures are effective crisis management tools to maintain the political regime in crisis, and have threat effects during peacetimes. It appears to have played a role in preventing centrifugal movements of the local leaders and maintained authority of the party Central.

However, as Deng Xiaoping himself had recognized, he was always facing uncertainty with conditions that were 'dangerous' that 'the fate of the party and the nation is in the hands of my own health'. (Yabuki 1990, pages 98) Furthermore, a highest leader would only take forcible measures for a short period of time in crisis, which did not have a strong enough impact to reform an institutionalized power structure. And during longer lasting normal times, the possibility that a highest leader would take forcible measures was very small; therefore it did not have much effect to prevent local and fundamental various-level leaders from becoming autonomous.

Vertical Structures of Profit Sharing Among Leaders

As various-level leaders of the central, local, and fundamental parties are also owners and the management of enterprises, they are motivated by increasing opportunities of their personal benefit. In order to secure their profits, the leaders would seek for mutual benefit between them and their superior leaders, and together established a network of profits sharing involving higher-level ministries and bureaus. Such networks of profit can be seen in the case study made by Yoshinari Kokubun (Kokubun, 1992, Chapter 2). This case introduced in his study was a conflict of interest between Beijing Municipality's 'regionalism' and Communist Party Central Secretariat's 'Urban Economic Construction Plan for the City of Beijing' for the construction project of 'Eastern Chemical Industrial Complex'.

The outline of the case, using the author's approach, is as follows. Aiming for construction, Beijing Municipality leaders and their subordinate Beijing City Chemical Industry Bureau established a profit sharing network with the Ministry of Petrochemical Industries of the State Council who was seeking for development of the petrochemical industry. In order to confront with the Party Center who was against the construction, they vigorously moved the project forward, by even performing illegal financing. While they were facing numerous interference such as receiving 'orders to ban the project' from the Party Center and dismissals of Beijing Mayor Lin Hujia and Vice Minister of Petrochemical Industry Li Guocai, the 'construction' became a known fact; and after a while the Party Center had to permit 'revival' of the construction.

From this case study, we can assume that benefit motivation structures in the superior-inferior leadership is a structure where the local and basis organization various-level leaders generate upward benefit and in return participate in policy decision process, rather than a vertical upward concentration of power. In the case of 'Eastern Chemical Industrial Complex', the profit sharing network established between Beijing Municipality leaders, Beijing City Chemical Industry Bureau and Ministry of Petrochemical Industries, was successful in pulling related ministries of the State Council on the side of the localities. As a result, Beijing Municipality leaders were able to increase their influence to the Center's policy decision processes. Such structures motivated by benefits created a new route for the local and basis various-level leaders to take part in the policy decision processes of the higher and central leaders.

Since the local and basis various-level leaders in China are owners and managements of local corporations, they have motivation for profit, and in a way they are business interest groups. In general, business interest groups take part in politics by lobbying and fund raising. The local and basis various-level leaders in China generally do the same. In most cases, however, the Chinese local and basis various-level leaders used illegal means of lobbying, such as bribery and 'Zou hou men' (back dorr operations). Such activities created a Clientelism relationship, which is a structure that generates mutual benefit among vertically lined leaders. Clientelism relationships were clearly key elements in establishing 'Structures to share business profit' and 'Network of profit sharing'.

Power Network Based on 'Pan' Connections

A power structure exists in China from the center to local, which is a leader-subordinate relationship based on strong 'Pan' connections. The tradition of 'Pan' goes back at least to the beginning of the QING Dynasty. 'Pan' is a tie of personal relationship among leaders of the same origin in hometowns, military service, party organization or state organization. There are numerous publications on 'Pan' and its historical backgrounds, namely 'Highest leaders of China/ Who's Who' 'Information on China/ People Encyclopedia' by Mitsubishi Research Institute and many others. For example, core members of Deng Xiaoping's 'Pan' were those who worked for him in the Second Field Battle Army during civil war. Hu Yaobang was one of them. And Zhao Ziyang, who was First Secretary of Sichuan Province Party Committee, Deng Xiaoping's hometown, was also a member. The principle that brings the power network of 'Pan' together is clientelism, an exchange of power and loyalty.

However, strong 'Pan' based power structures did not strengthen vertical centralization of power. It was because such power based on personal relationships were extralegal privileges, and helped the growth of autonomy and absoluteness power of local and basis various-level leaders. The following is an example:

> Despite repeated notices passed from the Central leaders to 'prohibit import of automobiles' and 'increase investment in agriculture' to local leaders, between the years 1987 to 1988, the Sichuan Province decreased agricultural expenditure to 1.5 billion Yuan, while foreign automobile purchase increased to 2.0 billion Yuan ('People's Daily' March 6, 1989).

There was, however, no press coverage that criticized or demanded penalties toward the Sichuan Province leaders. Moreover,

Province Party Committee Secretary Yang Rudai was promoted to Party Central Politburo Committee member. The reason behind this promotion was, that highest party leader Deng Xiaoping was a Sichuan Province origin, and that Party General Secretary Zhao Ziyang was former Sichuan Province Party Committee First Secretary.

We can find four vertical power systems in the political regime of modern China. However, none of its function was able to weaken the strong horizontal centralization of power. The dual structure of horizontal power centralization and vertical power centralization is not meant to have a function of mutual supplement. They are contradictory, and it is unrealistic to expect the two organizations to balance by equal amount of power, and become 'Strong power centralization in both horizontal and vertical aspects'.

We have found that the significance of a 'charismatic' highest leader and his discretion to use or not use forcible measures, have diminished the centrifugal directions that local various-level leaders were shifting to, due to multi-layered power centralization structures. They were also structural elements that were necessary in avoiding crisis of the political regime. Scholars have repeatedly indicated the instability of post-Deng Xiaoping brought by changes in highest leaders. They have also repeatedly indicated the risks of a political crisis. Deng Xiaoping himself had stressed 'the need to intentionally protect the party's core leader' for 'Sustainability of the Party Leadership'. When re-examined from the precedent lines, the situations appear even clearer.

Conclusion

In this Chapter I have made analysis on the structures of the 'state' and 'political party' that consists the state organization of modern China in the context of political regimes. These analyses confirmed the following. State organizations of modern China such as legislature, administration and judiciary have a horizontal power centralization structure that is multi-layered from central to local and basis administrative levels. These structures are horizontal centralization of power, where legislative bodies are predominant over administrative bodies in a legal sense, but is reverse in the actual power balance. These various-level Party Committees centralized state organization powers horizontally and multi-layered, and established 'multi-layered power centralization regime'.

The multi-layered power centralization mechanisms established by various-level party committees are as follows. First of all, the Party Committee, which is at administrative level of the Communist Party, the only ruling party, takes control over legislative bodies that are in the center of power concentration of all state organizations. While they are legally same-level administrations, the Party Committee takes control over the legislative body. Through its control the Party Committee controls various state organizations in the aspects of politics, organization and thoughts. Besides exercising control through legislative bodies, various-level Party Committees integrated themselves with administrative bodies, which are in substantial positions to lead various state organizations. And through this integration, it monolithically controls all state organizations in the same-level; legislature, administration, and judicial in the authorities of leadership, personnel, inspection and audit. In other words, various-level Party Committees monopolize power and information of same-level administrative bodies as the core of power centralization. They are, in fact, absolute leaders in their areas of jurisdiction.

In China, the legislative, administrative, and judicial organizations embody the state but are not independent actors. By integration of the Communist Party and administrative body, and by the Party's control over legislative and judicial bodies, the terms Communist Party and the State becomes a synonym. The two parties compose a single actor. This actor, however, is not a unified single actor from Central level to local and basis level. Centralized Power of the Communist Party Committee varying to numerous state organizations at various administrative levels demonstrates a plural-divided shape of power

At each administrative level, the Party Committee Standing Committee monopolizes leader positions in legislative, administrative, judiciary state organizations through 'Responsibility Sharing Institutions'. The Party Committee is not only 'A commission for the party organization', but rather 'committee' to control both party organizations and various state organizations. In order to distinguish this with the 'Commission for the party organization' and describe its 'committee' features which both controls the party and the state organizations, the former is called 'Party Committee' and the latter 'Leadership'.

The Party Committee Standing Committee lead both the administrative body and administrative organizations, People's Congress and People's Judiciary Council separately, by 'Responsibility Sharing Institutions. They resulted in monopolizing knowledge and information of the specific field, and thus became the most influential. State organizations demonstrate their influence under horizontal power centralization structures and through Party Committee Standing Committees.

The summary of this section is as follows; actors in the State structures in China are (1) 'The central leadership', (2) 'Local various-level leadership' such as 'Province, self-governing district, direct-managed municipality leadership' and 'City, Prefecture leadership' and (3) 'Township and village leadership' in farming villages and 'leadership in office organizations' in cities, and other 'basis organization leadership'. The actual governing organizations of the preceding are the Party Committee and its Standing Committee which is a monolithic control group consisting of leaders of the Party, administration, legislation, judiciary and major state organizations. In other countries, actors are recognized for vertical organizations or groups such as the State, political party, and interest groups. In the case of China, a multi-layered horizontal structure by central, local, and basis, better explains reality. Also, besides various-level leadership, the 'charismatic' highest leader is another actor. Vertically structured actors such as business and social groups seem to have raised their appearance since reform for market economy started in 1992. They appear to be, however, still secondary to various level leaderships.

Notes

1. In China, subsidies used to compensate for corporate deficit is considered to be one of the expenditures of the State budget. For example, in 1990, 57.888 billion Yuan, and in 1991, 55.672 Yuan respectively were subsidized from the annual expenditures. '*Fiscal Year 1990 State Financial Statements*', '*Fiscal Year 1991 State Budget*', China Research Institute *ed*, '*Annual Almanacs of China 1992*'. Also, Toshio Tajima '*Reform of State Owned Corporations in China and Economic Relations between Governments*' '*China Research Monthly*' China Research Institute, April 1990 page 20.

2. 'Corporate Bankruptcy Law' Articles 7-12, Chinese Daily *FA ZHI RI BAO* December 3, 1986.

3. Chinese scholars in Economics have also indicated that 'Localities (government) also function as basis unit of public ownership' Fan Gang and others '*General Principle of Corporate Ownerships' Shanghai* Publishing, 1990, pages 51-54.

4. Typical influence of regionalism is the so-called 'Feudal-Lords Economy'. Following papers are for reference: '*A Study on the Political Regimes in Modern China- Analysis of 'The Feudal-Lords Economy' Phenomenon*' '*Asia Research'* Volume 38, Fourth Edition, Asia Political Economy Academy, 1992.

5. Taiwan: '*Taiwan Daily'* September 1, 1992.

6. Yang Zhongmei, *Zhun Yi and Yan An*. Hon Kon: Ben Ma Press, 1989, page 401.

Communist Party Central Party Archives Research Center *ed*, '*Communist Party Archives No. 3'*, Communist Party Central Publishing/Internal Publication, 1982, page 117.

7. Tomoyuki Kojima analyzed the relationships between one party rule, profit general summary and intra-party disputes. Tomoyuki Kojima, '*Chinese Politics and General Public Lines- General Public Movement and Mao Zedong; Political Movements in Central and Local'* Keio Press, 1985, page 1085

8. '*Mao Zedong's General Conversations with Local Leaders'* Daito Bunka University Asian Culture Study Center *ed*, *'Important Materials on Revolution in Modern China'* Volume 3, 1980, page 1085.

9. Translated term 'Power Sharing' is also used. Yasugo Tusji '*Law and Society in China'* China Research Institute *ed*, *'Chinese Basic Law'* Japan Hyoron Publishing, 1988, page 473.

10. In his publication, Mastake Wakabayashi described ' An Agent *by the Party'* as one of the characteristics of Communist Party dictatorship in modern China, distinguished from Taiwan's People's Party dictatorship. '*Taiwan: A Divided Nation and its Democracy'* University of Tokyo Press, 1992, Introduction. Tomoyuki Kojima ' Act dictatorship *by the Chinese Communist Party'*, Tatsuo Yamada ed, '*Modern China in the Context of History'* Michikusa Publishing, 1996, pages 239-241.

11. Akira Ishii '*Changes in China's Foreign Policy Organizations-1949-1982'*, Kazuko Mouri *ed*, '*China in Mao Zedong Era: Studies on Modern China I'* Japan International Research Institute, 1990, pages 123-125, 137-139. ZHAO Hongwei '*Chinese Communist Party Central*

Foreign Affairs Leading Group', *'Chinese Communist Party Central Foreign Affairs Leading Group'*, *'Modern China Encyclopedia'* Iwanami Publishing, 1998.

12. Zhang Zhijian *ed, 'Personnel Management in Modern China'* (Beijing) Modern China Publishing, 1994, Volume I, pages 73-86. People's Bank of China Personnel Division *ed, 'Selected Documents on Human Resources Managment'* (Beijing) China Financial Publishing, 1985, pages 399-405. State Council Personnel Division *ed, 'Selected Documents on Human Resources Management'* (Beijing) China Personnel Publishing, 1991, Volume 13, pages 39-44. Chinese Communist Party Daily *'People's Daily'* May 17, 1995. Also reference; Tang Liang *'Principles of the Party Management and Personnel Management of a Administrative Body'* Political Science Journal, Keio University, Volume 15, December 1992.

13. Alan P.L. Liu, *Communication and National Integration in Communist China.* Berkeley: Univ. of California Press, 1971. Kazuko Mouri *ed 'China in the Mao Zedong era Modern China I'* Japan International Research Institute 1990

14. 'Non-public Newspapers' are mentioned in the following memoirs: Yan Jiaqi, "Bao Tong" Yang Zhongmei (Chinese Publication) *'Democratic China'* (Tokyo) The 40th Period, November 1992.

15. L.Pye took important notice of the 'loyalty' concept in Chinese politics; he indicated that it was a typical form of 'reaching mutual agreement' in China. Lucian Pye, *The Dynamics of Chinese Politics*, Cambridge, Mass: Odgeschlager, Gunn & Hain, Publishers, 1981, p51.

16. Shin Yabuki *'The Truth of the Tiananmen Square Incident'* Volume I, II Soso Publishing, 1990

17. ZHAO Hongwei *'The Origins of 'Pan' in Modern Chinese Politics'* 'Kyorin Socio-economics Research' Kyorin Socio-economics Academy, Volume 14, 2nd Edition, 1998. Zhi Yumin and Shao Yong, *Chinese Bang.* Shanghai People's Publishing, 1993. Chen Mingtong defined 'Bang' in Taiwanese Politics as a 'faction' and established its studies in the political science field. (transl Masashi Wakabayashi) *'Politics in Modern Taiwan and Factionism'* Toyo Keizai Shinposha 1998.

Chapter 4

Modern China's Political Regime and Social Structure

Actors can be split into two types: actors who deal with policy-making and implement; and the one who embody the interest. These two types of actors in modern China, are even categorized into the 'state' actors, the 'political party' actors, which form the state, as well as the 'economic' actors and the 'societal' actors, which form the society. So it can be said, that the study of political regime should cover the structure of both state and society, as well as dealing with each of the two types of actors for policy-making, policy implement or embodying interest.

However, up till now, the studies on China's political regime have been concentrating only on the state structure. These studies have always analyzed the structure of state or political party, which are the actors dealing with policy-making and implement. For example, in her *Modern China's Politics,* Mori Kazuko said, "the analyze of China's political regime needs first to explain the three factors of state, party and military, and then the interaction among the three factors' (Mori 1993, p.93). The weight of Mori's analysis is on actors of state structure, who deal with policy-making and implement. Although there are some studies on social structure, or the actors embodying interest (Goodman, D. 1984), few of them focused on political regime.

This chapter deals with the other aspect of political regime study. That is, 'the analysis on actors who make the society up'. The previous analysis on social structure was not highly evaluated because the studies on political regime basically were limited within the institutions of state study, and the studies were not dynamic. In this study, the 'social structure' is taken into the analysis frame of political regime. By doing so, the author looks forward to increasing the academic value of the study on political regime.

By taking the social structure into the analysis frame of political regime, a comprehensive study on political regime with two aspects of state structure and social structure becomes possible. Moreover, since analyzing the structure of actors that is related with policy-making and implement as well as embodying interest is explaining the structure of the power that drives everything in the policy process, so analyzing policy process from the angle of political regime would become possible. The relation between political regime and policy process, the mechanism of the interaction and the change of political regime would become new academic frontiers. Besides, since the social tendency and policy process are dynamic, studies on both these two subjects can change the previous political regime studies into dynamic ones.

According to Almond and Powell, 'embodying' interest is a process of individuals or groups expressing their demands toward factors that directly deal with political decision. Medias and various organized interest groups are the most effective ways (Almond & Powell 1966, p. 98). I have already analyzed the medias in Chapter three. So in this chapter, I will mainly analyze the structure of interest group. Part one in this chapter deals with the factors for economic policy making, part two deals with the factors for the non-economic interest-'social' policy-making, and part three deals with the structure of election which is regarded as the fundamental way of expressing citizen's common interest.

Section 1: The Structure of the Economic Policy Making Factor

Generally speaking, the economic policy making factor is considered as the organization that include industry group, related pressure group in the economic circle, or political supporting group. This organization is the economic interest group that represents its own interest while affecting politics. However, this type of economic interest group does not exist in socialist countries, because socialist countries are symbolized by public ownership and state-run economic activity. So it is necessary to explain the unique body that express economic interest in the socialist country.

It is believed that the dynamism for the establishment of and the action taken by an economic interest group originates in owning or managing an industry. So let us consider the industry related people in China as the factor for economic policy behavior. In the following, I will review the economic actors in modern China's political regime, by analyzing the ownership and the management structure.

The Structure of the Enterprise Ownership

In China, state run enterprise is divided into 'central governmental enterprise' and 'local governmental enterprise'. The former is also called 'ministry enterprise', belonging to each of the industrial ministries in the State Council. The latter is owned by local government such as province, autonomous region, cities under central government's direct judiciary, normal cities and counties. In addition to the state run enterprises, there are also public enterprises, called 'collective enterprise'. This kind of enterprise includes 'city collective enterprise' and 'township enterprise'. The 'city collective enterprise' is run by the CCP and the government's lower level agency, township office, police, law enforcement, military, school, research institute or even some state run enterprises. Except a limited number of private enterprises, the ' township enterprise' is run by the committee in township or village in the countryside.

As early as in 1975, Kojima has focused the structure of China's enterprise. In Kojima's study, the ownership structure of China's enterprise was named 'classic industrial system' (Kojima 1975, p. 204). Later in his study in 1988, he mentioned 'the variety of the style of China's enterprise according to its ownership', as well as the economic behavior in light of competition among various administrative agencies (Kojima 1988, p. 37-40).

Ishihahra Junichi has pointed out the Chinese enterprise' management in different administrative region, bringing out the multi-layered structure of traditional sector and modern sector, planning sector and marketing sector in China's enterprise. Moreover he mentioned about the friction in the multi-layered structure and the income gap among regions (Ishihara 1991, p. 18).

One of the indicators for the owner of an enterprise is receiving the allocation of the enterprise profit. In China, the profit of an enterprise is allocated between administrative agencies and the enterprise, in accordance with the management from the top administrative agency in the central government through local government and even lower level office all the way to the public enterprise (Chen Ru-long 1988, p. 374-375. Ma Jun-lei, Luo Li-qin 1994, p. 87-88). This can be named multi-layered profit allocation structure according to the enterprise ownership.

Up till 1993, China's enterprise profit allocation institution was mainly called ' financial responsibility institution', which was established during the financial reform in 1980, 1985, 1986 and in 1988 (Tajima 1994, p. 12-20). According to the 'financial responsibility institution', public run enterprise pays certain amount of its profit to the local government, but keep the rest portion of its profit. It is said that the local government usually has the right to receive more profit from the public enterprise than the central government. Under such a institution, local government and its sub agencies are given taxation power toward enterprise by the central government (Ohashi Hedeo 1995, p. 128 figure 4).

Since 1994, China launched its tax institution reform, implemented the so-called ' Tax Distribution Institution'. By a brief explanation of this institution, business tax, local enterprise income tax, individual income tax are taken as the income source of the local government. Surtax, stock exchange tax and resource tax are taken as special financial resource, and they are to be shared by both the central and the local governments with certain proportion. Obviously, local enterprise's income tax has been decided as the income of various local governments. According to the 'Tax Distribution Institution', the central government takes 40% share of the taxation income, while the local government takes 60%. According to an economist's study on the 'Tax Distribution Institution', "under the premise that local government's financial income relies on local state run enterprise, that central government shares the income with the local government, China's financial institution has never changed" (Tajima, p.22).

Before 1993, most of the public enterprises adopted the 'Enterprise Management Responsibility Institution' that started to be implemented as part of China's economic reform in 1986. Even the 'Tax Distribution Institution' in 1994 has inherited the characteristic of the 'Enterprise Management Responsibility Institution'. In other words, enterprise' profit plan, profit reserving rate for the enterprise and the amount of profit share for governments are decided according to governments sharing profit with their enterprises. Even the legal tax rate can be changed if it is necessary. And this characteristic has never changed.

Besides, local government can even partially change certain type of tax rate that is decided by the central government. This can be seen in the local governments' 'Favoring Tax-rate Policy' for the purpose of attracting investment. For instance, according to the 'Policy of Encouraging Investment' issued by the Sichuan Province in the end of 1996, the provincial finance is used to pay for the national tax on highway (The Sichuan Daily, December 28, 1996). This kind of tax institution has brought about unfixed tax rate among enterprises or local governmental agencies. It has also indicated that local government is the actual owner of the enterprises.

In addition to the regulated taxation institution mentioned above, there is also an 'Increase/Decrease Tax' toward public enterprise. According to this tax institution, public enterprise' after-tax-profit is managed by the government that owns the public enterprise. The institution is implemented either by demanding the profitable enterprise for contribution, or by providing financial subsidy to the deficit enterprise. Governments' demand for contribution from the public enterprises is widely known as 'Tanpai', or contribution ratio among enterprises. This kind of financial exercise has become more popular, instead of cooling down, despite the Central government's repeated ban (Economic Daily, November 5, 1986. Southern Daily, August 6, 1997).

A unified tax institution is the common sense for a government. However, from the above analysis, we know that China still does not have a unified tax institution. Also, since the public enterprise' profit is shared with all levels of governmental agencies to which the enterprise subordinate, it can be considered that the relation of subordinate between governments and enterprises equals to the relation of ownership.

The Structure of Enterprise Management

The structure of China's enterprise management is symbolized by joint management of the enterprise, central and local governments as well as various lower level administrations. Enterprises, local government and lower level administration can partially exercise managerial power toward the enterprise. And this is the result of the marketing institution established in the Deng Xiao-ping era, when the economic reform policy was implemented. In other words, it has become that enterprise, central government, local government and even lower level administration share the management power of the enterprise. And this means that all of the four parties play the role of representing the enterprise's interest, and they all have the nature of the economic actors. But the significance of the role and the way of playing the role are not the same among the four.

First, as an economic actor, the enterprise leadership has limited influence. In China, enterprise is prohibited from creating lobbying group. Enterprise itself originally is not organized to be a lobbying group. Furthermore, with few exceptions, enterprise cannot represent its interest. Second, central government, local government and lower level administrations play the role of economic interest group. But in each of every administrative district, there are specific 'enterprise administrations' created according to the type of industry. These 'Enterprise administrations' represent the enterprise' interest toward the their boss, which is the district leadership.

The 'Enterprise administration' means specific industrial ministry in the central government as well as industrial bureau in local level governments. These ministries or bureau are the very office that exercise central or local government's sharing management power on enterprise. For instance, reviewing enterprise' investment or production plan, signing contract with enterprise, appointing enterprise' boss, supervising enterprise' management and so forth are all the concrete responsibilities for the offices. Thus the enterprise administrations own multiple enterprises in each specific industry within the administrative district, creating 'interest groups' among different industries. And the interest competition takes place among the 'interest groups'.

The ' Enterprise administrations' never would give the management power to the enterprise. They are the very offices that keep the management power for various levels of local governments. However, in order to push forward the reform on marketing economy, in March 1998, the central government has decided to abolish the 'Enterprise administration' at every level of the central and local governments (Xinhua News Agency March 6, 1998). Chin was then facing the structural change in the state-enterprise-relation.

As the *De Facto* 'state' in the administrative district, the local governments play the role the interest arbitrator for the enterprise administrations. From the central government level all the way to the lowest local government level, every enterprise related administration is an 'economic interest group'. And these groups compete each other with the same level of counterpart. The financial control by the above-mentioned administrations and governments has strengthened the management toward enterprises, and has also consolidated the enterprises' dependency toward administrations and governments.

As the key component, all the different levels of administrative offices or local governments have formed up the multi-layered centralized regime. The financial sectors are kept under control of all these administrations. Each administration or government forces banks to provide loan to the enterprise that belongs to the administration. Due to the motivation to increase enterprise properties, each of the administration as the owner of the enterprise, tends to request as much of the bank loan as possible. However, since the administration is a governmental office, not the legal person of the enterprise, it does not need to assume the responsibility to pay the debt on behalf of the enterprise. From the perspective of the administration, getting the loan from national banks is nothing but competing for national capital against its counterpart in other administrative district. Therefore, each of the administrations will try to get as much of the loans as possible. No body even pays attention to the interest or returning the loans. The leaders of the administration consider returning loan as the thing would be done after their terms are over in the future. They would not care about the enterprise even in case the business do not run well, because the central government could have various policies or financial aids for debt reduction and business loss for public enterprises.

Further, local government or administrative office has the authority to get loan from the bank. According to an interview to a research fellow in The Chinese People's Bank, it is not at all a surprise that a bank is forced to provide loan under the pressure of political and administrative power (The author's interview, October 4, 1990). In order to improve the situation, as early as in 1979, the branch's personnel appointment power was removed from local government to the headquarter of the bank (Kaizuka, 1992, p. 80). This is an attempt to build up a vertically centralized power structure in the bank institution. But the reform was not thoroughly implemented. In the 'Resolution of the National Conference of the Chinese Communist Party' in 1985, it was regulated that local party committee and government have the authority to observe the bank (China Yearbook 1986, p. 166). So, the bank institution's separation from the multi-layered centralized regime was not permitted. Therefore, local governments have repeatedly set pressure on the bank branches, to try to get loan from the bank. In 1997, the central government emphasized the significance of the Asian Financial Crises. In the end of the same year, the central government decided to reform the bank institution. Under this reform policy, bank branches in every province except Beijing and Shanghai were closed. Instead, these closed branches were re-assigned into approximately ten districts (Asahi Shimbun, December 12 & 17, 1997). However, the Chinese People's Bank has not yet been independent at the central government level. It still is a ministry in the State Council. And this kind of the bank's position was legally regulated in China's first Bank Law in 1995 (People's Daily, March 23, 1995).

Let us take a look at a real example here. During the period from November 1989 to May 1990, The Li Peng administration used 195,9 billion Yuan as the additional finance to deal with the management crises of the big and intermediate size of state enterprises. This amount of money equals to two third of the national financial income for the fiscal year of 1990 (Yamauchi, Kikuchi edit, 1991, p. 10). The National People's Congress did not even review this decision. More over, the Light Industry Ministry spent 3.5 times of its budget to build gorgeous office. This incident suggests that even the budget get passed in the National People's Congress, it still can hardly limit the wrong-doing by the local administrative offices or banks.

Through the analysis on the ownership and the management structure of the Chinese enterprise, we can conclude the structure of the economic actors in modern China's political regime as the following. First, public enterprise is categorized into a few types including central government ownership, local state ownership and collective ownership, according to the administrative level where the enterprise stands. The ownership and management authority is partially controlled by the central, local and lower level administrations in the multi-layered way. Thus the multi-layered centralized power structure in public enterprise has been formed up.

Additionally, under such a power structure in the enterprise in terms of the ownership and management, the supervising sectors from the central government all the way to the lower level administrative offices have become the owner as well as the manager of the enterprise. The leaders of the enterprise are not the owners of the enterprise, but they are managers who have a part of the management power. Therefore, the economic actors are, China is formed up from central government, local government and even lower administrative offices as well as the leaders in the enterprise. Besides, in certain supervising sector, specific industrial ministry or department play the role of representing the economic interest of the enterprise, as well as the role of economic actors. These economic actors together form up the 'economic interest group', and they compete one another.

Finally I want to point out that while the leading sectors from the central government to the lower level administrative offices are actors dealing with policy making and implement, in the mean time, they are also the actors to represent the interest. In other words, the actors in the modern China's political regime have the multi-aspects nature. This would affect the factor itself in its behavior pattern.

Section 2: The Structure of the 'Social' Actors

Generally speaking, social actors means the organization including various pressure groups, political back-up group and others. These groups organize the people, expressing their own interest, and affecting politics. Labor union (which is the economic actors), women or young people's organizations, human right group or environment promoting group and other citizen's groups are for example. This Part Two will deal with the structure of the work unit, which is China's fundamental institution for the organization of its people. Part Two will also include labor union, the important social actors. I will try to explain the structure for expressing social interest in China, as well as the social actors in the structure.

The Structure of the Work Unit

In the beginning of Part Two, I have mentioned that the work unit is the fundamental institution for the organization of the people in China. In order to realize the structure of the social actors in China, one cannot avoid this key word of the work unit.

(1) What is the work unit?

In China, people call the place where they work ' women danwei' (=our work unit). Enterprise, governmental agency, school, research institute and hospital are for example. The Japanese researchers dealing with the Chinese studies often use this keyword in Chinese language. In English, the keyword 'danwei' is translated as Work Unit (Henderson & Cohen 1984).

The 'Work Unit' was used in the title of a book on the study of the 'danwei' by the American scholars. This book was published in 1984, so I presume it is the first study on the 'Work Unit'. In this book, the author described the insight of the work units in detail, based on his personal experience in a hospital in China. It is a very interesting book but its theoretical analysis cannot be considered as adequate.

As for the study on the 'work unit' in China, Lu Feng's publication in 1989 should be the very first one. According to Lu, the work unit is ' a unique organization type that is generally adopted by various organizations in China'. And it has become 'the basic of political, economic and social institution'. Lu analyzed the nature of the work unit, tracing the origin and the developing course of the work unit back to the experience of the revolutionary base of the Chinese Communist Party and the political process thereafter.

The relation between the work unit and the economic reform is also among the studies in China. As one of these studies has pointed out, the reform has brought about change that is 'not comprehensive and not fundamental either', 'the organization of work unit is still very powerful, it still maintains its fundamental characteristics as well' (Li Lulu, 1994, p. 5-16).

In America, the theory of 'the communist neo-traditionalism' has attracted researchers' attention toward the study of the work unit. According to this theory, the state run enterprise employees 'depend on the enterprise socially and economically', and 'depend on the managers politically', moreover, ' depend on their boss personally'. Since this type of dependency is 'characteristically owned by the communism', it can be conceptualized as 'the communist neo-traditionalism' (Walder 1986, pp.14-22).

By comparing China's study with America's, the former keeps the attitude of 'not mentioning the politics', which is probably due to the limit of political environment. The latter keeps mentioning the politics but putting the nature of the work unit into the general concept of the communism. Therefore, it can be said that the meaning of the Chinese characteristic 'work unit' is still not comprehensively elaborated.

In Japan, there have been quite a few publications on the study of the work unit since before. However, few of them have taken the work unit as their main research topic. Zhou Xiao-meng, a graduate student in the University of Tokyo (then) is the first one who completed a research paper with the main theme of the work unit. In 1997, another graduate student Shinyichi Tanigawa published his 'research note' on the work unit. From the viewpoint of the 'new institution theory', Zhou attached importance to China's political and economic institution that has created the work unit. Tanigawa presented his knowledge on the 'work unit' used as the vehicle for controlling the relations in the country or society. Thanks to both Zhou and Tanigawa, the 'work unit' has finally regarded as the main theme for academic studies. The 'work unit' is an important phenomenon, but the current situation in Japan is that there are still not very many research that focus on this phenomenon.

In this book, the 'work unit' is seen as one of the 'fundamental institution' in modern China's political regime. And I believe that the 'work unit' has several of its own institutions by which the Chinese people are kept under control. I also believe that the 'work unit' plays the role of the terminal-governing device for the political regime.

(2) The political institution of the 'work unit'

The political institution of the 'work unit' includes 'the centralized directing institution by the basic party organization', 'the working institution for ideology and politics' and 'the documenting institution'. First, 'the centralized directing institution by the basic party organization' has the following four characteristics: 1. Party committee or Party branch under the core leadership of party secretary is established in every 'work unit'. These party organs as the 'work unit leadership' has the centralized power towards everything in a 'work unit'. 2. This kind of centralized leadership exercise its power by the 'Responsibility Sharing Institution' implemented among the members of party committee or party branch. This means the members of party committee or party branch occupy administrative, economic and every other important positions.

Second, 'the working institution for ideology and politics' in a 'work unit' is a communication institution for mobilizing the mass by the communist party's policies and the communist ideology as well as promoting the ideological control. Its characteristics can be summarized in such phrases as dictatorship, mandatory and doctrinaire. The phrase of dictatorship indicates without the leadership or approve of the party organization in the work unit, any meeting or other political communication is not allowed. The phrase of mandatory indicates the requirement upon the 'work unit' employees to attend 'the meeting for political study', as well as to obey the party cadres' doctrine. 'The left behind' (=the looser) will be labeled to the people who show inactive attitude. Moreover, these people's carrier will also be negatively affected. The phrase of doctrinaire means the mass' ideological obeying rather than their action is regarded as the purpose of 'the ideological and political work'. It has been pointed out, that China's governmental control relies more on 'the ideological and political work' with the purpose of doctrinaire than the terrorism of the police (Townsent 1980, p. 16, translated by Kojima). The political control is carried out mainly by the party organizations in every 'work unit'. And it will result in strengthening the authority of the leadership of the 'work unit'.

Speaking bout the 'Documenting Institution', since there is special study on this topic (Saijo, 1984, p. 211-233), I will only analyze the characteristics from the viewpoint of 'the work unit institution' (ZHAO, Hongwei, 1990). 'Document' is the life long 'Record of political behavior' of every single employee except farmers. Its nature can be summarized into these phrases of political, secret, penalty, involvement, and lifelong.

(a) The phrase of political

Unlike the democratic country where the personnel appraisal record mainly concerns the achievement and skills of the employees, the 'document' in China mainly records people's political behavior. The main categories in the document include 'family occupational background' (it used to be family class in the Mao's era), 'political identification' (communist party member or counter-revolutionaries and so forth), 'political attitude' (including personal political action and opinion ever since 18 years old, party's investigation document, report from the information provider, relation with the relatives or friends who are counter-revolutionaries, the relation with the overseas relatives, with the friends or foreigners in foreign countries, and etc.).

(b) The phrase of secret

Cadres or party members' 'document' are kept by the Organization Department in the party committee. General employees' 'documents' are kept in personnel office. In either case, the party committee has the privilege to record in the document, there is no anyone else who has the privilege to read the document.

(c) The phrase of penalty

In case there are unfavorable records in the secret 'document' of someone, without his/her knowledge, he/she will be treated negatively through his/her life, in terms of employment, change of carrier, salary increasing, promotion and etc. It is also possible that the person will encounter troubles in his/her marriage.

(d) The phrase of involvement

This means the 'document' could bring about disadvantage not only to the documented person, but also to his/her children and relatives. For instance, in case one is recorded as 'counter-revolutionary' in his 'document', even after the death of this person, his children and relatives will encounter troubles for entering party or being promoted as cadre.

(e) The phrase of lifelong

This means the 'document' goes with the documented person for his whole life. For instance, if one changes his carrier, his 'document' will be transferred to his new work unit. The leader of the new work unit can either send an investigation letter to the person's previous work unit, or send a party cadre to investigate, if the leader thinks necessary. Thus, for the Chinese people, if one's penalty is recorded in his 'document', that is not a one-time-penalty, it means the person is put under condition similar to 'life in prison with parole'.

The 'document' with the above mentioned characteristics are used as the terminal-control-device for China's political regime. It plays two major roles for the leadership of the 'work unit', in terms of 'strengthening the forcing power' as well as 'increasing the controlling power'. The dangerous content of the 'document' may consequently bring about extreme instability. It is therefore definitely possible that the record in the 'document' will target in people's promotion, salary, housing application, the level of penalty for possible violation or political mistakes in the future, for the purpose of a political campaign' (Hashimoto 1990, p. 307). Because of this special nature, we have to acknowledge the fact that people are absolutely obeying the leadership in their 'work units'. Moreover, in case one wants to change his job, if his leader in the 'work unit' does not send the person's 'document' to the person's new 'work unit', then the person will not be admitted by the new 'work unit', and therefore he will not be able to change his job (Funabashi 1984, p. 20-22). In other words, the leadership of the 'work unit' uses the 'document' as a weapon to keep the employees in its 'work unit' under control. And it has driven its employees to a place where they can only obey to the leadership.

(3) The administrative institution of the 'work unit'

The administrative institution of the 'work unit' includes the 'household institution' and the 'work unit permit institution'. Japan also has household institution. But China's household institution limits

its people's freedom for moving. There appears the fundamental difference between the two countries on the household institution.

First, China's household institution divides the household into 'country household' and 'city household'. Converting the 'country household' to the 'city household' is prohibited. So the 'farmer's identification' is created, and the farmers are contained in the country. The only exception for the household converting is in case a student graduated from a college, or a military person who is beyond the level of the company commander. Most of the people will have to spend their entire life as farmers if they were born in a farmer's family. Second, China's household institution also limits people who have the city household from their moving to another city, especially from a small city to a bigger city (Wakabayashi Keiko 1989, p. 131).

Thanks to the economic reform since the late 1970s, the household institution shown certain relaxes in its implementation. For instance, in February 1998, the Guangzhou city government announced a policy on the change of the household institution for the purpose of aiding the constructive industry. According to this policy, the government will grant suburban district household to the people who have bought townhouse for seven years, as well as having paid 20,000 to 40,000 yuan RMB. And the suburban district household can be switched to the city household (The Japanese Economic News, or Nihon Keizai Shimbun, March 4, 1998). Thus, because of pursuing economic interest, the household institution is driven to be reformed.

With the characteristic of limiting people's freedom on their moving, the household institution contains people within a certain area, providing the administrative environment for the existence of the 'work unit institution'. Even in the case an inter-village-moving or inter-city-moving is exceptionally approved, 'the permit from the work unit' is necessary as a step of the procedure.

According to the so-called 'work unit permit institution', in case an employee of a 'work unit' contacts another 'work unit', or doing business within the domain area of the other 'work unit', he has to have a permit namely 'introducing letter' issued by his own 'work unit' with him. The authority of issuing this kind of permit indicates the legitimacy of the 'work unit'. For example, a village leadership has the authority to issue the 'permit' to a farmer (Nakao 1990, p. 69). Therefore it can be said that the village is the *De facto* 'work unit' for the farmers. There is even a saying on the necessity of the 'permit'. According to this saying, in the past days a food begging farmer in a city could be arrested by the police, had he not had a 'permit' in hand (Hayashi 1986, p. 121).

Thanks to the economic reform since the late 1970s, the household institution shown certain relaxes in its implementation. For instance, in cities, there appear people who are self-employed but they do not belong to any 'work unit'. In order to set a minimum control on these people, in September 1989, a new 'Citizen Identification Institution' was established, and the 'Citizen's I.D. Card' is issued for the entire people (The Institute of Chinese Studies 1997, p. 472).

The permitting authority of the leadership of the 'work unit' originates from the following structure, and it also represents these structures. First, most of the matters that require permit are related with the responsibility of the administration. Therefore it is clear that the 'work unit' is not just an enterprise, but it is an administrative agency that has the administrative power.

Second, the leadership of the 'work unit' has the physical controlling power toward its employees, which is beyond the administrative management. Due to the structure of centralized leadership by the party organization in a 'work unit', the leadership of a 'work unit' has the absolute controlling power and ruling power that surpasses regulations toward the employees of the 'work unit'. If the 'permit' of the leadership of a 'work unit' has to obey law or the guidance from the upper leadership, then the 'work unit' institution will decrease its importance. By taking this into consideration, one can understand that 'the supera-regulation ruling power is the most significant characteristic of the 'work unit permitting institution'. One can also understand that the supera-regulation ruling power has brought to the 'work unit permitting institution' the nature in terms of the physical controlling. The super-lawful 'permit' by the leadership of a 'work unit' is issued according to the 'interior regulation' as well as the willfulness of the member in the leadership. As the matter of fact, the leadership of the 'work unit' in China frequently creates 'interior regulations'. And many items of these regulations are against law or even the Central Committee's policy. Moreover, there are some other cases in which the 'permit' is issued due to the private connection, despite the 'interior regulation'.

(4) The economic institution of the 'work unit'

The economic institution of the 'work unit' is the institution for making up economic or living community in every 'work unit'. It keeps employees within a 'work unit', based on the 'living assurance provided by the work unit'. This institution includes two aspects of the 'work unit assignment' and the 'work unit welfare'.

The 'work unit assignment' is a mechanism by which people can only receive their salary from a certain work. This mechanism was brought about in the 1950s when the communist party has eliminated the traditional household business, pushed forward the 'collective economy in the rural area, while thoroughly implemented public ownership as well as finished the socialist convert for the economy in the city. Since then people's side work in the city was not allowed until the 1970s. And there was no opportunity for the side work. But due to the economic reform since the late 1970s, the 'work unit assignment' is no longer the absolute working opportunity for a group of people. For instance, since the late 1970s the household businesses were restored in the rural area, farmers' main income source changed from the work assignment by the village leadership to their own family businesses.

The 'work unit welfare' is a contrast concept in relating to the 'social welfare'. This is the mechanism by which people can only receive the welfare from one fixed 'work unit'. For example, since China unlike Japan, does not have the National People's Pension Institution, after retirement, one will receive pension monthly from where he worked, rather than the government or pension union. The establishment of various modern social insurance institutions has not become the important task for the reform until it has entered the 1990s.

There is a gap between country and city in terms of the 'work unit living assurance'. First, concerning the 'work unit welfare', farmers can only receive the extremely low level of welfare. The governmental Medicare institution or the pension institution has not yet established in the rural area. However city residents can receive relatively good welfare. This is especially true in the case of state run enterprise. According to a Chinese scholar, the enterprise provides various social welfare or social services including daycare, kindergarten, grade school, high school for the employees' children, as well as the employees' after-retirement-living assurance, their children's employment, the assurance of the employees' housing, medical insurance and service for the employees and their family, and recreation facility and activity for the employees' family.

Besides, there is difference between the country and the city in terms of the source of the 'work unit living assurance'. The majority of the entire farmers and their leaders cannot receive the assured welfare of salary, medical insurance and pension from the government. They basically rely on themselves, using the interior resources of their on 'work unit' for the 'work unit assignment' and the 'work unit welfare'. But in the city residents' case, people can expect the increase of the 'work unit assignment' and 'work unit welfare' by the interior resource, according to the profit of the 'work unit'. Even in case the 'work unit has encountered business loss, the employees can rely on the government's financial aids for their basic salary, medical insurance and pension.

Country and city share two common places. Firstly, the 'work unit living assurance' is the only source of the income or welfare for the member of the 'work unit'. Although the city residents receive the financial aids from the government, they have to receive them from their 'work unit'. Consequently, people have no choice but become a part of their 'work units' for the purpose of existence.

Secondly, the 'work unit living assurance' has become 'maintenance expense' for the 'work unit' leadership physically controlling its employees. The 'work unit living assurance' plays the role of economically containing the employees within the 'work unit'. Meanwhile, in return, it has to assume the responsibility to assure its employees' basic life. Therefore, the concept of the 'work unit living assurance' has two aspects of 'economically controlling' the employees and providing 'economic assurance' to the employees.

Additionally, in case the 'work unit' is unable to assure its members' basic life, or it has decided not to do so, the 'work unit' as a controlling device weakens, and its function declines. This is especially true in the rural area. Since the farmers' 'work unit' is responsible for both the 'work unit assignment' and 'the work unit welfare', its power is easily getting weak. This point can be supported by the collapse of the people's commune and the recovery of the 'family business' in the 1980s (Refer to Chapter Six). On the contrary, the 'work unit' in the city, such as state run enterprise can still exist even when encountering deficit, as long as the government can tolerate the financial burden and keep providing aids to the 'work unit'.

(5) The mutual supportive power structure among 'work units'

The relations among 'work units' are mutual supportive for the authority to control the employees in various aspects including politics, administrative, economic and ideology. For instance, without mutual respect among 'work units', no one can effectively control its employees, the involving nature and the life long validation of the 'document' will be meaningless. Since the 1980s, the interest motivation in every 'work unit' has been inspired by the development of the marketing institution along with the economic reform. In the reality, there are more and more 'work units' that ignore the household institution, the 'work unit permit institution' or the 'document institution' while hiring employees, in order to maintain skillful personnel and working force. In other words, along with the development of the marketing economy, the 'work unit institution' is more or less shaken by the mechanism of pursuing interest, and the institution is declining. To a certain degree, people's moving is gradually allowed. However, I want to insist that despite the reality of the weakening 'work unit institution', the fundamental structure of the institution has not yet been legally reformed; it is basically maintained.

Here, I would like to present the definition of the 'work unit'. The 'work unit' in China is a controlling device set in the terminal position of the political regime of the modern China. It is used to control the people in various aspects including politics, administration, economy and ideology. It is used to organize the majority of the people.

According to an opinion, the three levels of leadership of the 'commune', the 'production team' and the 'production group' in the country in the Mao's era should not be regarded as the 'work unit', and today's village should not be considered as the 'work unit' either. However these organizations are all equipped with the political regime, administrative institution as well as economic institution, for this reason I consider that all these organizations should be regarded as the 'work unit'. But due to the collapse of the people's commune institution as well as the recovery of the 'family business' in the 1980s, farmers' economic independency has reached to a certain degree. By this very definition, it can be said that the farmers have somehow got rid of the 'work unit'.

Concerning the relation between the 'work unit' and expressing interest, the above analysis has made it clear that the 'work unit' splits the society into isolated controlling blocks. And then it plays the role of hindering the development of the 'social' actors. However, as the 'living community' for the employees, the 'work unit' also represents the common economic interests of its employees to a certain degree, due to the perception of the responsibility for the employees.

Finally, along with the development of the economic reform since the late 1970s, there also economic and social bodies appeared. They are individual entrepreneurs, private enterprises, foreign joint ventures or foreign capital enterprises and etc. These enterprises have dismantled certain characteristics of the 'work unit'. But since the freedom of association is prohibited, so even these social or economic bodies can function like the actors in dealing with certain issues, they are extremely lack of the ability to represent interest.

The Structure of Workers Union

We can see from the above analysis, that generally speaking, there is not 'social' actors in China. Here, I want to review the structure of the workers union, which is regarded as one of the most important 'social group' in China.

(1) The organizational structure according to region

In China, the 'Chinese National General Workers Union' is the only union organization. Workers in the city especially the state-run enterprise employees automatically become the member of the union when they start to work. China's workers union has very unique organizational style. 'The Chinese National General Workers Union consists of two major institutions. The one is made up with the so-called regional workers unions, or the workers unions at every single administrative level (from the basic local governmental office all the way to the central government level). The other is made up with the so-called industrial unions, or the workers unions in every single enterprise. By looking at the regional workers unions, first, the township, country and city level 'unions' together form up the provincial 'general union'. And its upper institution is the 'Chinese National General Workers Union'. The provincial 'general union' also consists of unions for different industries (The Japanese Labor Association 1987, p. 214; also, refer to figure 4-1).

By looking at the above explanation as well as figure 4-1, it is difficult to differentiate the organizational style of China's workers union. However, (a) lower level union is facilitated in every enterprise; (b) its upper union is regional workers union; (c) the unions in every enterprise do not directly lead the workers, they are kind of sub-administration for the regional workers union. Therefore China's workers union can be regarded as regional style.

Chart 4-1: The Organization of China's Workers Union

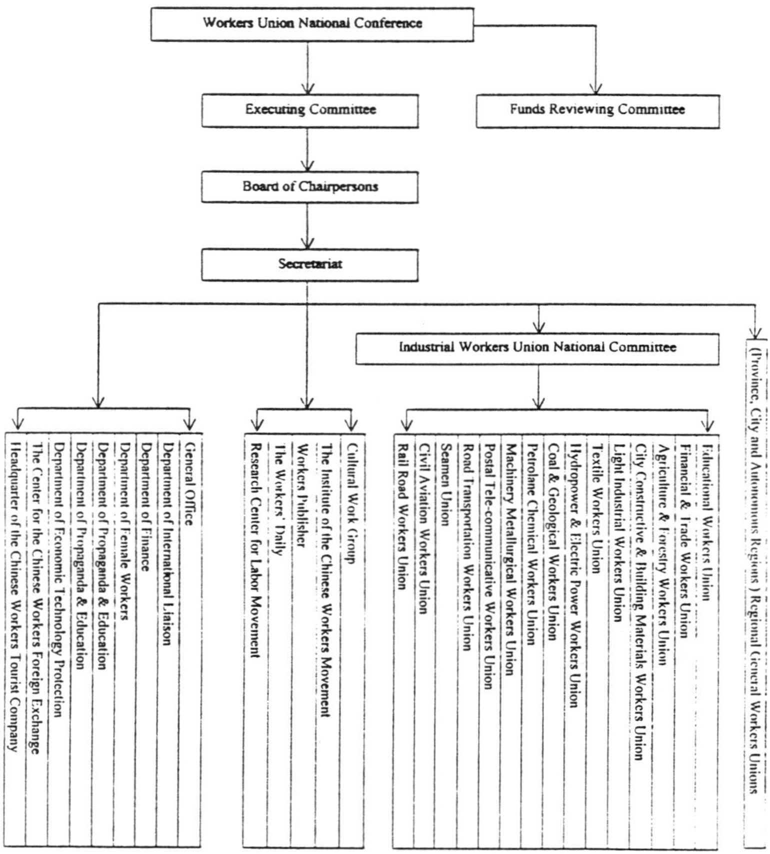

Source: *The Organizational Structure of China's Workers Union*, By Department of International Liaison, The Chinese General Workers Union. 1988.

Like the Central Organizational Department or Central Propaganda Department of the CCP (= Chinese Communist Party), the Chinese National General Workers Union is 'the institution directly under the leadership of the CCP'. Likewise, each local union is the 'direct institution' of each local party committee. But this is not officially announced to the public (Interview to the cadre of the Chinese National

General Union, May 3, 1992). Thus, China's workers union is put under the centralized leadership of the communist party committee at every level. And this has decided the nature of the union in China to be the regional organization in the multi-layered centralized regime.

(2) The 'work unit' and the workers union

From the perspective of that enterprise is a 'work unit', it is certainly true that the relation between the 'work unit' leadership and the union is decisive factor for the nature of the workers union. According to the 'Workers Union Law', 'Public Ownership Industrial Enterprise Law', and the 'Union Regulation' created by the Chinese National General Workers Union, the Chinese National General Workers Union is the only union that can be allowed to exist in a 'work unit'. Moreover, the workers union equals to the standing institution for the 'Workers Representative Conference' for reviewing and supervising the management of the enterprise (Workers Daily, October 23, 1983). It is regulated that the nature of workers union is 'the mass organization for the workers under the leadership of the communist party'. A standing member of the party committee shall assume the post of the director of the union, according to the 'sharing responsibility institution' in the enterprise' party committee (The Chinese National General Workers Union 1988, p. 69).

In general, the full-time cadre including the director of the union in state-run enterprise is the 'governmental cadre', that is the 'orderly'. Its personnel management is taken care by party committee (Kawai 1991, p.219). The union's activity expense and the salary for the full-time stuff of the union are not covered by the union expense, but they are paid by the 'non-production expense' of enterprise (the union of non-profit 'work unit' such as college receives government's financial aids for its expense). (Interview to a Chinese National General Workers Union cadre, May 3, 1992). In other words, the union in the enterprise is virtually a standing institution concerning workers' matter under the leadership of the 'work unit', rather than the so-called 'mass organization of workers'.

(3) Workers interest and workers union

Given the above-mentioned nature, does the union function as a 'social' actors, representing the workers' interest? Over a hundred years of continuous world workers movement has resulted in the establishment of 'the three rights', that is, the right for association, the right for group negotiation and the right for disputing (including the right for strike). These three rights guarantee the expression of workers' interest. However, let us review the Chinese workers situation in terms of their rights concerning their interest expression.

Firstly, concerning the 'right for disputing', it is mentioned in Article 45 of China's Constitution (1978) that 'workers have the freedom to strike'. But this has been abolished in the new version of 'The Chinese Constitution' (1982)(Takeuchi 1991). Secondly, The Chinese National General Workers Union is China's only legal workers union. But since this is the only union that can be established in an enterprise, it is hard to say that the Chinese workers have 'the right for association'. Moreover, concerning 'the right for group negotiation', there is no 'regulation' in the related law. Even in the reality the performance of this right, such as periodical negotiation between workers and managers in the enterprise, is not seen. Therefore, the Chinese workers do not have the rights for freely expressing their own interests.

Thirdly, concerning the function of The Chinese National General Workers Union, according to 'the union regulation', the union 'protects the workers' legal rights and interests, strengthening the ideological and political education as well as cultural and skillful education toward workers, fostering workers who is equipped with higher goal, morality and knowledge, who maintain the regulation as well' (The Chinese Workers Union News, Number 3, 1983). Obviously, the function of The Chinese National General Workers Union consists of both representing workers' interest and mobilizing masses for the communist party's political, administrative and economic purposes. The Chinese workers union thus is not just an institution to express workers' interest, but it is also the communist party's institution to mobilize masses.

When reviewing the reality of the Chinese workers' interest being expressed, according to a survey by The Chinese National General Workers Union in 1986, 60% of the workers have negatively evaluated the activities of the union in the enterprise. The more detail survey results are as following: 17% of the workers believe that the union's 'mobilizations are adequate but pragmatic activities are inadequate'. 24% of the workers 'cannot see the union's function except recreational or sports activities'. And according to the 8% of the workers, the union 'does not listen to the opinion or voice of the workers'. Another 8% of the workers believe that the union 'is kind of governmental agency rather than the masses' organization' (The Chinese National General Workers Union 1987, p. 454). We can see from this survey, that except recreational or sports activities, the workers union is not playing an effective role in expressing workers' interest. In China, 'recreational or sports activities' in an enterprise is categorized into 'workers welfare'. Therefore the union in the enterprise is generally seen as the department that handling welfare matters.

Under the situation that the Chinese workers do not have 'the three rights', there should be only one possible process for the union' s expressing the workers' interest. That is, the union representative (director) as one of the leaders in the 'work unit's leadership (standing committee member of the party committee in the enterprise) bring up his opinion at the meeting with the 'work unit' leaders. This process has a couple of characteristics: (1) the 'work unit' leadership expresses workers interest on behalf of the union, (2) the 'work unit' leadership rejects any interest such as political interest other than workers' welfare. But the 'rejection' is carried out by mobilizing and by ideologically controlling.

In the reality, the 'work unit' is more enthusiastic than workers towards the 'work unit welfare'. However, this chapter is not dealing with the analysis of the enterprise leadership. But briefly speaking, leaders of public-own enterprise are not the owner of the enterprise, and they have only a part of the managerial power. Therefore they are lack of the interest motivation concerning the capital increase. But they have strong desire on expanding consumption. This is way they are enthusiastic towards the 'work unit welfare'. Salary cannot be raised up without government's permit. Therefore in order to deal with this situation, the 'work unit' leadership would distribute cash and real commodities to the entire employees including leaders themselves, in the name of 'workers welfare'. To this very point of expanding 'welfare', the interest of 'work unit' leadership and the interest of workers agree.

With the analysis in Part Two, we can conclude that there is no 'social' actors such as a social interest group in China. The current masses organization let by the workers union is not a 'social' actors. The 'work unit' instead of various social interest groups or independent individual, has organized almost the entire people. To a certain degree, the leadership of the 'work unit' expresses the employees' economic interests such as work assignment or welfare. By this meaning it plays a partial role of the 'social' actors. However since it rejects other interest, especially the political interest or any interest expression other than the welfare, it is functioning as a terminal controlling device for China's political regime.

Section 3: The Structure of Election

Election is believed as the fundamental rule for expressing people's general interest. But to what extend does the structure of China's election perform this function?

Indirect and Multi-step Election Institution

According to Article Second of the Election Law, 'the representative of the People's Congress at the level of city (that has no administrative district), district that is under city's jurisdiction, county, autonomous county, township or township of minority people shall be directly elected by electorate'. But 'the representative of the National People's Congress, and the representative of the People's Congress at the level of province, autonomous region, municipality directly under the Central Government, city that has administrative district, or autonomous prefecture shall be elected by the right next level of the people's congress' (The Institute of Chinese Studies, 1988). Like I have mentioned in Chapter three, the direct election is not approved except the case of electing the People's Congress representative at the lowest administration level. The election of the representative for the National People's Congress must go through at least three times of indirect elections at county level, city level and provincial level. Moreover, the members of the standing committee of the National People's Congress need to be elected by the representatives of the National People's Congress. This kind of multi-steps indirect election is only seen in China.

According to Masamichi Kima, the concept of 'multi-step election' is not suitable for both constitution study and political science. But it is close to the indirect or semi-indirect election institution, so we can just call it 'indirect multi-step institution'. (1) In the Election Law, it is specifically regulated that candidates for the representative above the county level do not have to be elected by the right next lower level People's Congress (or local council). So even the trial of the direct election, a candidate may still be able to meet the qualification for people's representative by the rule of the indirect election. Therefore, among the people's representatives who have been elected from the county level, the number of candidates who have been directly elected by the electorate gets smaller at each of the upper level of the People's Congress, such as city council, provincial People's Congress and the National People's Congress. As the result, none of the National People's Congress Standing Committee members is elected directly by electorate.

Chart 4-2: The Structure of China's Direct Election of People's Congress under the County Level

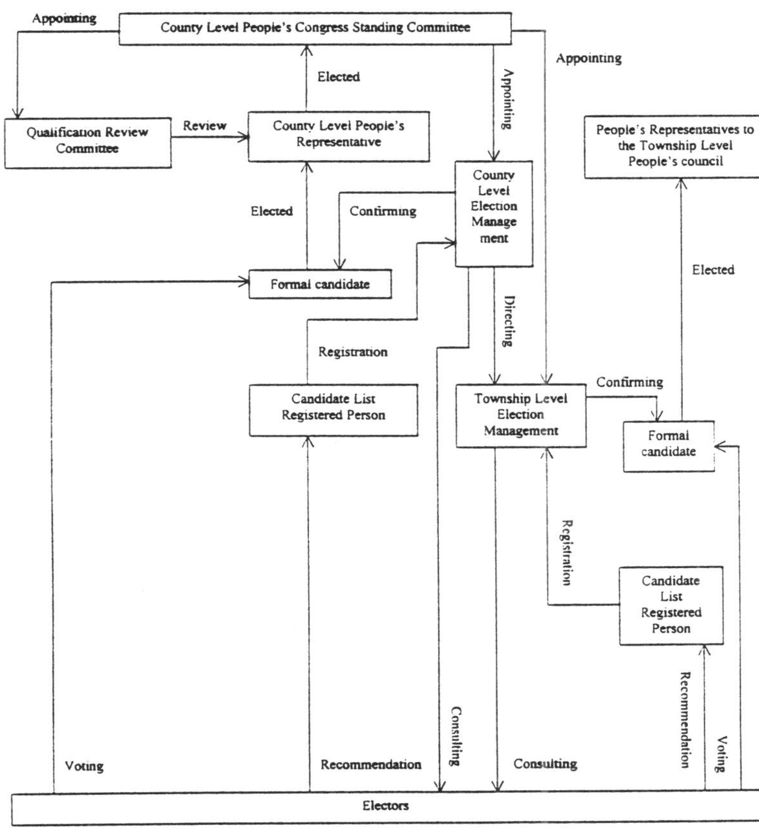

Source: *National People's Congress Election Law & Local People's Congress Election Law*, in Collection of China's Basic Laws, edited by the Institute of Chinese Studies, Nippon Hyoronsha, 1988.

Chart 4-3: The Structure of the Indirect Election of China's National, Provincial and Municipal Level People's Congress

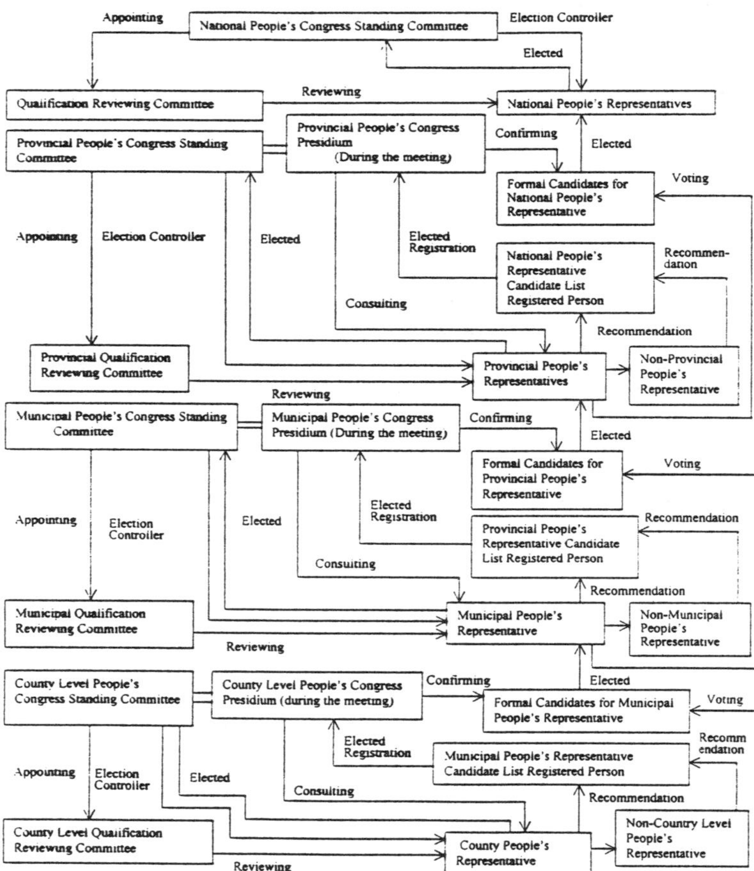

Source: Same as Chart 4-2.

This kind of 'indirect multi-step election institution' is implemented at central government, local government and every level of the lower level administration in China's multi-layered centralized regime. Therefore the electorates are kept under the leadership of the administration regardless the election step. For instance, when the representatives of the National People's Congress are elected, when the direct election, such as the election at the county or city council or the election by the electorates, is held, the provincial administration cannot direct the election. However, the indirect election at the provincial people's congress can be held under the supervision of the provincial government. Thus in China, even the election is structured into the multi-layered centralized power regime that consists of central government, local government and every level of lower level administrations. Under such an election institution, the election is kept under the supervision of the leadership from the central government all the way to the lower level administration. Therefore people's representative and members of the National People's Congress Standing Committee are not supervised by the electorates. The function of election is greatly weakened in expressing people's voice, as well as receiving the supervision from the electorates. Next, let me examine the process of election.

About the Candidates

Candidates are divided into 'Candidate List registered' and formal candidate. Candidates are to be recommended accordingly and to be confirmed before being decided as candidate. Candidates for National People's Congress or local council first need to be recommended by each political party, each people's group or ten electorates, and then becoming 'Candidate List registered'. The recommended candidates are recorded in the People's Representative List. Election committee cannot make any change on the list, it cannot add or drop the 'Candidate List registered'. The election must be carried out among multiple candidates (*The Election Law*, Article 26 &27; *The Regulation on Direct Election*, Article 10). Thus, it seems that the process of recommending candidate is freely independent. However, it does not mean that the recommended candidate can become the formal candidate immediately. The 'Candidate List registered' must also go through the decision process for the formal candidate. And this process can only be seen in China.

Let us take the lower level direct election (under the county level) as example (Refer to figure 4-2). The election committee presents the list of the 'Candidate List registered' to the electorates in every election district, let them sufficiently discuss or exchange opinion. Then the committee will decide formal candidates based on the opinion of the majority of the electorates, before publicly announcing the formal candidates decided five days prior to the election day (The Election Law, Article 28). However, it is against the principle of secret ballot that the election committee facilitates the electorates' 'sufficient discussion' and opinion exchanging. Although it is questionable whether the electorates express their true opinion or not, the election committee will change the candidate list, add or drop candidates and decide formal candidates based on the electorates' questionable opinion. Moreover, this kind of questionable opinion is even limited within the scope of the election committee's acquisition. So it does not objectively express the real opinion of the majority of the electorates.

For example, when a 'Candidate List registered' has been formally approved to be a candidate, the notice from the election committee is the only information the candidate can get. There is no evidence to inform the candidate about the detail voting outcome. In short, China's Election Law regulates the freedom for candidate, but in the reality, a candidate is decided by the administration at every level, and the decision process goes through two steps of the unique 'Candidate List registered' and formal candidate.

Organized Voting at Every Working Unit

According to Article 22 of the Election Law, election district for direct election under the county level can be set either according to the population in the residential area, or it can be set in various kind of working unit or company. Actually in China, most of the residential areas are formed by every working unit. For example, a village is under the leadership of the village office, company employee live in the company's apartment complex. Almost everything including the daily live are under the management of the working unit's leadership. Therefore election district is established in every working unit where the electorates belong.

This kind of election district setting has brought about the working unit's organized voting into the election. For instance, the election committee will collect opinion from every electorate group, in the order to decide candidates. However, since the electorate group is organized by the working unit, the opinion collecting actually is the leadership of the working unit trying to unify the opinion of the electorates in the working unit.

According to the deduction from the Organization Law of the National People's Congress, in the case of the indirect election above the county level, electorates or the people's representatives are mainly organized into every delegation from every administrative district (Sometime military is also regarded as a working unit) (Article Four, National People's Congress Law). This is fundamentally different from the congressmen's group in a democratic country, which is made up of various different party groups or other political organizations. Because China's delegations to the People's Congress are organized in every administrative district, they are under the powerful influence of the local leadership. These delegations are representing the administrative districts rather than political parties.

Election Controlling Agency

Taking the direct election under the country level as example (Article three, National People's Congress Law, and Article 45,Local People's Congress and Government Law), the election control agency is the election committee, it is responsible for (1) confirming candidates, (2) arranging election districts, (3) distributing the ratio of the representative, (4) to decide the election date, (5) opening ballot, (6) confirming the election to be valid. And (7) the election committee of the municipal district or of the city that does not have country or district shall direct township election committee in the administrative district. Most of these responsibilities influence the outcome of the election. Moreover, the above (1), (2), (3) and (4) are not seen in the election control agency in a democratic country. Additionally, there is a 'Representative Qualification Reviewing Committee' besides the election committee, which reviews and confirms the qualification of the elected people's representatives. However, there is no law on the standard for the reviewing.

Since the election control agency is very powerful, it is difficult to say that the agency can maintain the fairness. Here let us take a look at the make-up of the election control agency. First, according to the Election Law, the election committee is set in the city that does not have country or municipal district, or in the municipal district, as well as in the township. The members of the election committee are appointed by the country level people's council/congress standing committee. The standing committee of the people's congress at the level of province, autonomous region, city that is directly under the jurisdiction of the central government, or the city that has municipal district shall direct the election of people's representative under the country level. Moreover, the election of the representative for the National People's Congress is controlled by the standing committee of the National People's Congress. And the election of the people's representative at the level of province, autonomous region, city that is directly under the jurisdiction of central government, or the city that has municipal district is controlled by the same level People's Congress Standing Committee (Article Seven, The Election Law; Article One, The Regulation on Direct Election). In other wards, the standing committees in different level of the people's congress have the power to control the election. However, since the members of the standing committees will become the candidates themselves at the time of the election, as the result, the candidates will control the election.

Second, according to the Election Law, when local people's council elects people's representative for its one level upper people's council, the council directors group shall control the election (Article 32, Election Law). Just like what I have pointed out In Chapter Three, the council directors group that functions during the council meeting actually is the former standing committee with a different name. In other words, most of the people's representatives who are sent to the one level upper people's congress/council are standing committee members in their own congress/council. Therefore, the election under the control of the council directors group eventually becomes the election that guarantees the candidates who will elect themselves.

Further, when looking at the make-up of the Representatives Qualification Reviewing Committee that is set in the Standing Committee of the People's Congress/council beyond the county level by the Election Law, it is regulated that the member of the Representatives Qualification Reviewing Committee is the member of the People's Congress Standing Committee (Article Three, National People's Congress Law; Article 45, Local People's Congress and Government Law). This means that the members of standing committee of people's congress as the candidates during the election, will review and confirm their own qualification by themselves.

I have analyzed four characteristics of China's election structure in the above. It is clear that the election that originally should be the fundamental way to express people's general interest has been put into a multi-layered centralized regime across the leaderships in all levels. The election is used as the mechanism to control the entire society as well as to mobilize the people. Under such an election structure, it is impossible that the election fully expresses the people's interest. We cannot say that the elected people's representatives or members of standing committee of the National People's Congress have reflected the people's opinion, but we have to say that they are lack of the legitimacy in observing the responsibility for politics and law.

Conclusion

Chapter Four is concluded as following. Generally speaking, the economic actors and social actors can be considered as concrete examples for the actors that represents the interest. In China, these factors are horizontally organized by the leadership in central government, local and even lower level administration. In other words, the economic and social actors are organized into the state structure, and they have been institutionalized by the government. So, in China, the structure of the state and the structure of the society have merged into one organic whole. Moreover, the expression of the interest has the Chinese characteristic. That is, central, local government or even lower level administration play the role that is generally played by the economic or social actors.

Finally, I want to point out that along with the economic reform that started in the late 1970s, the social structure in China is in the process of change. Since the 1990s, economic groups or social groups and other similar organizations have rapidly increased in China. The Ministry of Civil Welfare in the State Council that in charge of the administration on people's association, is carrying out research while making up project teams (Wang Ying, 1993). Are these social groups in favor of the development of independent social actors that is against the work unit's control? Or they are just assisting the work unit's control? This should be a new task for researchers.

Notes

1. Kojima Reii: *China's Economic Statistics & Economic Law Review*, Institute of Asian Economy, 1989, p. 41.

2. Tajima Toshio: China's State-run Enterprise Reform and the Government Finance, in *The Chinese Studies Monthly*, April 1992, p. 20. Li Jie-sheng: The 'Mixing-up type' management in China's state-run enterprise – The case of the Beijing Iron & Steal Company, in

China Quarterly No. 22, 1993. In this paper, Le described the pattern of this system in detail.

3. China Mayors Association edit: *Introduction of the city economic zones in China*, China City Publisher, 1994. This book is a collection of documents on provincial or municipal policies for inducing foreign capital.

4. *People's Daily,* September 14, 1992. In this paper, there is a report on the Armed Police Troop using the profit of its own enterprise to improve its living condition. By reading this report, one can understand that the Armed Police owns its enterprise as well as the profit.

5. Lu Feng: Work Unit – A special type of social organization, in *China Social Science* (Beijing) No. 1, 1989. p. 71-78. The origin and development of the system of China's work unit, in *China Social Science* (Beijing) No. 11, 1993, p.66-87.

6. Zhou Xiao-meng: Marketing economic system as the key condition for a free society – The work unit in China. in *The Related Social Science 3, Conditions for a free society*, edited by Oniduka and others, The Shinsei Publisher, 1996, p.100-138. Taniguchi Shinyichi: A research note, The 'work unit' system in China – Reviewing political regime in the Mao's era, in *The Chinese Study Monthly*, The Institute of the Chinese Studies, March 1993.

7. Uchita Tomoyuki: The Chinese society in light of household control and the ration system, in *China in the Mao Ze-dong Era – Studies on Modern China*, edited by Mori Kaduko, Japan Institute of International Problems, 1990, p. 259. Tian Ming: The City-Country Relation under the Household System in China, in *Agriculture and Economic Issues* (Beijing) 1991 No. 3.

8. There is a paper by a Chinese scholar bringing up the issue form the viewpoint of 'social control', despite that this paper is not an argument on the relation with the 'work unit system'. Ding Shui-mu: Household Management and Social Control, in *The Society*, 1989, No. 3.

9. In China, instead of laws, the interior regulation or the leader's command are used to handle matters. The following paper presented a series of cases. Hatanaka Katsuo: The laws and the society in the modern China, in *General Theory on Laws in Modern China*, by Zhang You-yu, Amano Katsuo, The Law & Culture Publisher, 1989, p.210-211

10. Mo Shu-ben: A General Study on the Development of the Employee Salary in the past 35 Years, The Chinese Working Personnel Publisher, 1986, p. 305. Kisaki Midori: State-run enterprise in the modern China: a study on the interior structure, in The Series of Modern China Studies 32, Association of Asian Politics and Economy, 1995.

11. Kima Masamichi: The reform of election system in China – The 1979 election Law and the course before it came to the reality, in *Various Aspects of the 'Reform' in the Socialist Regimes*, edited by The Association of Studies on the Socialist Laws, Law & Culture Publisher, 1985.

Chapter 5

Categorizing the Political Regime of Modern China From a Comparative Political Science Viewpoint

Introduction

As indicated in Chapter 1, categorization studies of a socialists' regime is an area of studies not yet explored. In this Chapter, I would like to conduct a comparison of a democracy regime, authoritarianism regime and Soviet-socialism regime, upon verifying the results of analysis conducted in Chapter Three and Four on the internal structures and external relations of actors, using comparative political studies methods. The purpose of this analysis is to define the characteristics of the political regime in modern China. The comparative political studies method here refers mainly to categorization studies on the structures of actors. In concluding this chapter, I would like to summarize, characterize and define the structure analysis made on the political regimes in Modern China.

Section 1: Comparison of State Organizations

Comparison to Democratic Institutions

I indicated earlier in Chapter 3 that in the power relationships among state organizations in China, power is centralized to the legislative body on a horizontal basis. This structure where a legislative body is superior in a legal sense, is categorized as 'assembly system' in constitutional studies. This 'assembly system' is said to been adopted by most socialist nations. The 'assembly system' however, was not a system invented in a socialist nation, but was first introduced in the Swiss Constitution established in years 1848 and 1874 as one form of governing the nation (Saito 1986 pages 5-6). Then what could be the difference between the China-type and democratic Swiss-type structures of the 'assembly system'? Compared to that of democratic countries, the China-type 'assembly system' can be described as 'administrative'. It means that the Chinese legislative body introduced in Chapter 3 is not an assembly with Congress members of equal authority. Rather, it is remarkable that it is an administrative body where the assembly chairman and leaders of the legislative body lead the People's Congress Standing Committee Members (equivalent to Congress members) and representatives. Power relationships between the 'administrative'-type legislative, administrative and judicial bodies exposed a different structure compared to that of democratic nations. First of all, in an administered legislature, the legislation and audit roles agent by a small number of legislative body leaders have made the congress members de-powered. And such powerlessness of congress members diminished the authority of the legislature among the three bodies.

Second, legislative leaders playing the roles of congress members have reformed the power relationships between the legislative bodies vs. administrative/judicial bodies, to a small number of legislative leaders vs. leaders in administrative/judicial bodies. This made the legislative body appear superior, at least in a legal context. However, it actually lead to 'black box'-like policy decisions made only by a few leaders of the three bodies and ties of the three body leaders as a consequence.

Comparison with Authoritarian Organizations

In this study, Taiwan during the period of authoritarianism will be the comparison objective.[1] Not only do we have superior studies on Taiwan's authoritarianism regimes of the past that we could rely on, the Republic of China government in Taiwan was the former government of continent-China. The case of Taiwan is considered the ideal comparison objective. An authoritarianism is 'a political regime that is restricted, has a characteristic of pluralism where no one is committed to its responsibility, does not have a well-thought leadership ideology (it does, but only to the point where the nation is still making development), and while the leader (or in some cases a small group of leaders) formally has unlimited authority, he actually pursues authority only within a limited and foreseeable sphere of activity'. And Taiwanese style authoritarianism is also 'indeed a False-Leninism Party State which survived its isolation by support from the Unites States and by regulating clientism.'[2]

An authoritarianism nation basically does not have an 'assembly system' structure, and with a few exceptions, a presidential autocracy (or a similar reign system by the king or military chief) is usually adopted. In addition to Taiwan, Korea, and Latin American countries where Keiichi Tsunekawa conducted categorization studies, were also the same (Tsunekawa, 1986, Chapter 9). This was mainly because the leaders did not seek for mobility of the people of advanced political parties nor permanent legitimacy of the political power.

One of the reasons why many socialist nations including China adopt 'assembly system' structures is that they wish to prolong the legitimacy of dictatorship by winning 'support of the assembly'. However, leaders of authoritarianism nations, even leaders of Taiwan, the 'False-Leninism' Party State, stressed that 'party nation institution' (Single party rule structure by the People's Party) was a tentative structure before settling into a 'democratic constitutional structure' (Wakabayashi, 1992, page 5). The People's Party, therefore did not need to pretend that the current structures was 'a genuine democratic structure' by utilizing the 'assembly system' as used in the Communist Party.

Autocracy with 'assembly system' structure establishes its single party control over the Congress by a mobilized election process. In contrast, the authoritarianism control does not mobilize its people. Therefore, a supra-party president-type leadership was more suited than an advanced political party, which could mobilize people. Furthermore, an authoritarianism nation usually describes a power centralization structure at the center made by the autocrat. Descending to the local various-level administrations, we can find multi-polarization of power (though limited in some areas) in the local elected-congress, local administrative and judiciary bodies who try to be independent from the ruling party, and in inspection organizations such as the prosecutors, police, and secret police who maintain power centralization organizations independent from the local administrative organizations (Wakabayashi, *ibid*, Chapter 3).

Also, economic power centralization was not seen in authoritarianism nations as in China or The Soviet Union. Co-authors of 'Economic Institution', Kobun, Murakami, and Kumagai indicated that under an authoritarianism nation, 'it would not possible to enforce a collective order over an ownership', and therefore 'theoretically, a combination of collective power and private ownership does not make sense' (Murakami, *et.al* 1973, page 186). In an authoritarian nation, as long as has a private economy system, ownership and management of economic organizations by the state as seen in socialism nations is not possible. The state does intervene with private enterprises compared to democratic nations, however, not by state institutions as seen in socialistic nations. Enterprises are basically independent, form interest groups and function as economic actors. This means that while the entire society is run by state organizations in a socialist nation, the society is independent from the state in authoritarianism nations.

The precedent indications could be summarized as the following: In an authoritarianism nation, especially in Taiwan during its period of authoritarian structure, the autocratic leader ruled above the political parties and state organizations at the central-level and thus ruled over the nation by a power centralization structure. At the local level, there were characteristics in power structures such as 1) a certain extent of decentralization in state organizations and local political power, 2) economic Actors arising from private driven economy, 3) social independence that shows development with some restriction (Separation of social organization from a state organization and growth of independent social actors). The author takes these centralization of power at the central level and limited decentralization at the local and social levels as a characteristic of authoritarianism nation's power structure; namely 'senior level power centralization organization'.

Comparison with Soviet-type Socialism Organizations

When we compare China with Soviet-type socialism organization states, they appear to have the same interstate organization relationships (horizontally in legislature, administrative and judiciary) that has an administrative 'assembly system' characteristics. However, when we view the two from a vertical superior-inferior intra-state organization relationship perspective, the Soviet-type organization state has a 'centralized power' structure when in turn, the China-type has a 'multi-layered' centralized power structure. At first, I would like to review power relationships between vertical administrative organizations. In Chapter 3, I indicated that various-level administrative bodies hold authorities on both corporate management and administrative inspection besides general administration. When this is compared with administrative bodies in The Soviet Union, it becomes clear that power structures in corporate management differs among Chinese and The Soviet Union's administrative bodies.

Most corporations in The Soviet Union were controlled vertically by the Central various-ministries and by industry, and therefore the local various-level administrative bodies did not have the ownership and management rights of state-owned enterprises (Yuri *et.al,* 1990, page 120). For example, a data describes that out of 70 enterprises in Pochi, a small sized city in Georgia, 30 of them belonged to ministries in Moscow (Shimotomai 1987, page 76). In China, public enterprises are categorized by central state-owned enterprise, local state-owned enterprise, and township and village enterprise respectively. Each of these enterprises are horizontally owned and managed by industry ministries of central administrative bodies, local ministries, municipalities, prefecture governments, and by basis level township and villages.

Alec Nove who has been studying The Soviet Union's economy institutions, categorized its structure as 'power centralized multi-polarism. He indicated that, ownership and management rights of state owned enterprises concentrated to central ministries (central centralization of power), distribution of corporate profits to central ministries, and a multi-polarization principle created by 'interest groups' by each central ministry, is the structure's main characteristics (Nove, *transl.* Ohno 1986, page 59-64). In the case of China, ownership and management rights of public enterprises is centralized in 'multi-layered centralization of power' to various level administrative bodies by various administrative levels from central to local and basis, which is one of its characteristics. The other is 'regionalism', where public enterprise profit was divided by units of administrative regions, and by 'economic interest groups' formed by each administrative region. As seen from the preceding, ownership and management rights of public enterprises in China and The Soviet Union describe a structural difference, where one is 'The Soviet Union's vertical centralization of power by central ministries by industry' and the other is 'multi-layered horizontal centralization of power by administrative level of China'.

Furthermore, the power structure in competence of administrative bodies differs in China and The Soviet Union. In China, the vertical relationship among administrative competent authorities such as various level public safety, state defense, and examination authorities from central to local levels is an usual business relationship, and not a relationship of political-administrative leadership or that of personnel appointment. Such authorities lie in same-level local administrative bodies. In The Soviet Union, vertical relationships of competent authorities such as the Interior Affairs or the KGB is an independent vertical power system which describes a strict vertical centralized power structure from the central to local (Uda, 1989, Chapter 4).

Local competent authorities in The Soviet Union such as the local various-level Interior Affairs ministries and KGB were nominally organizations of local various-level administrative bodies. However, they were not subject to the same-level local administrative bodies in the actual political-administrative leadership nor in personnel related matters. This defines that structural differences in 'The Soviet Union's vertical centralization of power by central ministries by industry' and 'multi-layered horizontal centralization of power by administrative level of China' were also found in competent authorities of administrative bodies.

In Chapter 3 I have analyzed that in China, while there is supposed to be an intention for power centralization between central and local administrative bodies in a legal sense, in reality the local administrative bodies have a strong intention for autonomy. I have also indicated its reasons, that local administrative bodies taking ownership and management of public enterprises have enabled development of local administrative bodies themselves to grow into interest groups with strong profit motivation and economic strength. Another indication was that since local administrative bodies were in a position to control local inspection/audit authorities and information, they were not exposed to inspection or audit within its local jurisdiction by the higher administrative bodies and therefore their absoluteness of power was secured.

In viewing authority of local various-level administrative bodies in The Soviet Union under the above context, we could see that local administrative bodies in China have three authorities, namely in general administration, enterprise management and administration competence. The Soviet Union local administrative bodies had only two authorities, enterprise management and administrative competence, or even smaller portion of each. For this reason, the local administrative bodies in The Soviet Union could not perform a strong autonomy as in China.

Next point is the power relationship of the superior-inferior judicial bodies. Of the two organizations, the jurisdiction and prosecution, the structural differences of Chinese and The Soviet Union appears in the power relationships of superior-inferior inspection organization. In The Soviet Union, the prosecution orders from the central to local had its own power centralized regime in all areas of leadership, personnel, and operations. According to the 'Soviet Union Constitution (1977) (Article 164-169), the Union Secretary General held authorization to appoint prosecutors for the Union Republic States, Self-Governing States, and Provinces. And further, the appointment of district and city prosecutors by Union Republic State prosecutors required authorization from the Union Secretary General. All prosecution organizations are subordinated to the Union Secretary General, who exercises its authority (Miyamoto, *ed*, 1982). The Soviet Union tried to secure its independent prosecution authority with strict vertical power-centralization authority systems. Such systems are widely adopted in nations of democratic and authoritarianism structures.

In the case of China, as indicated in Chapter 3, according to the 'Law on People's Prosecution Council Organization', it is not the highest council or the superior council who has the authority to appoint and dismiss local various-level chief prosecutor, deputy prosecutor, prosecution committee member, prosecution member (a higher-level prosecutor) at local various-level People's Prosecution Council, but it is the National People's Congress or its Standing Committee of the same level. In regards to leadership authority of the prosecution body, there is no regulatory prescription that the Highest Prosecution Council or the Superior Prosecution Council should lead local various-level People's Prosecution Councils. It does, however regulate that local various-level People's Prosecution Council owes responsibilities to the same level People's Congress and its Standing Committee and thus receives their supervision. Since the Chinese Prosecution Organizations do not have independent power-centralization authority systems, structural differences in 'The Soviet Union's vertical centralization of power' and 'multi-layered horizontal centralization of power of China' in prosecution organizations becomes clear.

The structural differences in the administrative and judicial organizations in China and The Soviet Union has brought different type of administrative 'assembly systems' in their state organizations. In China, in various-level administrative levels from central, local and basis, administrative bodies lead by various-level judicial bodies hold authorities including the three, general administrative, enterprise management, and administrative inspection. Also authority of justice, lead by the judicial body, are imposed to jurisdiction and prosecution. This means that in China, an administrative 'assembly system' is properly established in various administrative levels.

On the other hand, in Soviet-type socialist organization states, and in The Soviet Union in particular, while the central administrative level had a similar system to China, it was different at the local various-level administrative levels. The administrative bodies in the Soviet Union held only general administrative authorities. Because the prosecution organizations of the judicial body exercised an independent power centralized system, despite that authority to lead administrative and judicial bodies were formally supposed to be centralized to local various-level legislative bodies, it was only on general administrative and jurisdiction organizations where they were able to enforce its authorities. The above describes that in The Soviet Union, a complete form of 'assembly system'-power centralization structure was not established. From these differences in power centralization structure of China and The Soviet Union at local administrative levels of state organizations, I have concluded that the 'multi-layered power centralization' is an important characteristic of power centralization structure of various state organizations in China.

When we compare the case of modern China to an authoritarianism nation's 'higher-level power centralization structured' state organizations, distinct characteristics are that China established a power centric structure to 'all' areas from local to society levels. If we added 'administrative assembly system' that are different from a form adopted by a democracy state, and 'multi-layered' characteristics that are different from the Soviet-type socialist regime, we would have to typify in details the power centralization structures of state organizations in modern China as 'multi-layered', 'administrative', 'collective', and 'assembly system'. In order to avoid being too specific, I would like to prescribe the power structures of state organizations in China as 'multi-layered power centralized structure', since among theses notions, 'multi-layered' is a unique characteristic seen only in China *(ibid* Chart 3-3).

Section 2: Comparison of Mutual Relationships in Actors

This Section, in addition to precedent comparative study on state organizations, is a comparative study on political regime in general, about actors in political parties, state, economy, and society.

Comparison to Democratic Regimes

Constitution Studies describes the case of 'assembly system'-like power structures in a Swiss-origin state organization. It explains that in general, in accordance with functions of the superiority in Congress, political gravity is likely to move to a smaller group of similarity (Saito 1986, pages 5-6). In a democratic state, taking majority of a Congress under the Swiss-type 'assembly system' –like organization was supposed to mean a rule over the three bodies. However, there were factors that the ruling party could not take control over, such as Congress members from opposing parties, direct elections, referendum, neutrality of public officials, and independent actors in the economy and 'society' areas; and therefore a multi-polarized politics continued to exist.

In the case of socialist state, the communist party is the single political party and therefore it becomes the single Congress ruling party. And due to functions of superiority in Congress brought by 'assembly system'-like power structures in the state organizations, the only Congress ruling Communist Party became an absolute power-reign who seized control over various state organizations. Therefore, in comparing socialist and democratic states, 'Single Party System' becomes the key term.

Comparison with Authoritarianism Regimes

Since many authoritarian states also employ a 'single party system', this alone does not differentiate socialist states from authoritarian states. In this section, I will conduct a comparative analysis of China and Taiwan during the period of authoritarian regime. Political regimes of China and Taiwan both have a party-state feature. As Masatake Wakabayashi pointed out, however, the party state of Taiwan is a 'False-Leninism-like party state' or 'authoritarianism-like party state', and not a 'perfect' party state (Wakabayashi, 1992, pages 5-8, 17). From Wakabayashi's writings, this imperfect-ness could be defined to the following points below.

(1) 'Agency-ism' by the People's Party, such as the party organization directly taking over administrative and public organizations, does not exit. Party control over the military is seen in some areas such as the party organization structure not being disclosed in the military, or 'political works factions' subordinating to supreme command factions. They are far from 'taking hold' compared to the political committee institutions of the Chinese Communist Party. Also supporting organizations such as Salvation group's area of activity is much smaller compared to that of communists' youth organizations.

(2) Taiwan needed to maintain a formal face of 'democratic constitution policy'. Therefore some development of a 'constitutional policy' was seen within the regime from the establishment of its state, such as conducting an election at the local political level with some freedom for competition. An opposing power called 'Exclusive of the Party' worked to create an authoritarian-like ' limited multi-polarism' in the People's Party state.

(3) Unlike totalitarianism states that have adopted a socialistic system, the fact that a market existed beyond the state-governing organization boundaries, could not resist rise of social elites. It enabled some level of independency for technocrats, who inside the ruling elite, could manage the market free from political loyalty, and on a long term not recruited for the party state in a state-society relationship.

By comparing Wakabayashi's indications to the Chinese political regime, the following discrepancies become clear. First, in the context of ruling party and state organization relationship, China is under integrated state control by the Communist Party through 'assembly system'-like structures of state organizations. To the contrary, in Taiwan, with no 'assembly system' or 'agency-ism' by the People' s Party, administrative organizations and 'public organizations' (The People's Congress and Judicial Council equivalent to the Legislative body) were to some extent independent from the People's Party. Rather than an integrated rule by the People's Party, it was a 'dual dictatorship' by Jiang Jieshi and Jiang Jingguo. And below this was a 'limited multi-polarization' power relationship between the People's Party, administrative and public organizations.

Second, in terms of relationships between the ruling party and other parties and public groups, there were no other political group in

China besides the Communist Party that had a 'political party' policy acting capability. There was neither 'social' policy acting groups under the 'unit control' of society. In Taiwan, on the other hand, rise of technocrats and social elites outside of the party state was made possible as a result of opening a competitive election at the local politics level, and also due to the presence of a market-driven economy system. This means that opposing political power with a 'political party' actor characteristic, and a social interest group with a 'social' actor characteristic could have existed.

In addition, in terms of relationships between the ruling party and economic actors, there are no economic actors independent from the Communist Party in the case of China where most of the businesses are state-owned and operated by the central and local-basis various-level party leaders from various-level party committees. And in Taiwan, independent economic interest groups apart from the People's Party and the state, under private economy systems, play the role of actors.

In summary, authoritarian regime in Taiwan was, compared to that in China, by far loose and limited, in integration of various state organizations, integration of various economic and 'social' actors, and integration of social-state structures that occurred as a result of these integrations. In China, the Communist Party's various-level committees totally controlled the state organizations, the economy and society, and the Party did not accept existence of any state/economy/'social' actors independent from the Party. It completed a literally 'party state' and 'party society', which was far beyond that of a 'party state' claimed by the Taiwanese People's State.

Comparison with Soviet-type Socialist Regime

Integration of various actors by the Communist Party, such integrations generating further state and social organizational integrations in China, are again 'multi-layered'. 'Multi-layered integration' by the Communist Party is a Chinese characteristic that is clearly distinctive from the Soviet Union and other Soviet-type socialist regime. We shall first compare structures of state organization, which were each integrated by the Chinese and Soviet Parties. In China, various-level party committees established at each administrative level literally take leadership of all state organizations under 'assembly system'-like power centralization structure in state organizations of the same administrative level. These committees have control over personnel matters and all of judicial inspection and audit organizations. They also have control over the Party's internal matters, the Party Regulation inspection organization, inspection and audit organizations for Party elections. As described, the local various-level leaders in China maintain absolute power and will never be subordinate to any sort of inspection or audit within its own jurisdiction.

In the case of the Soviet Union, similar to China, at the central level, the Communist Party Central took integrated and centralized control over various state organizations. At local levels, however, the Soviet Union did not deploy an overall 'assembly system'-like power centralized structure as done in China. Therefore, at the local levels, local political party committees could not control over all local Soviet state organizations.

The Interior Affairs, KGB, administrative audit organizations such as prosecutors and judicial organizations were not managed under leadership of various-level party committees' as was the case in China. Rather, it held an independent centralized power system from the center to local, and was able to exercise its authority to various organizations. Also, local business ministries in the Soviet Union turned to their respective central ministries, rather than their local party committees. It means that vertical power structures in the Soviet Union from the central to local and basis, and authorities of administrative inspection, prosecution and enterprise management at the local level is not integrated by the party's power system. Because each state organizations had power systems of their own beside the Party, local various-level party committees in the Soviet Union did not arise to hold absolute integrated power within their jurisdictions as seen in local various-level party committees in China.

Boris Yeltsin's autobiography gives us a hint. He wrote in his autobiography that while he was First Secretary of the Province Party Committee, he was observed from the Province KGB when he was supposed to lead them, and was put in a position where he would not be able to see their operations. He wrote that because he was able to maintain 'a good respectful personal relationship' with the KGB Province General, he was 'favorably informed of various matters', but at the same time 'knew that there were many matters that he was never informed of' (Yeltsin, *transl.* Ogasawara, 1990, page 79).

The relationship between the Party and State organizations in China and in the Soviet Union also showed discrepancies in the method of institutionalization. This can be explained in the management structures of the 'charismatic' highest leader. In order to institutionalize the position of a 'charismatic' leader, the Soviet Union addressed the Party Chief Secretary to become its highest leader in accordance with 'Party Regulations'. While in China, they took supra-legal procedures and made 'confidential decisions' to select their highest leaders. In regards to the leadership methods, the leaders in the Soviet Union mainly took legal authentic steps by using the Party and Party organizations, inspection organizations such as the KGB as prescribed in the Party Regulations. The leaders in China rather exposed direct personal leadership to all members of the party and the state and appealed for their submission, rather than to process through legal organization systems. These cases were very evident in the eras of Mao Zedong and Deng Xiaoping.

Furthermore, 'multi-layered integration' of state organizations by the Chinese Communist Party appears to have supra-legal colors compared to that of the Soviet Union. Stipulations in the Chinese Communist Party Regulations, the Constitution, and institutional laws of various state organizations all prescribe that vertical organizational structures of both the state and the party should reflect superior-inferior relationships of order. Therefore, the state structures in China were long considered to be 'power centralized'. However, the legal structures prescribed to have 'centralization of power' were almost never adopted in the actual organizations.

What actually did exist was a multi-layered horizontal centralization of power, which was brought by integrated control over various administrative levels by the Chinese Communist Party Committee. In the case of the Soviet Union, legal structures of 'centralization of power' were basically consistent with the actual structures, and did not have much supra-legal factors. It has become clear from the above that power centralization structures of state organizations built by the Chinese Communist Party are 'multi-layered' and 'supra-legal' compared to that of Soviet Union. It has also become clear that such power centralization structures enabled the various-level party committees in China to seize 'absolute' authority.

Next is a comparison in structures that integrated economic/social actors by Chinese and Soviet Parties respectively. In China, various-level leaders of the central and local and basis various-level party committees have the ownership and management rights of public owned enterprises by administrative levels. The leaders are economic actors who are required to generate profit as well as take control over these enterprises. In the Soviet Union, enterprises were managed based on a power centralization structure by central business ministries divided into industries. Since local various-level party committees did not have ownership and management rights, they did not bear the role of an economic actor with responsibility to generate profit of these enterprises. This means that in the Soviet Union, roles of economic factors were filled by each central business ministries, and not on a regional basis as in China.

China and the Soviet Union also displayed a different structure when integrating 'social' actors by the Party. For instance, the labor unions in China are organized by enterprise, by region, integrated and represented by administrative levels to local and basis various-level leaders, in accordance with multi-layered ownership and management structures of the public enterprises. To the contrary, in the Soviet Union, labor unions are formed by industries to be in line with each ministries ownership and management of enterprises on a centralization of power structure. These enterprises were more closely tied to central ministries and the Soviet Communist Party Central rather than local party committees (Kimura 1987, pages 128-130).

Furthermore, there were differences between the two countries in the structures of lowest unit control device that controls and integrates the People. The 'unit' in China bounds its people by workplace. It limits the people's mobility between workplace and regions, integrates people in all areas of politics, administration, economy and thought, an organization with strong monitoring-like color. The Soviet Union did have a system of 'control at workplace' over its employees', however the control system was vertical and power centric. It was possible for people to move vertically along the system and enabled mobility in workplace, in between cities, and in between rural and city areas. They were not tightly bound to their 'units' as seen in China.

The different integration structures of economic and social actors by the Parties in China and the Soviet Union displayed different characteristics to that of integration in state and social structures. As indicated earlier in Chapter 2, in China, local and basis various-level leaders integrate society. In the Soviet Union, however, the society is vertically integrated in line with structures of each central ministry under the central leadership. Therefore, while central-local relationship is important in China, the Soviet Union had its central leadership-central ministries relationships and inter-ministry relationship. These relationships hid two aspects, of inter-state power relations and state-society relations. Also in generating economic and social profit, local and basis various-level leaders were the actors in China, while in the Soviet Union, each central ministries acted as 'society' to the central party leaders and thus beard the responsibility to generate profit.

Finally, I have indicated earlier that the 'absoluteness' of power in China's local and basis various-level party committees is a characteristic different from the Soviet Union. The multi-layered integration structure of economic and social actors by the Chinese Communist Party displayed following characteristics to the power of local and basis leaders. First of all, I can refer to 'multiple sides' of power. The local and basis various level leaders are not merely a power organization of politics and administration, but play the role to generate profit as economic and social actors. The second is 'autonomy' of such power. Autonomy of power is subject to legitimacy, incentive and ability before it is enforced. As local and basis various-level leaders in China own and manage public enterprises, they have the legitimacy and incentive to pursue business profits and accumulated business knowledge. They have become a strong economy and social interest group in the local and basis reign.

As examined in this chapter, in the political regime of modern China, the Party central and local/basis various-level party committees reign as the core of power centralization above multi-layered power centralization structure in various state organizations. In addition, the boundary of power centralization was expanded to include all economic and social actors, which resulted in a 'multi-layered centralization of power' structure. And local and basis various-level leaders in China, reshaped by its multi-layered power centralization structures, have displayed its own characteristics, such as multiple-sided, autonomy, and absoluteness.

Conclusion

In this Chapter, referring to the analysis preceded in Chapters 3 and 4 where I have analyzed internal structures and external relationships of various actors, and through comparative studies on the democratic regime, authoritarian regime, and the Soviet-type socialist regime, I have made the characteristics of political regimes in modern China very clear. I would like to conclude by presenting a general summary on these categorization analyses and define the political regimes in modern China.

When we measure political regime in modern China by the four variables I used in Chapter 1, they are (1) the 'power centralization styles' is mainly a multi-layered horizontal centralization of power by each administrative level. (2) Inside the 'power centric core' is the 'charismatic' leader who is the core of a single ruling advanced political party with its various-level committees. (3) 'Numbers of political actors' who were integrated in state organizations are limited, in the sense that various-level leaders integrate all actors in state, political party, economy and society. (4) 'The strength of power centralization', is strong in horizontal directions, but relatively weak in a vertical centralization of power.

Supplementing to one of the characteristics that 'strength of power centralization is relatively weak in vertical directions', the strength of vertical power centralization in the political regime of modern China, should be defined as (1) 'relatively weak' compared to the multi-layered horizontal power centralization structure. (2) 'Relatively weak' compared to the Soviet Union and other Soviet-type socialist regime. (3) 'Relatively weak' during Deng Xiaoping's era compared to that in Mao Zedong's era. (4) 'Relatively weak' during peacetimes compared to a short crisis period.

From all earlier findings, I would like to present the following definitions. The political regime in modern China[1] has a 'state organization' with multi-layered centralization of power structure, where its power centric core is located in administrative region leadership consisting of various-level party committees of a single ruling advanced political party by each administrative level. It also has a 'social structure' consisting of economic and 'social' actors who are made into state organizations by[2] (a) ownership and management of major economic organizations, (b) overall control over society, c. 'unit control' to the people. It is a political regime that was structured by integration of these state and social organizations, a strong multi-layered horizontal power centralization structure by actors and a relatively weak vertical centralization. This book summarizes such political regimes in modern China in the concept of 'socialists multi-layered centralized regime'.

Also when we compare the political regimes of Soviet-type socialist regime and modern China's multi-layered centralized regime, a structure of horizontal power centralization with central level leaders in the core center, while vertical power centralization by each central ministries underneath the central are important characteristics in

Soviet-type. Such Soviet-type socialist regime should be summarized as 'socialists centralization regime'. The so-called authoritarian states, the political regimes of Taiwan in particular, has dictatorship at the central level, has limited authority among actors and state organizations, political party, economics, society and local levels. It also has a social structure that takes importance in privatized economy and society. From these characteristics, it has been defined as 'authoritarian superior centralization regime' (Chart 5-1).

Chart 5-1: Political Regimes Categorized by Power Relations of Actors

Political Regimes		Power Relations between Various Actors									
		Ruling Party	Administration	Legislature	Jurisdiction	Prosecution	Police	Policy & Police	Actors of Economy	Actors of Society	Mass Media
Socialist Multi-layered Centralized Regime (Contemporary China)	Central Level	◇	←	←	←	←	←	←	←	←	←
	Local Various Levels	↑	←	←	←	←	←	←	←	←	←
Socialist Power Centralized Regime (Former-Soviet Union)	Central Level	◇	←	←	←	←	←	←	←	←	←
	Local Various Levels	↑	←	←							←
Authoritarian Superior Centralized Regime (Taiwan)	Central Level	◇	←	□	←	←	←	←	◇	◇	←
	Local Various Levels	↑	←	□	↑	↑	↑	↑	◇	◇	←
Democratic Power Decentralization Regime	Central Level	◇	◇	◇	◇	◇	◇	◇	◇	◇	◇
	Local Various Levels	◇	◇	◇	◇	↑	↑	↑	◇	◇	◇

Note: ←horizontal centralization of power, ↑ vertical centralization of power, □ not perfectly controlled, ◇independent

Source: By author

Notes

1. The author's comparative analysis mainly relies on studies by Masatake Wakabayashi. Masatake Wakabayashi '*Taiwan-A Divided Nation and its Democracy*' University of Tokyo Publishing, 1992.

2. Definition of authoritarianism refers to, Juan J. Linz, 'An Authoritarian Regime: Spain.' In Erik, Allard and Stein, Rokkan *Eds., Mass Politics; Studies in Political Sociology,* New York, Free Press, 1970, page 235. Definition of authoritarianism in Taiwan refers to Masatake Wakabayashi, *ibid.* Page 17.

Chapter 6

Provincial Party Secretaries in the Political Regime of Contemporary China

Introduction

To understand the center-locality relationships in China, it is crucial to understand the power of Provincial Party Secretary (PPS), who is head of Administrative Region in direct contact with the Central Government. However, what kind of power does PPS have? How does a PPS exercise his power? What is the mechanism that produces and maintains his power? Despite the apparent importance to understand the roles of PPS, there has been conspicuous lack of research on this subject. One of the reasons is that no PPS has ever accepted interviews by researchers.

In 1990, one of the high-ranking officials in China called Xu Jiatun took refuge in the United States, who accepted an interview by the present author. Xu was vice-Party Secretary of Jiangsu province in 1955 and Party Secretary from 1977 till 1983. From March 1983 till February 1990, he served as Secretary of Hong Kong and Macao Party Work Committee and as Director of Hong Kong Brunch of Xinhua News Agency. Xu also published memoirs, so this article will utilize these basic materials to undertake a case study of PPS.[1]

Recently, memoirs and biographies of some of former PPS's were published.[2] Those included reminiscences by other former Jiangsu PPS's: Peng Chong who held the post in 1974 and his predecessor. Jiang Weiqing who served in 1956. So coincidentally, reminiscences of successive PPS's from 1950s till 1980s in Jiangsu Province have now become available. However, since these memoirs or biographies are published in China domestically, their writings are bound to be under political constraints. Moreover, completeness and reliability of these documents as representations of independent cases are questionable, since the writers could not be crosschecked by personal interviews. Therefore, I shall primarily employ Xu's document while using the others as supplements. In addition, since any of the reminiscences do not cover the 1990s, political movements in Guangdong Province leadership after 1998 were studied to fill in the gap. This type of case study is far from ideal, as it does not examine a large number of independent cases, but I hope a crosschecking of Xu's case with other sources will show certain generality in the study I present here.

Now, "political regime" mentioned in this article refers to an institutionalized but dynamic structure of actors who participate in the policymaking processes. Based on this definition and the approach of political regime analysis founded on the search for structures and behavioral patterns of actors, I propose the contemporary Chinese political regime to be called "Multi-layered Centralized Regime."[3] Under this Regime, the power of local leadership can be shown to have multi-faceted nature, autonomous nature, and absoluteness. This article will undertake a case study to examine the power of PPS from both macro and micro perspectives.

In the first section, characteristics of the power of PPS are considered in the context of macro political process. In contrast to local chief in general sense, a PPS is not only a local leader but a national politician as well. His political power has multiple dimensions for having such dual roles. (Here, a "national politician" refers to one who participates in the policymaking process at the State/Party center.) I will argue that the characteristics of PPS were legacy of the political tradition under Mao Zedong, which were subsequently strengthened under Deng Xiaoping. The second section is devoted to a macro analysis of the mechanism that produces and maintains the power of PPS. I will show that the power of PPS is shaped by the Multi-layered Centralized Regime, and that his ability to exercise his power is institutionalized. The third section re-examines the result from the macro analysis in the previous sections from a micro-perspective. In actual practice, how does a PPS exercise his power? To what extent can he participate in the policymaking process at the center? To what extent can he maintain autonomy? In general, the ultimate substance of political power is ability to make policy. A PPS has a role perception[4]as head of local government a PPS certainly takes orders from the central authority, but he is also able to participate in the policymaking process at the center, for he is a national politician as well. This section will show that although there are certainly limitations in his autonomy as head of local government, his own autonomy as being a national politician is well legitimized. This study focuses on Xu Jiatun's case, at the same time drawing on those of other PPS's.

Section 1: A Man of Power as Local Leader and also as National Politician

Starting from the time of liberated areas under control of the Chinese Communist Party (CCP), the basic characteristics of the power of PPS, both as head of local government and national politician, gradually evolved by the end of the Mao Zedong era in 1976. During the era of Deng Xiaoping, PPS's authority over economic matters had been reinforced till 1994. However, as a result of the deepening market reforms during the Jiang Zemin era, the previous pattern of feedback of power from the center to localities, and from the localities to the center, was disrupted. A structural change has been introduced to break the pattern, where the power, mainly the economic authority, was deprived both from the center and locality, and was delegated to the market.[5]

Tradition of the Mao Zedong Era

"Monolithic leading Institutions by Party Commission" was the basic system of the Multi-layered Centralized Regime, and in China its prototype emerged and developed under the peculiar political environment in the liberated areas during the war. After the founding of the nation in 1949, Mao Zedong fully established the Monolithic leading Institutions by the Party Commission, and built up a pattern of policymaking in which PPS's play important roles. Under such circumstance the multi-layered Centralized Regime gradually evolved and the unique characteristics of the power of PPS developed, both as head of province and as national politician at the same time.

Since the founding of the nation until the 1980s, one common feature existed for local leaders. That was, they all had experience in establishing and managing liberated areas by the CCP during the extended Liberation War period from 1927 to 1949. Their experience in the liberated areas gave rise to two characteristics: one was a strong autonomy in the management of their own jurisdiction, while the other was a strong willingness to participate in the policymaking process at the center. Liberated areas were military bases that scattered around the extensive townships and were often surrounded by enemy forces. They were almost "local autonomous bodies" with a very high level of independence, because they had their own army, own administrative body, and control over the economy and the society of the region. The base leadership accepted full responsibility for the existence and development of the base where they could not rely on the central leadership.

Successful base leaders were rewarded for their capability. During the Liberation War period, the CCP itself was made mainly of Liberation Bases, and since the "party center" really was just one of the bases, local leaders were ranked high up in the CCP Central. Moreover, participation of local leaders was well justified, since the central leadership needed to collect information from the local bases and make policy in accordance with diverse situations of individual bases, and also since local leaders demanded that they should be able to participate in the policymaking at the Party center. The CCP Central established Party Committee at each Liberation Base and entrusted all the local authority to it. This was to ensure the loyalty of many base leaders in various regions, who were highly dispersed over the vast country. Later, Mao was to conceptualize this type of institutions under which the powers of the regional Party Committees were concentrated horizontally as " Monolithic leading Institutions by Party Commission." Concentration of all the power to the Party Committee had a function to strengthen the power of the Party Secretaries of locality.

Just after the founding of the nation, China imitated her predecessor of centralized political regime, the Soviet Union, in building a socialist nation. For instance, various industrial bureaus at local levels were to become direct subordinates of the Central Government. Administrative bureaus were supposed to receive "dual leading" from both the Party central and the Party local, but the former had more say, and thus the leading from the local committee was considered secondary.[6] Introduction of the Soviet style centralized political regime was a reform to diminish significant potion of the administrative power of PPS, and aimed at transforming the regime inherited from the Liberation Base era.

Political conflicts arose between the first generation of the local and the central leaderships just after the founding of the nation. In 1952, Ye Jianying, Secretary of Huanan Bureau of Communist Party, was criticized for "localism" by the center. In 1954 was seen a "struggle" between "Gao Gang and Rao Shushi Anti-Party Union." Gao Gang and Rao Shushi were charged for attempting to make Dongbei and Huadong, which were their jurisdictions, into "independent kingdoms," and also for disrupting the Party and attempting to seize the highest power. The grand administrative region was abolished this year, and Province became administrative region directly reporting to the center.[7]

However, Mao Zedong was not in favor of the Soviet style centralized political regime. He had been a base leader himself, and then was the Party Chairman at the top of the whole Nation/Party organization. Mao demolished the grand administrative region, as it tended to give rise to "independent kingdoms." However, he initiated a policy change to strengthen the power of the Party Committee. In other words, he reinstated the traditional Monolithic leading Institutions by Party Commission. Around 1957, the Soviet style centralized political regime was reformed and Multi-layered Centralized Regime was re-established as the fundamental institutions of the Monolithic leading Institutions by Party Commission.[8]

After the reform, Mao Zedong launched a Great Leap Forward (GLF), counting on the motivation of the local leadership. According to Asanuma, behind the launching of the GLF there was a political disagreement between the center and localities. The Central Government was in favor of a redistribution policy that aimed to integrate various regions with wide economic gaps into a nation. However, some provinces were opposed to the policy. Mao Zedong politicized the disagreement by collaborating with southern provinces, aiming for a policy change.[9]

Moreover, in the political process of amending the GLF policy, autonomous moves of the PPS's played a significant role.[10] The Lushan Conference in 1959 represented a re-emergence of the pattern of policymaking process in which Mao and PPS's collaborated closely. Initially the purpose of the Lushan Conference was to amend the leftist tendency in the GLF policy. During the first half of the conference, Mao held three meetings repeatedly with Hunan Province Party Secretary Zhou Xiaozhou and Executive Secretary Zhou Hui. Hunan Province was where Mao was born, but it was reluctant in taking part in the GLF movement. As a result, Hunan minimized the economic damage of the GLF to become the only province that did not experience major famine in 1959. Zhou Hui looked back the role of PPS in the policymaking and implementation of the GLF movement as follows: "It was PPS who went to the 'Imperial Court' to do proceedings, and implemented policies after coming back to the Province." "Even Chairman Mao needed to talk to PPS when he came to Province."

According to the orthodox studies of the GLF, the reason Mao shifted from the leftist to the opposing rightist tendency was that he did not want to bear the responsibility of the policy failure, and also because he could not face up to the criticism by Peng Dehuai. However, there actually was the following process behind the scene. Mao did want to amend the GLF policy, but did not want to take responsibility at the same time. This was in line with the interest of the majority of PPS's, who actively supported the GLF. However, Hunan PPS and those on his side furiously criticized the supporters of the GLF, resulting in a serious division among PPS's. Under such circumstances, Zhou Xiaozhou and Zhou Hui visited Peng Dehuai to ask him to suggest Mao to support them. Peng promised to write a letter to Mao. Mao interpreted this letter as a sign of deepening division in the central leadership due to the conflicts among PPS's. So he thought it was no longer possible to "amend the GLF policy without taking responsibility." In response, he collaborated with the supporters of the GLF, and thus shifted from criticizing the leftists' to the rightists'.

In the amendment process of People's Commune Institutions started from 1961, PPS's acted quite autonomously.[11] From February 1961, the Party Central held several meetings with PPS's and drafted a policy document called "People's Commune Work Ordinance and Trial Run" over five months. At the same time, many PPS's formulated reform proposals and experimented freely within their own jurisdictions. Anhui Province First Secretary Zeng Xisheng presented a policy that was to become the prototype of "Household Responsibility

Institutions" adopted in the Reform and Opening- up Period seventeen years later. In 20 March, Ceng wrote a letter to Mao, and met him personally in July. Ceng reported on the Anhui institutions under which farm households were responsible for the management of the farm production. By autumn 1961, this institutions spread to 85.4 per cent of the Provinces. However, Mao announced in December that he did not approve of this institution, making it clear that work unit was to be the basic management unit as defined in People's Commune Work Ordinance and Trial Run. From Ceng's case, we can infer that a PPS had right to formulate a unique policy and implement it in his own jurisdiction. Even more, PPS could make policy recommendations to the Party/State center directly. Although Mao made clear that he did not approve of Ceng's proposal in the end, either had he not interfered while he was actually experimenting on it. Lastly as is well known, Mao initiated the Cultural Revolution in collaboration with Shanghai City Leadership and received severe opposition from the Beijing City Leadership.[12]

We can summarize the ways in which PPS's exercised power during Mao era as follows. PPS's perceived autonomy in their provinces and their political participation at the state center as interrelated rights. They took these rights for granted because they saw themselves both as head of provincial government and as national politician at the same time. PPS's made moves independently and formulated unique policies to implement in their jurisdictions. Moreover, they participated in the policymaking process at the national level with their unique policies. Over this background the central leaders collaborated and confronted with PPS's, and center-locality and locality-locality relationships became politicized. This type of policymaking process had turned into a pattern.

Characteristics in the Deng Xiaoping Era

In the Deng Xiaoping era, which is characterized by a rapid economic and slow political reform, the power of PPS's carried on the tradition under Mao. However, economic development of their provinces became the prime responsibility required on them. As their authority over the economy was reinforced significantly, so their autonomy in policy-making process was increased.

The first step of the economic reform was that of the People's

Commune Institutions by the introduction of "Household Responsibility Institutions." As mentioned earlier, Anhui Province First Secretary Ceng Xisheng devised the prototype of this institution by 1961. In winter 1977 in the same Province, the reform of the People's Commune Institutions started after farmers in a certain village revitalized the institutions experimented 16 years earlier. Ceng Xisheng's idea must have had a long lasting impact.

Next year, Anhui PPS Wan Li expressed approval of the Household Responsibility Institutions, and afterwards the Sichuan PPS Zhao Ziyang and the Inner Mongolia Autonomous region PPS Zhou Hui joined in support for the institutions. Zhou Hui had just been appointed to the post in July twenty years after his fall at the Lushan Conference. According to Zhou's memoirs, although "Reform and Opening-up" had not been proposed by anyone and no central leadership was showing signs of approval, he thought that someone had to take an initiative.[13] PPS's recognized that they were in the new era of big policy change and saw their role perception in participating in the policymaking process by initiating policy change earlier than the central leadership.

The Deng Xiaoping era can be symbolized by a word "*fengquan rangli*" (to transfer power and profits). During this period power and profits were transferred to local leadership at various administrative levels, especially to the provincial. Basically, the reform-oriented leadership at the center collaborated with PPS's to initiate economic reforms. As Deng said, "I will primarily consult with the PPS's," reform-oriented leadership at the center and PPS's dominated the Chinese politics around this period.[14] Autonomy over provincial government budget and management of enterprises made significant impact on the power of PPS's, who therefore felt satisfied with these reforms.

Although the transfer of power and profits made local economy so active that a high economic growth resulted, irregular phenomena called "*Zhuhou Jingji*" (little empire economies) became widespread, manifested as investment competition and market partition by local leaders. The phenomena caused the cycle of overheating and recession of economy since the 1980s.[15] According to Xu Jiatun, one of the PPS's behaved as follows during the time of overheating and recession.[16] Since 1989 the centralized economic management was reinforced for some time, and Hubei Province Party Secretary Xing Chongzhi, who complied with the central authority, strictly controlled the private enterprises by demolishing a shopping street with many privately owned shops by bulldozers. After economic reforms were resumed in 1992, Hubei Province went into a recession and Xing Chongzhi lost his post. In contrast, Shandong Province Party Secretary Jiang Chunyun encouraged the development of non-State Owned Enterprises (SOE's) such as Township and Village Enterprises (TVE's). Later Jiang Chunyun was promoted to member of the Committee of the Politburo of the CCP and Vice-Premier of the State Council for making the GDP of Shandong Province highest in the nation.

As seen from these cases, political life of a PPS largely depended on his ability to autonomously manage the economy but not on doing what he was asked by the Center to do. In fact, this trend can be found from the beginning of the Deng era. In the case of the reform of the People's Commune mentioned earlier, two pioneers, Zhao Ziyang and Wan Li, were promoted to Premier and Vice-Premier respectively for increasing agricultural production in Sichuan and Anhui. In the Deng era, the most important factor governing the behavior of PPS's was their responsibility to the economic development in their jurisdiction. So their behavior was quite different from that in the Mao era, when "*Zhengzhi Diyi*" (Politics comes first) and loyalty to the leader was most important. Because of this change, autonomy of PPS's was strengthened.

To sum up, during the Deng era, PPS's participated more in the policymaking process at the center, as a result of which they saw themselves as pioneers of policy changes, and concern for the economic development became the prime factor governing their behavior. In this connection, transfer of power to the local leadership was an important political agenda in this period. PPS's therefore collaborated with the reform-minded leaders at the state center to increase their authority over the economy. As a consequence, the Multi-layered Centralized Regime was strengthened during Deng's era, and PPS's increased their autonomy of power under this Regime.

Changes in the Jiang Zemin Era

Market reform and administrative reform progressed under the leadership of Jiang Zemin, and this structural change significantly altered the power of PPS. Policy environment had shifted towards more centralized policymaking well before Ye Xuanping, the last leader from the Liberation War and the Head of the Guangdong Province, retired in the 1990s, or before Deng Xiaoping proclaimed the "completion of power transfer" to Jiang Zemin in 1994. The reform objective to pursue economic development was translated into a policy objective of establishing a market-oriented economy. Jiang Zemin also needed to avoid recession from an over-centralization, so the policy needed to be oriented towards soft-landing of the overheating economy. Market reform meant transfer of property and managerial rights not to the Central or Local Government but to individual enterprises. The soft-landing of economy meant balanced distribution of the economic benefits among players in the state center, provinces, and enterprises. It also meant establishment of rules in the market. It did not, however, mean to initiate yet another economic contraction policy by a centralized means. Under such circumstances, the Jiang Zemin Leadership negotiated with local leaders and his orientation towards centralization was focused on balancing of benefits for major economic players and establishment of market rules.

However, balancing of the benefits and establishment of the market rules by nature did not increase the authority of the central government. Rule of law was thus emphasized. This is apparent in Jiang's speeches, where the keyword shifted from "defending the authority of the Center" towards "governance by (the rule of) law" and "establishment of law."[17] Under these trends was it formally decided that SOE's were to be privatized through an introduction of the stock market in the 15th Party Congress in 1997.[18] This was a reform to transfer the property and the managerial rights from various levels of the government to the market. This meant that the economy was no longer to be controlled by the government but by the market. This reform broke off the cycle of an overheating of the economy caused by investment races at various levels of local authorities and a recession as a result of contraction policy by the Central Government in response. It should have become possible to make economy healthier and fit to the market.

The administration was also reformed structurally to accommodate market economy.[19] In 1997, all the Industrial Ministries under the State Council were abolished. For instance, the Ministry of Coal, which once used to be in charge of the world's largest coal industry, was downgraded to a Bureau, its manpower being reduced from about 650 to 90. In 2000 industrial bureaus at and below the Provincial level underwent a similar reform. Some argues that the reason full autonomy of enterprises could not be achieved by previous reforms was that the industrial bureaus at various levels clung to the managerial rights of the enterprises. However, with this downgrading of the Industrial Ministries, the Multi-layered Centralized Regime was transformed structurally.

Section 2: Mechanism that Produces the Power of PPS

This section will show that the Multi-layered Centralized Regime shapes the basic characteristics of the power of PPS, whereas the market reforms provided PPS's with motivation to act dynamically. In addition, the institutionalized policymaking process enables PPS's to actually exercise their power. It is an organic interconnection among these three factors that produces the power of PPS.

The term "Monolithic leading Institutions by Party Commission" was no longer used under Deng, but effectively the institutions was still in place. Provincial Party Committee still had a monopoly over legislation, administration, and judicial and personnel decisions (except for the Leaders of province, who was appointed by the Party center). More significantly than ever, they gained property rights and managerial autonomy over SOE's. During the Mao Zedong era, large part of managerial rights were delegated to the provincial leadership, while local leaders at various levels were given authority to establish and manage local SOE's, collective enterprises, and agricultural industry. In addition, fiscal autonomy and managerial rights were delegated to the Province during the Deng Xiaoping era.

A local leadership's power, with its authority even over the economy, was transformed as a result of the deepening market reforms during the Deng era. During the Mao era, outputs from the local SOE's were distributed as rationed goods. However, the market reforms enabled the local leadership to earn profits from the outputs of those enterprises. This motivated them, especially Provincial Party Committee and its Secretary, to act as if they were the owners of the enterprises and they thus turned into an interest group motivated by profits. Therefore, in the policymaking process PPS's not only needed to be conscious of the Party Central but also to watch the market carefully. In other words, the Party Central had become not the sole "superior" to PPS any more. Thus, first the "Monolithic leading Institutions by Party Commission" endowed PPS's with the power over their jurisdiction, and then emergence of the market gave them profit-motive and dynamism to exercise that power automatically.

Now let us take a look at the relationship between the institutionalized policymaking process and the power of PPS. First, in Party Committee a "Responsibility Sharing Institutions" is institutionalized. These institutions enable monolithic leading institutions by the Party Committee and guarantees PPS's to hold solid power. The Party Committee exercises power through its internal Responsibility Sharing Institutions as follows. In the case of province, each Standing Member of the Provincial Party Committee holds posts such as Head of Provincial People's Congress or Head of Province. Such a Responsibility Sharing Institution contains in itself a mechanism by which some absoluteness is rendered to the power of PPS.

Generally speaking, hierarchic relationship between the center and the local is supposed to be a relationship of leading and implementation, and that for communication of information. However in reality, because all the power is concentrated to the Provincial Party Committee through the Responsibility Sharing Institutions, the ties between central institutions and their affiliates are easily disconnected. For instance, in the policy implementation processes, various institutions in a provincial government report to the Provincial Party Committee about orders from the State Council. They implement the orders only after being approved by the Provincial Party Committee. Alternatively, orders from the Center are communicated to the Provincial Party Committee as orders from the "Party Central" or the "Party Central and the State Council". In China, joint document forms of the latter are encountered frequently.

Regarding the communication of information, since any political systems start functioning from input of communication, those who control it can naturally affect a political system to a great extent. In China, important local information is processed and approved by the Provincial Party Committee before being passed on to the center. In 1997 the following news report appeared, for instance. In order to prevent spreading of corruption within the Party, the CCP Central instructed Provincial Committee of Discipline and Instruction to report important cases of corruption not only to the Provincial Party

Committee but to its affiliated higher level Committee of Discipline and Instruction.[20] This news report reveals that previously the Provincial Committee of Discipline and Instruction could not directly report to the higher level or to the center.

In most of the countries, information is passed on from a state institution at lower levels to upper ones. In addition, central authorities mobilize various inspection and auditing institutions independent of local authorities so as to diversify information sources and to crosscheck information. In China, however, the Provincial Party Committee has a monolithic control over inspection and auditing institutions and other state apparatus, so that the state center does not have its own inspection and auditing institutions in provinces, with no other means available to collect information independently. The state center has to rely on reports from the Provincial Party Committee or provincial government institutions with an approval of the Provincial Party Committee.

Second, it is important to understand the conference institutions in the policymaking process in China. In the case of a legislative body, People's Congress, the representatives of people, are elected on provincial bases and each province forms a representative group for the Congress. A PPS is the head of such a group, who hosts deliberation meeting of provincial representative groups at the People's Congress. Moreover, PPS has the right to speak for his group at the plenary session.

A similar conference institution is employed within the Party. In the National Congress of CCP, which is the highest institution for policymaking, Province is the basic unit as above. In each province representatives are elected, a representative group for the Congress is organized, and deliberation meetings are convened, just like in the case of the People's Congress. The Central Committee, which is Standing Committee of the National Congress of the CCP, holds deliberation meetings on "regional" bases such as Dongbei or Huabei that consists of several provinces, because they have too few members of the Central Committee or Committee candidates in each province. However, a PPS chairs the meeting as in the case above. Moreover, PPS automatically becomes a member of the Central Committee, while Minister of the Central Government does not necessarily become one. Therefore PPS is generally regarded as more highly ranked in the Party than ordinary Ministers. As to the Committee of the Politburo of the CCP and the Standing Committee of the Politburo, which are the Central

Leaderships of the CCP, at least some current PPS's are the members of the former. Although no current PPS is member of the latter, most of its members were PPS before. An experience as a PPS is thus one of the "prerequisite" to be promoted to the Party Leadership.

In addition, important policies are made on meetings called "Central Work Conference" which are held on demand. The central leadership invites PPS's and others to make policy in these conferences. In most cases, important policies are discussed, benefits to related parties are balanced out and policy are made prior to the Congress in the Central Work Conference. For instance in the Mao Zedong era, the GLF policy was formulated in a series of work conferences chaired by Mao, from January to April 1958 with PPS's at Nanning, Chengdu, Wuhan, and Guangzhou Conferences. Later in August at an Extended Politburo Conference, it was decided that the GLF was to be advocated and People's Commune Institutions was to be introduced. In Extended Politburo Conference, Politburo Committee members as well as PPS's are invited to decide on policies.[21]

In the Deng era a certain pattern of policymaking emerged. First, PPS's were assembled in Central Work Conference where they formulate policy proposals, which are then formalized at the Plenary Session of the Central Committee. Before the third Plenary Session of the 11th Central Committee Meeting, which was to be remembered as the commencement of the Deng era, Central Work Conference took place over more than a month, and a series of policy were in large part made in these conferences.[22] Apart from the Central Work Conferences held before the Central Committee, work conferences on various policy themes were also convened frequently. In the Jiang Zemin era, Rural Work Conference and Economic Work Conference took place every year, and work conferences on other themes were also called as required. Just after the Asian Financial Crisis in 1997, a work conference on financial sector was convened at the end of the year.[23]

Lastly, we have to look at the "*Shidian Zhidu*" (Test Institutions). To carry out a "*shidian*" is to experiment a policy in one or more provinces before it is formally introduced at a larger scale. As early as in the Mao era, the need for "*shidian*" was advocated and it became a "*gongzuo fengfa*" (method of implementation) for CCP. Local leaders were generally keen to be selected for "*shidian*," because he can actively participate in the policymaking process at the center by implementing a test case by their own hands. Moreover, if the experiment turned out to be success, he would be seen as one of the pioneers of the reform. For instance, Hainan Province was selected for a test case of the political reform for "small government." Many of the achievements were called "*shidian jingyan*" (experience of the test case) and were publicized.[24]

To the local leadership, "*Shidian Zhidu*" provides a means and an excuse to pursue their own original policies and to influence the policymaking process at the center. For instance in 1998, seven Provincial Party Committees made requests to include election of heads of Townships in the agendas for political regime reform to the Party Central. In December a direct election for a head of Township in Sichuan was implemented using the term "*shidian*" as an excuse. Generally the Center does not hold anyone responsible for implementing a test case, and therefore the person in charge of this direct election was not made accountable to the Center.[25]

On the one hand, although the power of PPS is guaranteed by the institutions mentioned above, it is nevertheless restricted. Institutions that limit the power of PPS are the "Monolithic leading Institutions by the Center", the "Collective Leading Institutions", and the "Personnel Institutions". The Monolithic leading Institutions by the center stipulates that the local party and the government institutions receive monolithic leading from the Party Central, or from the State Council. The Collective Leading Institutions advocates collective leading to prevent PPS to become dictator in the Party Committee. The Personnel Institutions empowers the Party Central to decide appointments and dismissals of higher-ranking officials in Provinces. We will look into these institutions in more details in the next section by examining concrete examples.

Section 3: Provincial Party Secretary's Authority to Make Policy

This section assesses the power of PPS by examining their authority to make policy under the "guarantees" and the "constraints" identified in the previous section. In general, PPS's manipulate the institutions that guarantee them power and they are relatively successful in making restrictive institutions ineffective. So in general they secure autonomy in policymaking within their provinces.

Original Policy in Jiangsu Province

In the memoirs of three Jiangsu PPS's, including Jiang Weiqing, Peng Chong, and Xu Jiatun, we find that all of them are commonly proud of initiating their own original policies independent of the center. Their sense of pride indicates that PPS's have role perception in participating in the policymaking process as heads of province as well as national politicians, and are personally trusted by individual leaders in the center. Jiang Weiqing looks back on the "Struggle Against Rightists Movements" started in 1957. In July, Mao Zedong visited Nanjing and scolded him, "Why aren't there any Rightists elements in the Party Committee in your Province? Why aren't there any exposures? Are you going to do it or not?" In response, Jiang answered back by saying, "Please fire me and then let my successor do it." In August Mao sent Peng Zhen to Nanjing and pushed Jiang to expose Rightists elements, but he snapped back by saying, "There might be some Rightists here but I have not found one yet." In the end it turned out that the Jiangsu Province was the only province where no "Rightist element" was detected in Party Committees higher than county.[26]

On the GLF, Jiang Weiqing and Peng Chong express almost the same opinions. Both of them think that the GLF movement was wrong in general, but they both recognize its contribution to the long-term development of Jiangsu Province. They think that in the long run development of the local and collective enterprises in this period enabled Jiangsu to become a province with the highest GDP per capita in China.[27] Their opinions are supportive of Asanuma's argument that the policy of the GLF was decided by the collaboration between Mao and the southern province PPS's who had their own interests. Moreover, their opinions show that the cultivation of local and collective enterprises was a long-term policy held by Jiangsu PPS's until Xu Jiatun period.

Since Xu Jiatun was in charge of the agricultural policy in the 1960s, he was pushing forwards his original economic policy. Even during the Cultural Revolution period he writes, "Jiangsu Province did not participate in banning of rural free markets." In other words, they did not take part in the so-called 'Cutting the Tail of Capitalism

Movement'. This was overtly out of line with the policy of the Party Central."[28] On his promotion of "*Shatui Qiye*" (changed its name to Township and Village Enterprise in 1982), Xu said, "To be honest, I was attempting many things to find a loophole in the State Policy."

Since the "*Shatui Qiye*" is one kind of the "collective ownership," there was some autonomy allowed for management, thus after remitting 51 per cent of the profit to the State, the other incomes could be used for investment by our own accord. Because of this, the Provincial Party Committee actively engaged in the development of the collective enterprises, and "*Shatui Qiye* " in the rural area and collectively owned enterprises in the urban area became a locomotive of the industrial growth instead of SOE's. As a result of putting emphasis on Small and Medium sized enterprises (SME's), the share of the SME's in the total number of enterprises in Jiangsu Province reached 98 per cent, of which 60 per cent were collectively owned. These policies were successful, and by the end of the Cultural Revolutions in 1976, economic situation in Jiangsu Province was clearly better than in other provinces. Although the National economy was on the verge of collapse, the growth of industrial output in Jiangsu Province averaged more than 10 per cent, and that of agricultural products was 5 to 6 per cent during few years until 1976.

Based on this economic success, Xu initiated a policy aiming for an even higher economic growth. As a result, the total value of agricultural and industrial productions in Shanghai Municipal City and Liaoning Province leaped to the top of the whole country by 1979, and the Provincial GDP doubled in six years till 1983.[29] Behind this scene, however, Xu conflicted with Chen Yun over the economic policies.[30] Xu was advocating multiple cropping, of which Chen Yun criticized him several times. In *Chen Yun Wenxuan* (*A Collection of essays by Chen Yun*) we find an essay entitled "Why single cropping is better than double cropping," which was on critique of Xu.

At the similar period, Xu was going to build a small-scale chemical fertilizer factory at each county in Jiangsu Province. Chen Yun dispatched his secretary Zhou Taihe for an inspection, and communicated his opinion to Xu. "A small scale chemical fertilizer factory is inefficient in comparison with a large plants, and so is illogical." According to Xu, however, a large scale chemical fertilizer plant must be imported from abroad, but not only the Province did not have the foreign exchange but it was very difficult to get an import approval from the center. In contrast, constructions of small-scale factories can Province authorize. Moreover, it can be managed at county level within their own financial and technological capacities. In *Chen Yun Wenxuan*, we find an essay entitled "Quicken the Development of Nitrogenous Fertilizer Industry" which contains criticism against Xu.[31]

Chen Yun's criticism towards the multi-cropping and the small-scale chemical fertilizer factory is not merely disapproval of individual policies. Given the economic policy of the center that placed emphasis on restriction of economic growth and "balancing of the national economy," it was likely that Chen, who favored the State policy and large-scale enterprises, was an advocate of the central policy. Especially Chen Yun was Head of the CCP Finance and Economic Leading Group who has the highest authority on the Chinese economy. All of Xu's original economic policies were totally out of the line with the State policy. Xu, however, did not subvert to the criticism.

To understand why Xu dared to oppose Chen, *A Selected essays of Deng Xiaoping* is essential. In an essay entitled "A Talk in Beijing After Seeing Jiangsu," Deng mentioned that in Jiangsu Province, "people were full of smiles and there were many newly built houses. Officials were very proud of themselves."[32] In 1982, Deng announced a plan to quadruple the national economy by the end of the century, which encountered with many skeptics. Because of the oppositions, Deng went to Jiangsu Province where the economy was developing rapidly. Xu Jiatun guided Deng around the province personally, and explained the reason for the rapid development and his original economic policies in detail. As a result, Xu gained personal support of Deng, which enabled him to ignore the criticism of Chen.[33]

Xu mentioned that there were three motives/goals for a PPS to implement his original policies in his own province. He pointed out that a PPS would participate in the policymaking as a national politician "by pursuing their legitimate autonomy," "to enhance benefit to the province," and "to create experience locally and let the results speak for themselves nationally".

First, "if there is a policy at the top, there would be a counter-policy at below." In such a large country as China, local autonomy must be respected, because regions are diverse. So it is only natural for locality to act independently. Therefore, this phrase aptly describes resistance of localities against conservative attitudes, standardized policy, and selfish behavior of the center that ignores their creativeness.[34] Second, as head of locality, a PPS must consider the benefit of his province. Desires of the masses and lower governmental bodies for development were very strong. In order to respond to them, Xu created a phrase "*paobu qianjin.*" In Chinese there is a conventional phrase with the same phonetics but with a different character for "*bu*" (run forward). Xu exchanged "run forward" with another "*bu*," meaning "ministry." His new phrase thus meant running around the Central Ministry to demand investment funds or deregulation and to pursue further "progress" of the local development.[35] Third, during the interview, Xu quoted Mao and emphasized that the "biggest contribution a locality can make is to provide policy experience for the center."

At first, the original economic policies in Jiangsu's Province were criticized as "going too far," but in the end, they were all acknowledged as "advanced experience." "Sunan Model" was among such policies. Some say that all the modernization policies in China are simply mimicking the West. However, the way of modernization by developing "Xiaochengzhen" (small cities), which was implemented in Jiangsu to promote commerce and industry by development of TVE's in rural areas, was originated in China. He gained reputation as a "creative and energetic man," and therefore was sent to Hong Kong.[36]

Section 4: Xu Jiatun at Hong Kong and Party/Government Institution of the Center

PPS's and cabinet members at the center are formally ranked at the same level, but the status of the former is higher than the latter. Under such circumstance, PPS's collaborate with the Center at one time and make conflicts at others. Now Xu was sent to Hong Kong, but it is still possible to use his case to consider the relationship between PPS and the center, because his status as the Secretary of Assignment Committee was equal to PPS, although the Hong Kong post was quite unique. While he was assigned to Hong Kong, he nullified constraints on his power such as the "Monolithic leading by the Center,"

"Collective Leading Institutions", and "Personnel Institutions." Indeed, he was able to take a lead in the policymaking process at most of the time. However, he fell from the position as he lost trust of the central leadership.

Xu explained the power relationship surrounding Hong Kong assignments as follows (Chart 6-1).

Chart 6-1: A Structure of the CCP Hong Kong and Macao Work Organisation (1983-1990 : While Xu Jiatun was in Hon Kong)

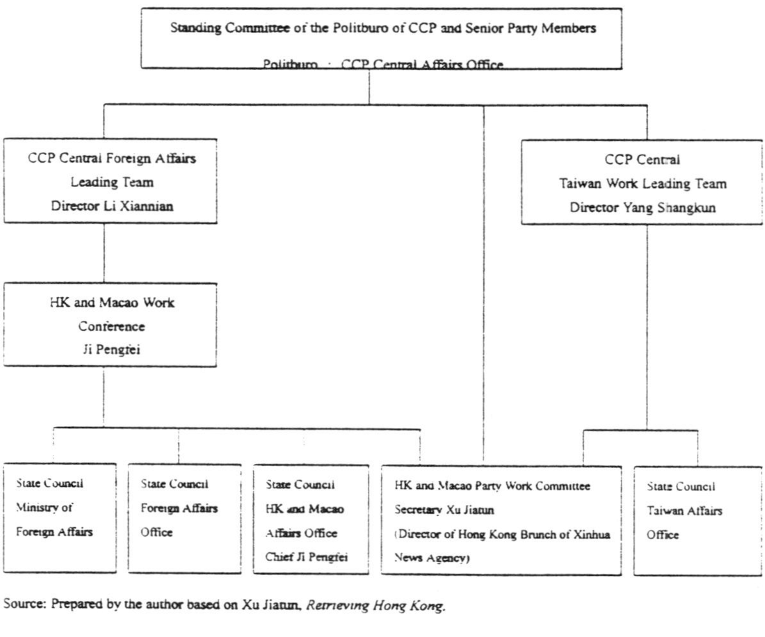

Source: Prepared by the author based on Xu Jiatun, *Retrieving Hong Kong*.

Party Work Committee of Hong Kong and Macao was an equally ranked institution as Ministry at the Central Government. However, the Party Work Committee of Hong Kong and Macao belonged to the Party, while Ministries were administrative bodies. So Xu did not need to report to and receive orders from the Ministries at the Central Government. Instead, Xu was accountable to the Party Central whom he reported his activities to and received orders from. Since the Work Conference of Hong Kong and Macao existed only during the conference (Diagram), Xu's direct superior was the CCP Foreign Affairs Leading Group and the Central Politburo. However, he needed to report to the CCP Central Affairs Office first, to ask them to which section he should report to or to ask for an order on a specific matter.

According to Xu, a PPS sends reports to the CCP Central Affairs Office in general. When CCP Central Affairs Office received a report, it redirects it to other party sections or Ministries under the State Council according to the content. Xu was conscious of the special nature of Hong Kong post so he paid particular attention to maintaining good relations with the Ministries under the State Council. He therefore addressed the report to the CCP Central Affairs Office as well as to the Ministries. However, the CCP Central Affairs Office Chief Hu Qili told Xu that it was not necessary for him to write (the address), and if necessary, they would send the document to related ministries."[37]

For instance, in one case Xu was ordered to "report the progress of his work to the Party Central three months after he started the post." In September 1983 after his arrival to Beijing, Xu was told by the CCP Central Affair's Office, Chief Hu Qili, that General Secretary Hu Yaobang had ordered the CCP Foreign Affairs Leading Group to hear the report. At that time the head of the CCP Foreign Affairs Leading Group was President Li Xiannian and the associated head was the State Council Premier Zhao Ziyang. Xu reported on the state of affairs in Hong Kong, analyzed the situation, and drew a policy implication.

After questions were asked and a discussion session was held, he was approved of the policy by Li and Zhao on the spot. Some people from related Ministries such as Hong Kong and Macao Office attended the meeting, but no comments were heard from them. Xu was leading the policymaking process, because he was the most informed person at the meeting. As Hong Kong and Macao Office and other related Ministries were not Xu's superior and were less informed than Xu, they could not take leadership in the meeting. From this example it is apparent that a PPS can limit the "Monolithic leading Institutions by the Center" by his official position in the Party and by controlling information.[38]

After Xu went back to Hong Kong, he held a "General Meeting of Hong Kong and Macao Work Commission," decided on the policies approved by the center, and started preparing for their implementation. The process of the General Meeting mainly consisted of Xu's congress report, sub-meetings among representatives, and a general summary by Xu.[39] According to Xu, the "recapitulation" has crucial importance to the power of PPS. In committee meetings such as General Assembly and smaller scale meetings, policies are decided not by vote but by his "general summary".[40] Therefore, this "recapitulation" curtails the collective leading by the Party Committee. According to Xu, "PPS is the key person. They talk about collective leading institutions but 'Yes' of PPS is the ultimate decision in reality."[41]

PPS's can control information not only because they are closer to the information sources but also because the center does not possess an effective institutionalized information channel. In the case of the visits of Chen Yun and Deng Xiaoping to Jiangsu Province, for example, Chen used his secretary to get information from the field while Deng went there himself.

In April 1984, Xi Zhongxun, a Committee member of the Politburo, disapprovingly said, "Liao Chengzhi (a person in charge of Hong Kong assignment) does not report to the center: he monopolizes the information, " during a conversation with Xu. In response to the problem the center resorted to an irregular means, according to Xu. "There was a breach of the party rule. The Party Central sent 'Visiting Scholars' to Hong Kong and created a channel that directly transmits information to the center."[42] This episode indicates that even though the Party Central faced a problem of "information monopoly" by the lower level, it could not penetrate the barrier without breaching the "party's organization rules."

Conflicts are internal to the power relationship between PPS's and Ministries under the State Council. From 1983 till 1990 while Xu was holding office in Hong Kong, Xu and bureaucrats of the State Council were struggling against each other. Soon after the "Xu Jiatun Report," Hong Kong and Macao Office, which represented the State Council, convened a national level meeting called "Hong Kong and Macao Economic Work Conference."[43] Related Ministries and local authorities were invited. In the conference, a document entitled "Nine Notes" was distributed. This "Notes" effectively prohibited Chinese enterprises from launching a business in Hong Kong. Deng Xiaoping, Chen Yun, Li Xiannian, Hu Yaobang, and Zhao Ziyang agreed with the contents as indicated by circle marks on the document placed by them.

It is important to note the background of this incident. Before Xu left for Hong Kong, he was shown a notification from the Hong Kong and Macao Office to carry out an order. The document was jointly written by the Hong Kong and Macao Office and the State Economy and Trade Commission, and stipulated that every Ministry and Province must not establish a branch institute in Hong Kong, and that any exiting institutes must be closed. From his experience as Head of Jiangsu Province, Xu thought that it was necessary to have a branch institute in Hong Kong in order to carry out reform and opening-up. So at that time, Xu answered that first he had to see the situation in Hong Kong himself in order to decide. After he arrived in Hong Kong, he called upon an officer of the State Economy and Trade Commission to undertake a joint research. Xu convinced State Economy and Trade Commission with his superior information, and subsequently blocked the order quite effectively.

According to Xu, it was customary for a PPS to convince government officials from the center by using the information superiority. In 1977, when he was undertaking a construction of "*Shetui Qiye*" in cotton industry, he was pinpointed by Li Xiannian, the Vice-Premier in charge of economy and was criticized that it was "inefficient and confuses the National Plan." However, he later invited a Minister of Cotton Industry to Jiangsu Province, personally showed him around in an inspection tour, and talked him over.[44] "Talking over" is thus one of the ways in which a PPS and officials from the central government form a co-operative relationship.[45]

There was little co-operation between Xu and Ministries in the Hong Kong assignment. Apparently, "Hong Kong and Macao Economic Work Conference" was a retaliation of the Hong Kong and Macao Office against Xu. After the conference, Xu visited Premier Zhao Ziyang and explained about the situation in Hong Kong and Provinces. He gained understanding of Zhao and proposed that "the document used in the conference should not be notified over the nation, and conference participants should not communicate the content." At the end, the policy plotted by the Hong Kong and Macao Office was aborted.

Conflicts between Xu and ministries did not arise simply from the differences in policy. A special circumstance in Hong Kong at that time was significant. Before Xu took office in Hong Kong, posts in the government station in Hong Kong had traditionally been occupied by officials from the Ministries. However, the station was upgraded to a Provincial level in 1983 and Xu, who had been Head of a province, was assigned to the new post. So Ministries in charge of foreign affairs, such as Hong Kong and Macao Office, Ministry of Foreign Affairs, and Foreign Affairs Office, tried to recover their lost stake. A "big fight" between two sides took place in the autumn of 1986.[46]

Ji Pengfei assembled all members of the Hong Kong and Macao Work Committee including Foreign Affairs Office, Ministry of Foreign Affairs, and Hong Kong and Macao Office to hold a "*Tanxinhui*" (meeting to disclose one's heart). In essence, that "*Tanxinhui*" was a meeting to denounce Xu. Continuous criticisms by heads of four institutions lasted as long as three days, and conference reports were sent to the central leadership everyday. This was an information war to force Xu out of office by showing Xu's mistakes. However, Xu relied on the personal trust of Deng he had gained since his visit to Jiangsu and Deng's favorable assessment of his Hong Kong policy. He disseminated his side of information by visiting the central leadership himself. As a result, he gained support from Deng and defeated Ji Pengfei. Xu produced a report on his Hong Kong policies, insisting that the Party center should notify it in the form of "CCP Central Document" so as to end the debate.

"CCP Central Document" is the most formal official document in China. The present case indicates that local leaders do participate in formalizing it. Moreover, in some cases a local leader may autonomously draft a policy document and request the Party center to label it as "CCP Central Document." Xu indeed participated in issuing of another one. In 1988, the CCP Finance and Economic Leading Group Secretary Zhang Jinfu entrusted Xu to draft a "CCP Central Document" called "Utilize the presence of Hong Kong in economic development of the coastal region," which was then collectively revised by the Group.[47]

During the interview, Xu repeatedly emphasized that the relationship between PPS's and Ministry officials was analogous to that between politicians and bureaucrats. According to Xu, in general, a new policy is formulated by politicians or/and researchers. Politicians in particular have to take into account various benefits to the economy and also the society in general, but they have to take responsibility for their own decisions on the other hand. So courage as well as accuracy is required for them. In contrast, bureaucrats are people who take care of logistics, for whom conservative attitudes or inaction are their own way to survive. So a PPS must not be a 'yes man' to the officials in the

Ministries: he is destined to fight with bureaucrats over policies.

Jiang Zemin and PPS's

According to the memoir of Jiang Weiqing, Deng Xiaoping said, "Mao Zedong always discussed policies with PPS's. He always consulted with PPS's and asked for their opinions even on small matters. I am going to revive this method."[48] As this quote and previous discussions show, participation of PPS's in policymaking processes was important. However, this has significantly changed in the Jiang Zemin era.

According to Xu's reminiscences, behind the disagreement between China and Britain on the construction project of the new airport in Hong Kong, there was the following process behind the scene. Xu thought that even if Britain had a political motive behind the construction project, a new airport was certainly desirable, and the project was financially feasible. So Xu told his opinion to Jiang Zemin, and promised to send a survey report as soon as possible. However, Jiang did not wait for the report, and publicly denounced the construction of the airport. He said that "*Ni qingke, Wo huichao?*" (Why should I pay money when you are the one who is giving the feast?) This had made Hong Kong people indignant. According to Xu, Jiang was not thoughtful enough as the head of nation in making a statement that implied an eventuality of the financial problem immediately after the new airport plan was made public. Moreover, "I" in a "Why should I pay" meant the Chinese government; but it was of course the people of Hong Kong who had to bear the increased tax burden when financial problems had really occurred, for which the Chinese Government needed not take any responsibility. So Jiang would have received well by Hong Kong people had he worried not about himself but about the burden they should bear. Xu criticized, "Jiang Zemin must have took words of people surrounding him for granted in making such statements."[49]

Jiang Zemin placed more importance on the opinions of bureaucrats in the State Council than information from local leaders, in contrast to Mao and Deng. Jiang did not experience the Revolutionary War, and by the time Deng announced that a transfer of power to Jiang had completed in 1994, all the previous heads of the liberated area during the war had disappeared from the central and local leaderships. Jiang changed the style of governance from collaboration with local leaderships towards utilization of modern bureaucratic organizations. As mentioned earlier, Jiang's tendency for centralization in his policy may be a manifestation of this general change in the method of governance.

Xu said, "The level of autonomy of a PPS largely depends on his personal trust from leaders in the center."[50] Indeed, his case supports this hypothesis. Importance of personal trust arises from a personnel institutions which authorizes the central leadership to dismiss top leaders of Provinces. Xu used to nullify Chen Yun's criticism by the personal trust he earned from Deng Xiaoping, Hu Yaobang, and Zhao Ziyang. However, he lost the trust of the central leaderships at the Tiananmen incidence in 1989, as he took side of Zhao Ziyang.[51] The central leadership could dismiss a PPS any time, of which Xu's removal from his office was a typical example.

Some incidents in the 1990s provide good materials to study the relationship between the personnel institutions and the autonomy of PPS's. The dismissal of the Beijing Municipality Party Secretary Chen Xitong and the appointment of Li Changchun to Guangdong PPS are such cases. Sasaki has already analyzed the dismissal of Chen from the point of view of the center-locality relationship, so the latter case I will examine here.[52]

At the beginning of 1998, a few important positions in Guangdong's Province were filled by those appointed by the center. Wang Qishan, who was the President of the China Construction Bank, was appointed Vice-Provincial Head in charge of economic affairs. In 2 March, China Central Television broadcast that the Guangdong PPS Xie Fei had left office and the Henan PPS Li Changchun took his place. On the same day, all the leaders at the administrative levels above municipality in Guangdong were assembled, where Zhang Quanjing, the Division Chief of the CCP Central Organization, reported the decision of the Party Central and praised the great achievements of Li Changchun. This was in marked contrast with the political tradition in the province. Guangdong leadership had been selected within Guangdong Province for the past twenty years, but this time the leader was assigned from outside. Moreover, unlike previous decisions on personnel's, it was openly publicized this time. These suggest that the

Party center showed its intention to increase control over Guangdong Province, which had been strongly autonomous by means of delegating a leader.

Although this incidence appears to merely represent Jiang's policy stance for centralization, there was actually a fundamental change in Jiang's policy towards localities around 1998. Previously, the main instrument used to control localities was political campaigns. After 1998, formal modification of power structure became the most important instrument in introducing a change. For instance, there was a progressive reform of the power structure in the financial sector. People's Bank of China (PBC), the central bank of China, used to have a branch in every province, but under the new system, some of the branches were merged so that there now remain only nine branches in the whole nation. An official in the Chinese government disclosed, "The reason for the massive outstanding debts is that local governments used to force the PBC branches to lend. The aim of the new system is to prevent local governments from intervening PBC activities."[53]

This change in the policy stance was decided at the 15th Party Congress in September 1997. So the decision at the Congress had an effect as early as a year later. Another important decision made in the Congress was the abolishment of all the industrial ministries and bureaus at the center as well as localities. From the perspective of the center-locality relationship, neither the center nor the locality gained increased economic authority from this change. Instead, behind the decision was a policy stance that relied on legal system and market mechanism. Behind the change in Jiang's policy stance towards the localities, one could find an idea that "governance by the authority of a leader is not needed anymore, but we need rule of law."

This policy stance that places importance on the rule of law was apparent in the liquidation of the Guangdong International Trust and Investment Cooperation (GITIC) started in October. The liquidation of the GITIC was initially thought to indicate an increased control of the center over the strongly autonomous Guangdong Province, but later was it shown not to be so. It was the President of People's Bank of China Dai Xianglong and the Vice-Provincial Head Wang Qishan, not the officials from Guangdong, who repeatedly stated from the outset that repayment of debts to foreign investors would be prioritized. They provided against hindering future foreign investments to Guangdong. However, their statements were soon to be turned over.

On 10th, 16th, and 21st of January 1999, high-ranking officials from the center and Guangdong Province held press conferences, and then on 27th Dai Xianglong himself stated in a press conference that the government was not going to be responsible for the repayment of the foreign debts accumulated by domestic financial institutions. More importantly, they stated that all the creditors will be treated equally according to the bankruptcy law, and foreign creditors would not receive preferential treatments. They also stated that the lenders needed to consider the balance sheet and the trust of the company they are lending money to more carefully, and that they should not count on a government bailout.[54]

As the Party center appoints and dismisses provincial leaders, PPS's are of course required to obey the center. However at the same time, bringing benefits, especially an economic development, to their jurisdiction is their prime responsibility, and thus their performance is assessed mainly by the economic situation of their province. As this example shows, local leaders' behavior depends not only on the personnel institutions, but also on local benefits. Although Wang Qishan was not originally from Guangdong, he feared that the foreign investors might be discouraged to invest in the future so he advocated priority settlement of foreign debts. The total value of exports from Guangdong province is about 40 per cent of China as a whole, and majority is created by foreign enterprises. The Center had to take this reality into account. Dai Xianglong expressed the same opinion as Wang precisely for this reason.

Another example can be given for local autonomy. In 1997, the state center started to tighten control over illegal flows of capital and goods between Guangdong and Hong Kong. In response, local leaders overcame this "crisis" by taking advantages of weaknesses of the policy, saving at the same time the face of the central leadership by various measures. For instance, the center ordered to impose a fine on illegal enterprises, from which Guangdong province collected about 50 billion yuan (about 730 million US dollars). Enterprises in Shenzhen showed loyalty to the center by collecting 20 billion yuan, which was twice the target amount set by the center. However, the fines were not the source of this revenue. Municipal leaders, wanting to avoid panic that examination of enterprises may provoke, settled the matter by collecting the money widely and thinly. They decided to charge 100 yuan per employee to all enterprises in Shenzhen. Local taxation bureau even prepared examples of document for the fine payment and gave guidance to enterprises individually on how to produce the documents.[55]

In these two examples, PPS Li Changchun did not play active roles, but since vice Provincial Head Wang Qishan was his right-hand man, and as Shenzhen Municipal Secretary is a member of the Provincial Party Standing Committee, Li must have been aware of the situation. In any case, Guangdong Province Party Committee tried to protect individuality and autonomy of the province so as to maintain and enhance economic benefits of their province. Lastly, it was because the center had to consider the economic development of Guangdong that the initial policy on ITIC of Guangzhou City had to be abandoned. Premier Zhu Rongji stated that there would not be any bankruptcy of any financial institutions other than the GITIC. In Guangdong, a rescue package for ITIC of Guangzhou City was announced.[56]

The preceding case study shows the following points. A PPS has a role perception as a politician who represents local socio-economic benefits, and is motivated by profits to maintain power and autonomy of multiple dimensions. He introduces original policies in his jurisdiction independently, and also participates actively in the policymaking process at the center. A PPS utilizes his position at the center and information advantage at the locality to limit the effectiveness of the "Monolithic leading Institutions by the Center," which is a device to curve local powers, and to gain an influence in the policymaking process at the center. As we have seen, PPS's sometimes take a lead in the political process. A PPS also can limit the "Collective leading Institutions," which is a device to prevent "dictatorship by a secretary," by having a control over the "recapitulation" of meetings. Thereby a PPS can hold final policymaking authority, so his power is said to have absoluteness in this sense.

We have also seen the importance of personal trust of the central leaders for the autonomy of a PPS, since personnel decisions are made at the center. The deeper the personal trusts he earns, the greater is his level of autonomy. However, there is also a limit in the personnel institutions to control a PPS. In Xu's example, some of the leaders were critical of his policy while others were supportive, so his autonomy was strengthened as division within the central leadership went deeper. In Li Changchun's case, once he was assigned to PPS, he had to protect the local interests; he therefore maintained the face of the center while keeping his autonomy.

Conclusion

Historically speaking, the characteristics of the power of PPS were originally formed in the era of liberated areas under the control of the CCP. By the end of the Mao era in 1976, the basic characteristics of the power of PPS, as head of province as well as national politician, evolved under the Multi-layered Centralized Regime. In addition, the economic authority of PPS was reinforced during the Deng Xiaoping era. In the Jiang Zemin era, however, the previous pattern of power exchanges between the center and locality was disrupted and the power became neither centralized nor delegated to localities. A structural change in the political regime has thus emerged, as much power has been delegated to the market.

Structurally, the Multi-layered Centralized Regime based on the "Monolithic leading Institutions by the Party Commission" determines the power of PPS, so that he has central authority to control legislation, administration, judicature, and the economy as top leader of the Provincial Party Committee. Such power of PPS is guaranteed by several institutionalized devices, most notably among which are; "responsibility sharing institutions" of the Provincial Party Committee, "conference institutions" that institutionalizes participation of PPS to the policymaking process in the center, and "test-case institutions." Such institutions built into the Multi-layered Centralized Regime constitute a mechanism that produces and maintains the power of PPS.

Actual policymaking processes show that the autonomy of PPS as local leader is constrained by the "Monolithic leading Institutions by the Center," "Collective Leading Institutions", and by the "Personnel Institutions." However, as a national politician his autonomy is well respected. Through his active participation in the policymaking process in the center, he can personally reduce the institutional constraints on his power. Specifically, so long as he preserves personal trusts of some central leaders and keeps face of the central leadership in general, he can maintain and sometimes reinforce his autonomy to exercise power in practice. Significance of the multi-faceted nature, autonomous nature, and absoluteness power of PPS should not be underestimated in today's China.

Notes

1. Main references of this articles are as follws; Xu Jiatun, *Honkonn Kaishuu Kousaku* (*Retrieving Hong Kong*) (Tokyo: Tsukuma Shobou, 1996), Xu Jiatun, *Xu Jiatun huiyilu yu suixianglu* (*Reminiscences and Essays by Xu Jiatun*) (Hong Kong: Mingjing chubanshe, 1998) and an interview of Xu Jiatun by the author on 22th May 1996 at Xu's house in Los Angels.

2. Jiang Weiqing, *Qi shi nian Zheng Cheng-Jiang Weiqing huiyilu* (*70 years of Journey-Reminiscences by Jiang Wei qing*) (Jiangsu: Jiangsu renmin chubanshe, 1996). Zhu Tonghua *et. al.eds.*, *He Peng Chong zai yi qi de ri zi* (*Days spent together with Peng Chong*) (Jiangsu: Jiangsu renmin chubanshe, 1997). Quan Yanchi and Huang Lina, *Tiandao-Zhou Hui yu Lushan huiyi* (Justice-*Zhou Hui joins the Lushan Conference*) (Guangdong: Guangdong luxing chubanshe, 1997). Shi Dongbing, *Zui chu de kang zheng-Peng Zhen zai wenhua dageming qian xi* (*The First Confrontation-Peng Zhen on the Eve of the Cultural Revolution*) (Beijing: Zhonggong zhongyang dang xiao chubanshe, 1993).

3. Zhao Hongwei, *Chuugoku no jiyusou shuuken taisei to keizai hatuten* (*China's Mutilayered Centralised Regime and Economic Development*) (Tokyo: Tokyo University Press, 1998). Zhao systematically discusses political regime of contemporary China discussed and models "Multilayered Centralised Regime." (Chapter 1 Theory of Political Regime and Contemporary China. Chapter 2 Establishment of the Contemporary Chinese Political Regime. Chapter 3 The Contemporary Chinese Political Regime and the Structure of the Nation. Chapter 4 The Contemporary Chinese Political Regime and the Structure of the Society. Chapter 5 A Model of Contemporary Chinese Political Regime. Chapter 6 Contemporary Chinese Political Regime and PolicyMaking Process. Chapter 7 Contemporary Chinese Political Regime and Policy Implementation. Chapter 8 Mechanism of Political Regime Shift in Contemporary China.)

4. Suleiman, Ezra N. 1974: Politics Power, and Bureaucracy in France: The Administrative Elite, Princeton, Princeton University Press.pp.204-211.

5. See Zhao Hongwei, "Chuugoku no gyousei kaikaku," in Japan Comparative Political Science Society (ed.), *Sekai no gyousei kaikaku* (Tokyo: Wasada University Press, 1999), pp.153-174 ["Administrative reform in China", *Administrative reforms in the world*].

6. Masao Fukushima, *Chugoku no jinmin minshu seiken-sono kensetu katei to riron* (*People's democratic government-its construction process and a theory*) (Tokyo: Tokyo University Press, 1965), pp. 515-516.

7. Zhongguo xingzheng quhua yanjiuhui (China administrative boundary research group), *Zhongguo shengzhi* (*China's Province System*) (Beijing: Zhongguo dabaike quanshu chubanshe, 1995), pp4-5.

8. Zhao Hongwei, *China's Mutilayered Centralised Regime and Economic Development*, pp.41-43.

9. Kaori Asanuma, "Chuuou-chihou kankei no seijika-1958nen wo jirei to shite" in Tatumi Okabe (ed.), *Greater China no seiji henyou* (Tokyo:

Keisoushobou, 1995), pp49-53. ["Politicisation of the centre-local relationship: a case of 1958," *Political Changes in Greater China*]

10. Quan Yanchi and Huang Lina, Justice-*Zhou Hui joins the Lushan Conference*, pp.160,178-185, 201, 204, 277, 288.
See also Li Rui, *Lushan huiyi shilu* (A Record of Lushan Conference) (Hong Kong: Tianditushu, 1993).

11. Zhang Hongru, *20shiji Zhongguo dashi quanshu* (*A book of big events in 20th century China*) (Beijing: Beijing chubanshe, 1993).

12. See Shi Dongbing, *The First Confrontation-Peng Zhen on the Eve of the Cultural Revolution.*

13. Quan Yanchi and Huang Lina, Justice-*Zhou Hui joins the Lushan Conference*, p.73.

14. Jiang Weiqing, *70 years of Journey-Reminiscences by Jiang Wei qing*, Vol. 2, p566.

15. Zhao Hongwei, *China's Mutilayered Centralised Regime and Economic Development*, pp.181-208.

16. Xu Jiatun, *Retrieving Hong Kong*, Vol. 2, pp.252-253. Also from the interview with Xu Jiatun.

17. A speech given by Jiang Zemin at the 4th Representative Members Meeting of China Law Society, *PR tuushinn* (Tokyo: *PR News*), 22 January 1997. See also "The 15th Party Congress Report," *Chuugoku Tuushin* (Beijing: China News), 25 September 1997.

18. *ibid.*, *PR News*

19. Liu Zhifeng, *Di qi ci geming-1998 Zhongguo zhengfu jigou gaige beiwanglu* (The Seventh Revolution-a memorandum of the administrative reform in 1998) (Beijing: Jingji ribao chubanshe, 1998), pp.65-101. Also by an interview with Wang Shengming (Chief, National People's Congress Legislation Work Committee Division of the Civil Law) in Tokyo on 29 September 1998. See also Guo wu yuan (ed.), *Zhongyang Zhengfu zhuzhi jigou* (*Central Government Organisatinal Structure*) (Beijing: Gaige chubanshe, 1998). And Wang Jinnian (ed.), *Zhongguo da jingjian* (Shandong: Jinan chubanshe, 1998). and *Nihon keizai shinbun* (*Japan Economic News*), 20 January 2000.

20. *Renmin ribao* (*People's Daily*), 27 January 1996.

21. Zhang Hongru, *A book of big events in 20th century China*, pp.49-51. See also Li Jian, *Guanjian huiyi qinli shilu* (*Historical record of Important Conference*) (Beijing: Zhonggong Zhongyang dang xiao chubanshe, 1998), Vol.1, pp.271-285.

22. Li Yan, *Zaisheng Zhongguo-Zhonggong 11 jie 3 zhong quan hui de qianqian houhou* (*China revived-before and after the 11th Central Committee Meeting 3rd Plenary Session*) (Beijing: Zhonggong dangshi chubanshe, 1998), pp.339-372.

23. Tokyo: *PR News*, 21 November 1997.

24. Zhongguo shehui kexue yuan Hainan zhengzhi tizhi he shehui tizhi gaige yanjiu, *'Xiao zhengfu da shehui' de lilun yu shijian-Hainan zhengzhi tizhi yu shehui tizhi gaige yanjiu* (*Theory and practice of 'small government, large*

society'-A Research on political and social regime reform in Hainan) (Beijing: Shehui keyue wenxian chubabshe, 1998).

25. Naruki Oohara, "Chuugoku gouchou chyokusetu senkyo no jitukenchi wo tazunete," Tokyo: *Ajiken World Trend*, June 1999, pp44-45 ["On a visit to an area experimented a direct election of the head of the Township"].

26. Jiang Weiqing, *70 years of Journey-Reminiscences by Jiang Wei qing*, Vol. 2, pp.415-418.

27. *ibid.*, pp462-463. Quan Yanchi and Huang Lina, Justice-*Zhou Hui joins the Lushan Conference*, pp.102-105.

28. Xu Jiatun, *Retrieving Hong Kong*, Vol. 1, p.11.

29. *ibid.*, pp.10-13. [1] *ibid.*, pp.285-289.

30. *ibid.*, pp.285-289.

31. Chen Yun, *Chen Yun Wenxuan* (*Selected Essays of Chen Yun*) (Beijing: Renmin chubanshe, 1986). Xu Jiatun, *Reminiscences and Essays by Xu Jiatun*, pp.69-70.

32. Deng Xiaoping, *Deng Xiaoping Wenxuan* (*Selected Essays of Deng Xiaoping*) (Beijing: Renmin chubanshe, 1993), Vol.3.

33. Xu Jiatun, *Retrieving Hong Kong*, Vol. 1, pp.7-13.

34. *ibid.*, pp.25-26.

35. The interview with Xu Jiatun.

36. Xu Jiatun, *Retrieving Hong Kong*, Vol. 1, p5.

37. *ibid.*, p.241.

38. *ibid.*, pp.63-69.

39. *ibid.*, pp.69-74.

40. Xu Jiatun, *Reminiscences and Essays by Xu Jiatun*, p.193. Also from the interview with Xu Jiatun.

41. Xu Jiatun, *Retrieving Hong Kong*, Vol. 1, p.24.

42. *ibid.*, pp.18-19.

43. *ibid.*, pp.282-291.

44. The interview with Xu Jiatun.

45. Xu Jiatun, *Reminiscences and Essays by Xu Jiatun*, pp.69-70.

46. Xu Jiatun, *Retrieving Hong Kong*, Vol. 1, pp.242-254.

47. This CCP Central Document was publishing it on *Qiushi*, a journal of the CCP, in Xu's name. Xu Jiatun, "Utilise the presence of Hong Kong in economic development of the coastal region," Beijing: *Qiushi*, Vol. 1, (1988).

48. Jiang Weiqing, *70 years of Journey-Reminiscences by Jiang Wei qing*, Vol. 2, p.566.

49. Xu Jiatun, *Retrieving Hong Kong*, Vol. 2, pp.201-203.

50. The interview with Xu Jiatun

51. Xu Jiatun, *Retrieving Hong Kong*, Vol. 2, p.113.

52. Tomohiro Sasaki, "'Chuuou no kengen wo mosaku suru Kou Takumin seiken," Tokyo: *Ajiken World Trend*, December 1995. ["Jiang Zemin administration in a search for an 'authority of the centre'"]Also see "Pekinshi toshi sai kaihatu wo meguru chuuou to Pekin no kankei," Ministry of Education (ed.), Tokyo: *Shirizu Chuugoku ryouiki kennkyuu*, Vol. 6, 1997 ["Relationship between the centre and Beijing surrounding the re-development of Beijing

City," *Series of China Studies*].

53. Tokyo: *Nihon Keizai Shinbun*, 25 December 1998.

54. Zhao Hongwei, "Tsihou Seiji," in Tokyo: Tyuugoku Kenkyuujou(ed.), *Tyuugoku Nenkan 1999*, (1999) ["Local Politics,"*China Yearbook*].

55. Tokyo: *Nihon Keizai Shinbun*, 5 January 1999.

56. Tokyo: *Nihon Keizai Shinbun*, 16 March, 10 April 1999.

Chapter 7

The Reforms and Transformation of An Administrative Organ

Introduction

Once an administrative organ is established, it begins to act autonomously as the actor bearing a certain sense of duty while it fulfills the duty. If such a general argument applies to China, the administrative organs in China may also have an aspect of an autonomous actor, while being restrained in the socialistic regime. Then, what characteristics of the Chinese administrative organs have been derived from their autonomy and the mechanism of autonomy formation?

During the fifty years since 1949, Chinese administrative organs have kept changing, sometimes expanding and sometimes shrinking. These changes brought about transformations of the administrative structure in some cases and little impact in other cases. They were also substantially transformed by political changes without an attempt of reforming. This section retrospectively discusses how the characteristics of the Chinese administrative structure elucidated in Section 1 have been transformed by administrative reforms and other factors, what changes have been brought about in the national structure, and what are the dynamics that have driven the processes.

Section 1: Administrative Reform in Mao Zedong Era

As stated in Chapter 2, after the transition period from the foundation of the country in 1949 thorough 1953, the constitution ("54

Constitution") and related laws including the government organization law were promulgated in an attempt to establish a Soviet-type centralized regime. However, pressed by heightened dissatisfaction of local party committees, who had lost most of their hold over the administrative organizations, the party Chairman Mao Zedong promoted, on behalf of the interest of the local party committees, promoted return from the Soviet-type centralization to the "monolithic leading institutions by the party committees," which had been the practice in the time of liberated areas. The resulting transformation of the administrative structure was completed by around 1957. This was the first administrative reform, which mostly comprised the transfer of rights to locality, such as the transfer of the control of most state-owned enterprises from the central government to local governments rather than changes in the numbers of administrative organs. The major dynamic of the reform was the center-locality relationship.

In the process of the first administrative reform, other factors also acted as dynamics. Firstly, the concentration of power from local administrative organs to central administrative organs under the Soviet-type centralized regime implied a change in the traditional route of power centralization from local party committees to the party central through the power system of the party, suggesting strengthened autonomy of the administration. This presumably alerted caution of the power system of the party led by Chairman Mao Zedong. In other words, the factor of the party-government relationship can be cited as the second dynamic.

Secondly, the struggle for leadership between the CCP and the Soviet Communist party that arose in the world communism movement after the death of Stalin in 1953. The CCP denied its experiences derived from the Soviet Union, such as the centralized regime, and began to grope for its own way. Mao Zedong began to try to assume leadership of the post-Stalin communistic movement in the world.

Lastly, incentives for development also served as a dynamic. Mao Zedong stressed the 'policy of walking on two feet' by operating two kinds of incentives, central and local, stressing" and maintained that power should therefore be transferred to locality.[1] Some theories of political development and developmental economics attach importance to the role of bureaucracy to replenish immature market in developing countries. In China as well, the natural conditions of the vast expanse of land and the daunting prospect of support from the Soviet Union heightened the importance of the role of local leaders for development, and attempts were made to give them incentives.

After restoring the regime, Mao Zedong promoted the Grand Leap Forward (GLF) for industrial development and People's Commune movement for agricultural development based on the incentives to local leaders and the resulting public mobilization. However, monolithic leading of all local power organs by local party committees implied that the party central loses means to check local activities. The unexpected outcome of the "monolithic leadership institutions by local committees," i.e., the weakening of control by the center and the strengthening of local autonomy, began to manifest themselves in 1958. At the end of the year, the failure of the GLF and People's Commune movement became evident, subjecting China to the industrial recess and nationwide famine, which began the following year and lasted for more than 3 years.[2]

In these circumstances, centralization in the sense of strengthening of planned economy was re-strengthened by mainly returning many of the enterprises whose management rights had been transferred to local governments under control of the center.[3] This was the second administrative reform. It should be noted that it does not mean a simple return to the Soviet-type centralized regime. Up until the mid-1960s, a regime whereby the equilibrium between the centralization and local autonomy is achieved was sought for, mainly by the planned economic control regime.

Nevertheless, when the "monolithic leadership institutions by the party committees" was maintained, it was natural that local leadership named local party committees acquires, as a self-contained power, autonomy independent of the central leadership in the center-locality relationship. Moreover, in the party-government relationship, the administrative organs that connotes a mechanism of behaving autonomously as an actor having a certain consciousness of duty, particularly the central government, became more autonomous independent of Mao Zedong's party central while continuing to expand in the process of strengthening the planned economy control regime. The second administrative reform was actually led in the frontline by President Liu Shaoqi, the top of the administration instead of Mao Zedong, who failed in the GLF and People's Commune movement.

Mao Zedong began to prepare the "Cultural Revolution" in 1964 and implemented it in 1966. The "object of revolution" then was no longer the Soviet-type centralized regime in the 1950s but the leaders conducting the administrative practice including Liu Shaoqi, Deng

Xiaoping, and Zhou Enlai on the center level and the local leadership that Mao referred to as "independent kingdoms."

The third administrative reform was brought about by the Cultural Revolution. Every central and local organs assuming power was dissolved and then restored. The "monolithic leadership institutions by party committees" was stipulated as the policy of the reform. Drastic simplification and involvement of workers, farmers, or revolutionary servicemen were prerequisites to ensure royalty to Mao and the center.

Major contents of the reform included the following: The post of the President was abolished, and the priority of the Communist Party was established in the constitution ('75 Constitution), which implied that Mao Zedong, the Chairman, was virtually the ruler of the state; The management rights of most enterprises owned by the center was transferred again to the locality[4]; The local governments were renamed "Revolutionary Committees," which were subject to leadership of the local party committees. By these changes, the reform succeeded in concentrating the power to the Chairman, strengthening the authority of the party organization, and weakening the government organs, but it is clear that it did not structurally reform the "monolithic leadership institutions by party committees".

Section 2: Administrative Reform in the Deng Xiaoping Era

Following the death of Mao Zedong in 1976, each government organ nearly restored its pre-Revolutionary name and organization concomitant with the reassuming of power of national leaders who had lost their positions during the revolution. This process of restoration, which continued until the revision of the constitution in 1982, is counted as the fourth of all administrative reforms and the first reform in the Deng Xiaoping era.

Deng and other leaders who succeeded in restoring their positions resumed the attempt of seeking a regime whereby the equilibrium between the centralization and autonomy of locality is achieved, which had been sought up to the middle of 1960s and then suspended by the Cultural Revolution. However, there was a change in the dynamics of administrative reform in the 1980s, producing a different kind of impact on such reforms.

As stressed by Deng by saying "Economic development is the

central issue of all work," the necessity for economic development produced the strongest impact on not only the administrative reform but also the contents of every reform implemented in the Deng era. In an attempt to seek the equilibrium between the centralization and autonomy of locality, the leadership of China was divided into two groups. The group led by Deng Xiaoping, the supreme leader, placed importance on the incentive of local leaders for development, whereas the group led by Chen Yun, a senior member and virtually No. 2 in the party, put stress on the role of the planned economy regime for balanced development and, in relation to this, insisted on concentration of power on the central government.

Whereas the Chen Yun group mainly consisted of members from the State Council, Deng Xiaoping group mainly consisted of those from the center and local leadership. This indicates complex interests among factors derived from the center-locality relationship and party-government relationship as the dynamics of administrative reform. The State Council, which involved an inclination towards autonomy, tended to support the planned economy regime that would lead to strengthening of their power. On the other hand, local leadership insisted on the rightfulness of the "monolithic leadership institutions by the party committee," which would hinder interference of the central government, in quest of the expansion of the independence of local leadership in the center-locality relationship. The party central organs kept pace with local leadership to maintain their superiority and check the autonomous tendency of the State Council. The organization of the communist party in economic reforms was not so conservative as is generally considered but played a role of checking conservative administrative organs that inclined towards strengthening of administrative power and maintenance of various economic rules in China, which has no democratic-party politics.

For China in the Deng Xiaoping era, maintaining the nation stable is a crucial political subject next to economic growth. Deng Xiaoping intended to legislate the method of ruling including administrative control. When compared with the era of Mao Zedong, the charismatic leadership of the Communist Party and its leader was weakened in the Deng Xiaoping era, while the social interest became diversified as the market economy developed. The struggle for leadership between the Chinese and Soviet Communist Parties no longer existed in the global communistic movement. Rather, democracy, which denies the orthodoxy of the ruling of communism, was a factor that produced an impact on the reforms in China including administrative reforms. In these circumstances, ruling based on legal systems became essential instead of casual ideas of the party organization and its leaders as in the era of Mao Zedong. Since ensuring stability and the legislation of administration for stability would lead to autonomy of administrative organs, such organs actively promoted it.

In the area of economic reform, the reform up to 1982 included the expansion of the rights for local finance and business management by the Local Finance Responsibility Institutions, expansion of management independence of public enterprises by the Business Management Responsibility Institutions, and achievement of independence by dissolving the Household Responsibility Institutions and People's Communes and restoring township and villages.

Central and various levels of local governments in China are characterized by their possession of the rights of ownership and management of enterprises in addition to the rights of administration in the generic sense of the term. A number of industrial offices were established by 1997 for managing enterprises in the governments, such as the Ministries for Coal Industry and Electronics Industry.

In regard to legislation for administrative ruling, the administrative organs were restored nearly as they had been before the Cultural Revolution, and additional government organs were established to ensure stability of politics and society, such as improvement of government offices for economic and social administration and establishment of the Ministry of State Security. As a result, the swell of the government became a notable phenomenon characterizing this period. Legislation of administrative ruling influenced by democracy was also found in this period. The rule of prohibiting three consecutive terms for the state council premier and the restored President was a reform that produced a particularly strong impact on the subsequent Chinese politics.[5]

The strengthening of the independent rights of the local leadership and swelling of the administrative organs, as well as the resulting strengthening of the autonomy of both up to 1982 led to the fifth, sixth, and seventh administrative reforms in 1988, 1993, and 1998, respectively. In the political status in the period between 1982 and 1988, the posts of the General Secretary and Government Premier were assumed by Hu Yaobang and Zhao Ziyang in the Deng Xiaoping group, who carried out transfer of rights to the locality, which satisfied the local leadership to a great extent. In this sense, the center-locality relationship was favorable.

In the aspect of the party-government relationship, the economic development increased the complexity and specialization of administrative offices, which strengthened their autonomy along with their swell in size. This intensified the friction with the party organs. In these circumstances, the leadership of the State Council strongly criticized the "Party instruction" to the economic operation by General Secretary Hu Yaobang as "inappropriate intervention" and schemed to get rid of him. According to the proposal by Yao Yilin and Li Pang, the vice ministers in the centralization-oriented Chen Yun group, Premier Zhao Ziyang himself wrote a letter to Deng Xiaoping and Chen Yun in 1984, in which they complained that the intervention by the secretariat of the party central was causing difficulty in the operation of the State Council and asked that these problems of the party-government relationship "be solved while the senior revolutionaries were still alive and well," while strongly criticizing Hu Yaobang for "violating the party policy of collective leading." Moreover, when Zhao Ziyang met Deng Xiaoping together with Hu Yaobang at the end of 1986, he blamed Hu Yaobang for causing the demonstration by university students in December demanding democratization and criticized him as being "timid in opposing liberation of the Bourgeoisie."[6] After all, Hu Yaobang was forced to resign in January 1987 for his three misdeeds: "violating the collective leadership policy of the party," "being timid in opposing liberation of the Bourgeoisie, " which were posed by Zhao Ziyang, and "being interviewed by Lu Keng, a reactionary reporter in Hong Kong without permission."[7]

Zhao Ziyang, who assumed the office of the General Secretary succeeding Hu Yaobang, proposed a plan for political and administrative reform in 1988 according to the political reform policy decided during the 13th National Congress of CCP in October 1987 featuring "government-party separation" and "government-enterprise separation."[8] However, in the atmosphere of agitated activity for democratization by the educated and university students, who were furious about the dismissal of Hu Yaobang, the sudden death of Hu Yaobang in April 1989 triggered a large-scale movement for democratization as if adding fuel to oil.

For Premier Li Pang and Vice Premier Yao Yilin, the recurrence of democratization movement was an opportunity of dismissing Zhao Ziyang following Hu Yaobang. After the dismissal of Zhao Ziyang in May and suppression of the democratization movement in June by the

"6.4 Tienanmen Incident," the "party-government separation" policy was counted as one of the misdeeds of Zhao Ziyang for being the cause of democratization movement by weakening the role of the party. The "government-enterprise separation" policy also receded in the centralized economic operation carried out mainly by Premier Li Peng. Thus the fifth administrative reform ended up with no particular results.

However, the centralized economic operation by Premier Li Peng brought about the economic stagnation up to 1991 instead of "balanced development" it aimed. In these circumstances, Deng Xiaoping made "Nan xun jiang hua" in March 1992, in which he clearly advocated a concept of "market-oriented economy" for the first time, directly giving a "great command" for "bold pursuit of total reform and opening-up" to the local leadership to realize the concept.[9] The Chinese economy then began to exhibit a high economic growth primarily by the initiative of the local leadership. In 1993, ZHU Rongji, who had been selected a Vice Premier from the position of a secretary at Shanghai City, was put in charge of economic operation in place of Li Peng.

Drastic reform was required for the State Council, which had retained centralized planned economy regime while continuing to swell, as the market-oriented economy grew. In 1993, Premier Li Peng submitted a reform plan to simplify the State Council and increase its efficiency.[10] However, the plan included unification and abandonment of only limited numbers of offices, while retaining most offices in charge of economic planning and industrial management in the planned economy era. It therefore scarcely achieved a structural reform to deal with market-oriented economy. This plan met an unprecedented large number of votes against it. This was the sixth administrative reform of all time and the third reform in the Deng Xiaoping era.

Section 3: Administrative Reform in Jiang Zemin Era

The economic stagnation began to be overcome in 1992 primarily by the initiative of the local leadership. However, the economic growth was not what resulted from normal market operation, causing overheated economy without an increase in economic efficiency – the Chinese "bubble" economy. An economic recess resulted from an inclination towards centralized policies and an economic over-heat resulted from an opposite inclination in the center-locality relationship. Such a phenomenon is not limited to this case but has repeatedly been observed since the 1950s, and the period of such economic cycles has been shortened since the 1980s. This was because the local leadership could not carry out rational management appropriate for the market, though their profit motive was strong as the owner/management of public enterprises.

Nevertheless, the policy environment had already been changed. The central purpose of reform was shifting from the pursuit of economic development towards a policy objective of achieving a market economy. Also, General Secretary Jiang Zemin had to include "soft landing" of the bubble economy in the policy objectives in order to avoid economic stagnation, which had been concomitant with centralization. Achievement of soft landing of the bubble economy meant transfer of the ownership and management rights not to the central government or local government but to individual enterprises. Soft landing of bubble economy required a technique of tightening economy not by the conventional centralized approach but by coordinating the interests between the center and locality to make it suitable for market economy. In these circumstances, the centralized tendency of the policy of Jiang Zemin and ZU Rongji converged towards coordination of interests suitable for market economy and establishment of market rules in the negotiation between them and the local leadership.[11]

It was officially decided in the 15th national congress of CCP in 1997 that publicly owned companies be transformed to stock companies. This was a reform meaning the transfer of the ownership and management rights not to the center or local leadership but to enterprises and markets. The separation of the management rights of public enterprises from various levels of local leadership, or "government-enterprise separation" in the party terms, meant to let the market among stock companies "adjust" the economy by themselves instead of adjustment by the center-locality relationship. Only this enabled the economy to have the opportunity to depart from the swing between overheats resulting from investment led by various levels of local leadership and recesses resulting from tightening by the center and become a sound one suitable for a market.

Moreover, structural reform of administrative offices was also carried out on an unprecedented scale to make them suitable for a market economy. According to the vote at the national congress of CCP in 1998, the functions of the offices related to economy in the State Council were adjusted, and the offices related to industrial management were all abolished (Chart 7-1).[12]

Chart 7-1: Reductions of Ministries in State Council Reform 1998

No. of ministries and committees reduced from 40 to 29; 80,000 staff members halved

Former	Reorganized as
Ministry of Power Industry Ministry of Coal Industry Ministry of Metallurgical Industry Ministry of Machine Building Industry Ministry of Chemical Industry Ministry of Domestic Trade	Bureau of State Economy and Trade Commission
Ministry of Posts and Telecommunication Ministry of Electronics Industry Ministry of Radio, Film and Television	Ministry of Information Industry
State Physical Culture and Sports Commission	All-China Council of Physical Culture and Sports
Ministry of Forestry	State Bureau of Forestry directly under State Council

For instance, the branches of People's Bank of China (central bank) equivalent to a department of the central government, which had formerly been placed in each province, were abolished, and large branches were newly placed to be in charge of several provinces.[13] This reform was intended to achieve complete independence of local branches from local leadership. The Ministry of Coal Industry, which had administrated the world's largest coal industry, was reduced to a bureau, while the staff was reduced from over 650 to 90.[14] The management rights of public enterprises had not been brought down to the enterprise level in the earlier reforms. This is reported to be because the industrial government offices at each level of administration in the center and locality retained such rights. These offices were all abolished in this reform.

Finally, the rule of forbidding three consecutive terms of national leaders in the "'82 Constitution" began to take effect in the Jiang Zemin era. When dealing with a tough problem of the party-government relationship, Mao Zedong abolished the post of the President to make the president of the party virtually the president of the state. Though Deng Xiaoping revived the post of the President while "systematizing" the administration, he did not assume the position but controlled the party and government by reigning over the General Secretary and President as the most influential person without a crown. Jiang Zemin officially assumed the posts of the General Secretary and President, as he was not charismatic enough for behaving like Deng. However, the establishment of the rule of "no three consecutive terms" in 1982 caused an unexpected situation. Jiang would have to resign at expiration of the term of office in March 2003 in line with the flow towards "legislation." The supreme leader of the party and state is no longer a lifetime post. This is a significant step ahead for China in its political regime.

Section 4: Dynamics of Administrative Reform

The administrative structure of China incorporated ownership and management rights of public enterprises as part of the socialistic administrative system, and the government included an economic department for each industry to operate such enterprises. Also, the administrative structure was formed to practice the liberated areas of CCP since the end of the 1920s based on the long pre-modern political history. For this reason the "monolithic leading institutions by the party committees," peculiar to China, were formulated, and the administrative rights were concentrated on multiple layers of the party committees on various administrative levels. The autonomy of the local leadership from the central leadership and the autonomy of the government from the communist party organization were generated under these conditions, and these were strengthened in the process of development of market economy.

The administrative structure experienced about seven reforms during the last 50 years. In the administrative reform of the Mao Zedong era, major dynamics were generated from the center-locality relationship and the party-government relationship related to it. The major subject was the distribution of administrative rights, mainly rights of economic management, between the center and locality. In the administrative reform of the Deng Xiaoping era, the paramount purpose was the pursuit of economic development, which generated dynamics from the center-locality relationship and the party-government relationship related to it, with an administrative structure suitable for economic development being sought. Since realization of a market economy was set as the objective of economic development in 1992, an administrative structure suitable for a market economy was pursued in the Jiang Zemin era. This marked the beginning of a structural transformation of the state in terms of departure from socialism and multi-layered centralization in the center-locality relationship and party-government relationship.

Conclusion

A view of the processes of administrative reforms over the last 50 years reveals that the center-locality relationship and party-government relationship related to it have been generating the major dynamics of reform. Accordingly, such dynamics will continue to bring about transformation of Chinese administrative structures in the new century as well. An active scenario of the political development of China may therefore be written as follows: "The progressive shift from the system whereby public order is attained and maintained by organizing a pyramidal structure of administration to the system whereby it is attained by mutual coordination of independent bodies present in multilateral forms – the so-called network structure"[15] may apply to the case of China. In the center-locality relationship, the conflict between the centralization and the multi-layered centralization may lead to a democratic power structure based on a sort of local agreement. In the party-government relationship, the "monolithic leading institutions by party committees" may be "legislated" into a national structure of autonomy and mutual watching among the party committees, government offices and People's Congress.

Notes

1. Mao Zedong "Treatment of Ten Big Relations" *Mao Zedong Selection*, China: Vol. 5, pp. 275-2
2. About the actual circumstances of the failure, Yasugo Tsuji *Famine and Poverty in Contemporary China – Testimony for the Incident of Death from Starvation of Two Thousands Million People* Japan: Kobundo Publisher 1991, Reference Book.
3. Shi Jiuqing *Political Processes in Contemporary China,* China: Shandon People's Publisher 1993, p. 477
4. Wang Song *The People's Republic of China and Politics,* (Beijing) Chinese Communist Party School Press 1995, pp. 297-300
5. *The Constitution of the People's Republic of China –1982* articles 79-87.
6. Wu Jiang *Passages of 10 years – Days Associated with Hu Yaopang* (Hong Kong) Jingbao Cultural Enterprise, August 1995, pp. 198-211
7. Lu Keng, translated by Masako Aoki and Zhao Hongwei *Autobiography of a Prodigious Reporter – Testimony for the History of the 20th Century* Japan: Chikuma Publisher 1999, referred to chapters 13 and 14.

8. Tatsumi Okabe and Masashi Ando edit. *Original Text of Contemporary History of China – Handbook to China Research* Japan: Iwanami Publisher 1996, p. 412, 416

9. Deng Xiaoping 'Lecture on Round Tour in the Southern Area' *Deng Xiaoping Selection*, (Beijing) Renmin Press 1993, pp.370-382

10. General Office of the State Council, Secretary Bureau edit. *Organizational Structure of the Central Government* Beijing: Chinese Development Press 1994, pp. 3-14

11. For example, Jiang Zeming "On Lecturing on Politics" *Qiushi* Beijing: the organ of the Chinese Communist Party, July issue 1996

12. (Beijing) Xinhua Press 6th March, 1998. *Yomiuri Press* 7th March, 1998

13. *Asahi Press* 12th and 17th December, 1997.

14. From the interview by this author in Tokyo as of 29th September, 1998 with Wang Shengming, Chief of Civil Law Chamber, Legislative Affairs Committee, National People's Congress

15. Akira Morita *World Administrative Reform,* Japan: Waseda Press 1999, p.15.

Chapter 8

The Possibility of the Chinese-style Democracy

Scholars are divided on whether China, as it moves away from Communist ideology and toward a market economy and the rule of law, can be viewed as moving toward authoritarianism or democratic organization. Many Japanese and American Sinologists label modern China as authoritarian, or at the very least moving in that direction. For a time in 1988, China was said to espouse a "Neo-Authoritarianism", as even Deng Xiaoping was heard to claim (Lu Jun 1989.Yabuki 1989, pp.85-86). Professor Wang Huning of Fudan University, who became known for espousing a "Strong Nation, Strong Government" doctrine, was invited by Jiang Zemin in early 1995 to join the Party's Central Policy Research Laboratory. In 1997 it was rumored that Jiang was putting forth a concept of 'Benevolent Authoritarianism' (Jiji Press 1997,4,29).

However, as I have already noted in Chapter 1, the modern Chinese political regime was neither authoritarian, nor moving in that direction. Regardless of the wishes of the Chinese leaders, due to the unique relationship between Central and Provincial authority, modern China was (as I have previously shown) already moving toward marketization and since its highest leaders were restricted by term limitations, conditions did not exist whereby an authoritarian structure could support massive centralized power or a leader or group of leaders with absolute authority.

In China the on-going economic, social and political changes certainly require reform of the Multi-layered Centralized Regime. Reforming this Multi-layered Centralized Regime will not occur by some mysterious process. What will be necessary is first, the establishment of a 'checks and balances' system through division of the three branches of government, and second, cutting off the central and provincial government from the rights of ownership and management of businesses. Achieving these two goals will mean changing at every level the character of these power concentrations and the groups that profit from them. Is it therefore possible to foresee the establishment of a Chinese democratic regime that can grasp these points?

Until now, research on the development of the Chinese politics has focused on putting forth established political science theories such as the Civil Society theory (shiminshakairon) or the Political Elites theory (elite-seijiron). Generally the conclusion is that due to the under-development of civil society and the lack of understanding of democracy by the political elites, there was little hope for optimism. This conclusion was supported by those who claimed that authoritarianism was required to move from an undemocratic regime to a democratic one. However, both historically and in actuality, those policymakers who had power to create political change reside in the provinces. Additionally the single most pressing political concern is the resolution of the relationship between central and provincial authorities. Therefore any attempt to assess the possibility of a Chinese-style democratic regime must not be based on pre-existing theory, but rather must be based on this history and these actualities.

First, since the time of Mao, although the central authorities have alternately strengthened their power and yielded it to the provincial leaders, this has failed to solve the problem, which remains today. During the era of Deng's economic reforms, as a result of economic power having been ceded to the local authorities, economic liberalization for individuals and enterprises has not been achieved. When the reforms have led to an overheated economy, the center has then moved to reclaim the initiative from the local authorities. This has often failed to have the desired effect. Instead of restoring power to individuals, it has merely removed it from the local authorities, inviting recession.

Also, around 1990 as the central and local authorities relationship was changing, the establishment of the Party's 'leadership core' and the legal codification of the political process regarding the central/local relationship, as well as the move toward a market economy and away from Communist ideology, indicated the direction of future reforms. Even as Jiang Zemin was advocating a system of "centralization plus a market economy", in actuality due to the greater understanding and agreement between central and local authorities and the systematization of their relationship, remarkably Jiang's own position in the 'leadership core' became subject to an 'expiration date'. This clearly worked against central consolidation of power.

Moving to a market economy is in itself incompatible with centralization, as central controls are removed to allow for the action of market forces. Moving away from Communism will clearly reduce the attractiveness and authority of the center. It is said that at the People's Congress in the spring of 1995, a plan was created by the local representatives to send several delegates from each province charged with the task of balancing the benefits (*China Yearbook* 1996,p.68). This movement was actually an attempt to change the current system of the Politburo being the highest decision-making body, and with this the local authorities signaled their desire to create a framework for a type of 'regional democracy'.

Actually such a system whereby political decisions are made with the consent of local authorities already exists. The majority of the Politburo is made up of members with experience at the local level. This experience is one of the conditions by which promotion to the Politburo may be achieved. At the 15th Party Congress, the five new members of the Standing Committee that were chosen were at the time local party secretaries. This may be viewed as the central government co-opting talented local authorities, or it could be explained as local leadership penetrating the central leadership against a backdrop of increasing local power, and directly participating in central decision-making.

Next, the Central Work Conference as well as various other national Work Conferences that are often held are notable for being gatherings of primarily local-level decision-makers. Whenever the Communist party needs to make an important decision, a working committee is held, and once a year before the Central Committee Meeting is held the Central Work Conference is opened to discuss the matters before the Committee. Also, the majority of the representatives on the Central Committee, the People's Congress or the Party Congress are all from groups made up of the local leadership. These local groups have great power in the policy-making process, especially when voting on personnel assignments by secret ballot. There are even cases, though rare, where the candidate chosen by the central government failed to achieve a high number of votes or even failed to be elected.

Since such an event will inevitably lead to a loss of face for the central authorities, the understanding of the local leadership is key both before and during the conference.

In addition to the importance of 'regional democracy' for the advancement of market liberalization, I would like to focus on the changes brought about in the relationship between the Party, the State Council and the People's Congress. As shown in chapter 3, the Standing Committee, which acts as a legislature, is being transformed into an administrative body. A bureaucracy has formed within the Standing Committee, and these bureaucrats perform tasks, such as drafting new legislation and amendments, that are not usually performed by bureaucrats in a democratically elected legislature. As the function of the bureaucracy becomes more specialized and complicated, the bureaucracy's "autonomy as head "(Suleiman 1974, pp. 204-211) gains inertia. The administrators accumulate power as they become the sole possessors of specialized knowledge and information. China's development toward a market economy continues to provide a mechanism for the accumulation of power by the People's Congress and the State Council.

Since 1995, "Sandakuai" (The Three Powers) has been a popular catch phrase among Beijing's politicians. As the functions borne by the People's Congress and the State Council have become more specialized and complicated, the Party has become unable to deal effectively with legal and policy matters based on their lack of information. Laws are adopted only on the basis of explanations provided by the Politburo's Standing Committee and the Politburo. As a result, beside the Communist Party Center, power has accumulated in the People's Congress and the State Council, forming the so-called Three Powers. The balance of the Three Powers has given rise to another new issue for China.

China must now find a new way of balancing the relationship between the central and local authorities and the Three Powers. As countries around the world adopt democracy, they must each find a way to reconcile this democracy with existing historical conditions if the new political regime is to last. In China's case, one possibility is 'regional democracy' at a national level. "Regional democracy" does not conflict with the basic values of democracy. Previously the "Cosmopolitan Model" of democracy has been suggested by the world's politicians, meaning a multi-tiered democracy where domestic and national democracy develop in tandem (Held 1995, pp.96-120).

Although this is meant to be applied to international politics, it may have use for China, which must not only manage 1.2 billion people but must also deal with the claims of the 'provinces' of Taiwan, Hong Kong and Tibet.

Under a national 'regional democracy' it is of course hoped that local democracy will also flourish. Because at the time when Hu Yaobang was party secretary, municipal elections were held to determine congress representatives, it is possible to say that the basic conditions already exist. In China, a multi-level democratization consisting of local democracy plus national regional democracy is a meaningful choice for political development. In short it may be possible to move from 'multilayered socialism' to 'multilayered democracy'. Of course, certain groups will be necessary to foster the creation of 'Chinese-style democracy'. Two I would like to mention here are an elite and a citizenry steeped in certain unique Chinese processes (Yang 1997).

In China the death of Deng Xiaoping spelled the end of the power of the politicians from the revolutionary era, and the start of the take-over of the second generation leaders. But, as those revolutionary leader represented by Mao and Deng had held power for so long, Jiang Zemin and the second level leaders were already old men in their 70's. Therefore when Jiang's era ends five or six years from now, the task of the creation of Chinese-style democracy will fall to the third generation.

The third generation leaders were mostly born between 1947 and 1960 and are now in their late 30's to their early 50's. They passed their formative years during the Great Cultural Revolution, and are therefore known as the 'GRC generation'. In general the GRC generation did not receive formal education and are thought of as a 'ruined' generation, but that is not actually the case. They are a generation that has experienced both extreme freedom and extreme repression. Many of them were 'sent down' to the country. The film director Jiang Wen recalls this period this way:

> Because we have experienced the Cultural Revolution, we have become concerned with finding ourselves rather than finding our relationship to society and others. As its name implies, the Cultural Revolution was about destroying the old system of authority. For those of us who grew up during this period, we have come to believe more in ourselves and our rights, than in the Communist Party (*Nihonkeizaisinbun*. 1997, 4, 12).

Growing up in an era filled with power struggles, this generation has managed to free itself from the constraints of ideology. The anti-ideological character is the primary characteristic of the GRC generation. An artist contemporary of Jiang Wen put it this way:

> Rather than be fooled again, we would rather be known as a despairing, cheerless, dangerous, cynical and lazy generation. We don't want to be thought of as having anything to do with that way of doing things. No matter what sort of ideology, after questioning it one hundred times, we will reject it and throw it on the garbage heap (Fang Lijun 1996, p.15).

This generation, whose imagination and behavior was forged during the Cultural Revolution, is a generation with a strong sense of identity and mission. After the GRC ended, the elite of this generation went on to university or foreign study. Those who remained in the country and had experienced both revolution and its end again had to contend with the upheavals in 1989 brought on by the Tiananmen Massacre, but they have recovered and are miraculously in the position of carrying forward the current economic reforms. Since the late 80's, this generation, which has shown itself so full of imagination and so active, has quickly come to dominate not only politics, but every area of society. This is the generation of film director Zhang Yimou ("Raise the Red Lantern") and author Jung Chang ("Wild Swans"). Many of the Chinese scientists working in western laboratories also come from this generation.

In the political arena on the anti-government side, those thought to be behind the Tiananmen demonstrations were all from this generation. On the other hand working within the government, this generation dominates the in the mid-level positions and is vigilantly biding their time until they can take over from the generation of Jiang. In 1997 this group again caused a stir with further calls for democracy (Li Li 1997, p. 322. Fang Jue 1998, pp. 6-8).

From the Sixties through the Nineties, the Third Generation had extremely difficult experiences that are almost impossible to describe. Today they have become prominent in every field and are representative of China to the world. "Our generation may yet make some mistakes, but we are certainly not ordinary," is a sentiment that is strongly felt (Yang 1997, 214). Unconstrained by ideology, these are the people that will tackle China's challenges and create a new order.

Bibliographies

Japanese Sources

Akio, Kimura, *Nation and Politics in Contemporary Soviet,* Kyouikusha, 1987.

Akira, Morita, *Authorization Public Administration and Bureaucracy,* Iwanami Shoten, 1988.

All-China Federation of Trade Union, International Information Section, *The Organization Structure of Labor Union,* (Beijing) 1988.

——, *The Documents of 8th National Congress of CCP*, (Beijing), Foreign Languages Press 1956.

——, *The Communique of 3rd Plenum of the 11th CCPCC, Beijing Review,* no 52, 1978.

——, *The Documents of 12th National Congress of CCP,* (Beijing) Foreign Languages Press, 1982.

——, *The Documents of National Representatives Congress of CCP*, Foreign Languages Press (Beijing), 1985.

——, *The Documents of 13th National Congress of CCP,* (Beijing) Foreign Languages Press, 1987.

Almond, G.A./ Hideo Uchiyama (trans.), *Contemporary Politics and Historical consciousness,* Keisou Shobou, 1982.

Atsushi Asai, *The Point under Discussion of Chinese Constitution*, Houritsu Bunkasha, 1985.

Blus, W. / Michiaki Sato (trans.) *Politics and Economics in Socialism,* Iwanami Shoten, 1978.

CCP, *The Regulations of CCP,* CHINA PRESS, 29 September 1997.

Chen, Mingtong / Masatake Wakabayashi (comp./ trans.) *Contemporary Politics in Taiwan and Factionalism,* Toyo Keizai Shinposha, 1998.

Chofu, Nunome, *A Study of SUI-TANG History,* Oriental History Seminar, 1968.

Chuzo, Ichiko, *Politics and Society of Contemporary China,* University of Tokyo Press, 1977.

Daigakukyouikusha (eds.) *Contemporary Politics Dictionary*, Brain Shuppan, 1991.

Dong, Biwn, *Dong Biwn-The Top of The Supreme Court of Justice's Report of 8th National Congress of CCP*, The Documents of 8th National Congress of CCP, (Beijing) Foreign Languages Press, 1956.

Dyuveruje, M. / Fukuharu Taguchi and Eiji Taguchi (trans.) *Political System*, Hakusuisha, 1964.

——, Chihiro Yokota (trans.) *A Guide for Politics,* Misuzu Shobo, 1967.

Eatman and Llyd, E/Shin Ueda and Yoko Fukao (trans.), *Society of China,* Heibonsha, 1994.

Fang, Lijun / Tamako Akiyama (trans.) Fang, Lijun*: An Image of Man in The Time without story,* International Cultural Exchange Fund Asian Center, 1996.

Fumio, Uda, *Soviet Union: Structure of Political Power,* Chuokoronnsha, 1989.

Gen-nosuke, Amano, *A Study of Agricultural History in China,* Nogyo Sogo Kenkyusho, 1962.

Gen Tsukamoto, *Concerning a Study of 'The Military Clique' in U.S.A.* CHIKAKINI ARITE no.13 1988.

——, *The Present Condition and The Subject of a Study of Chinese Modern Military Clique*, Academy of Chinese social culture (eds.) China Society and Culture no.4 1989.

Guo, Hualan / kinji Yajima(comp./ trans.) *A Study of History of CCP,* Shunjyusha, 1988.

He, Bingdi /Takanobu Terada and Shinichi Chikusa (trans.) *Imperial Examinations and Chinese Society in Modern ages: The Steps of Success in Life,* Heibonsha, 1993

Hidenori, Ijiri, *Contemporary American Intellectuals and China,* Minerva Shobo, 1992.

Hide, Yokoyama and Son Terachi (trans.) *Some Aspects of Chinese Social History,* Keiso Shobo, 1988.

Hideo, Ohtake, *Policy Process,* University of Tokyo Press, 1990.

Hideo, Ohashi, *Financial Relation to Central and Localities in Contemporary China,* Tsukuba Housei No.2, vol.18, March 1995.

Hikota, Koguchi (eds.) *A Guide of Chinese Law,* Sanseido, 1991.

Hiroaki, Yokoyama, *A Study of R.O.C History*, Sanichi Shobo, 1996.

Hiromasa, Nakayama, *Things Agriculture in Soviet*, Nihon Hoso Shuppan Kyokai, 1981.

Hiromasa, Nalayama (trans.) *Perestroika and Economic Reform,* Iwanami Shoten, 1990.

Hisashi Sito, *A Study of Sructure of Socialist Constitution,* Nihonhyoronsha, 1986.

Ichisada, Miyazaki, *'Imperial Examination'*, Chuokoronsha, 1963.

The Institute of China Study (eds.) *New Yearbook of China,* 1978-1984, Taishukan Shoten.

——, *China Basic Laws*, Nihonhyouronsha, 1988.

Ibenshtayn, k. / Kouji Soto and Tsuyoshi koji (trans.) *An introduction for Comparative Constitution,* Houritsubunnkasha, 1980.

Isamu, Fujita and Kazuo Hatanaka, *An Introduction of Soviet Law*, Yuhikaku, 1983.

Isamu, Ogata, '*House' and State in Ancient China—Order Structure under Emperor dominance*, Iwanami Shoten, 1991.

Japan Labor Association, *Things Labor in China,* Kousaido, 1987.

Jin,Guantao and Liu Qingfeng / Masatake Wakabayashi, Yujiro Murata (trans.) *The Super-stable System in Chinese Society,* Kenbunsha, 1987.

Jin, Nakakuni, *Document Tiananmen Incident*, Bingeishunjyu, 1979.

Jyo, Yamaguchi, *Political System, University of Tokyo Press,* 1989.

Katsuhiro, Ohta, *The Great Cultural Revolution and Contemporary China*, Iwanami Shoten, 1986.

Katsukiyo, Fukumoto, *A Commune Tragedy — Movement for Elimination of Counterrevolutionaries (1930-1917)* Research Institute of China (eds.) A Monthly Report for Chinese Study, May, July, September 1992.

——, *An Elegy of The Chinese Revolution,* Aki Shobo,1992.

Kazako, Mouri, *A change of System and 'Reform' of China: Significance of 'Tiananmen Incident'* Contemporary China no.64 Academy of Contemporary China in Japan, 1990.

——, (eds.) *A Period of Mao Zedong, A Theory of Contemporary China 1,* Japan Institute of International Affairs, 1990.

——, *Contemporary Chinese Politics,* University of Nagoya Press, 1993.

——, (eds.) *China of Market-oriented Economy,* Japan Institute of International Affairs, 1995.

——, (eds.) *Chinese Policy-making,* Japan Institute of International Affairs, 1996.

Kazankai (eds.) *China Almanac,* Every Year Version

Kazuo, Yamauchi, *Economic Reform in Contemporary China,* Gakuyo Shobo, 1988.

—— and Michiki Kikuchi (eds.) *New Aspect of Chinese Economics,* Housei University Press, 1991.

Kazutsugu, Nakakane, *A Theory of Chinese Economics Political Economics of Agriculture and Industry Relationship,* University of Tokyo press, 1992.

Keiichi, Tsunekawa, Authoritarianism and Development-Dictatorship A View Point From Latin America, SEKAI, Iwanami Shoten, September 1983.

——, *The Structure of Latin America Crisis,* Yuuhikaku,1986.

——, *Political Economic Study of Dependent in Mexico,* University of Tokyo Press, 1988.

——, *Rural Districts in Third World and Political System: The Present Condition of Theory and The Subject of a Study,* An Annual Report of Academy of Japan Politics.

——, *Political Development in Third World,* Iwanami Shoten, 1988.

——, *Enterprises and Nation,* University of Tokyo Press, 1996.

Kougo, Tsuji, *Starvation and Poverty of Contemporary China Testimony for the 2 ten million people Starve to Death Affair,* Koubundo, 1991.

Kouichi Nomura (eds.) *Iwanami Lecture Contemporary China 1: Political world in ContemporaryChina*, Iwanami Shoten, 1989.

——, *Iwanami Lecture Contemporary China The Another vol.1 Democratization and Chinese Socialism,* Iwanami Shoten, 1990.

——, *Iwanami Lecture Contemporary China The Another vol.2 A Guide for a study of contemporary China,* Iwanami Shoten, 1990.

Kunitoshi Ohnishi, *World' Constitution*, Seibundo, 1971

Kyouichi,,Ishihara, *Multi-structure of Chinese Economics,* Research Institute of Asian Economy, 1991.

Masakake, Wakabaybashi, *Taiwan: Divided Nation and Democratize,* University of Tokyo Press.1992.

Masamichi, Kima, *Reform of Election System in China Election Law in '79 and Realized Process,* Study Seminar for Socialism Law (eds.) Some Aspects of 'Reform' in Socialism, Houritsu Bunkasha, 1985.

Masao, Fukushima, *People's Democracy in China: Process and Theory for Construction,* University of Tokyo Press, 1965.

——, *Law and Politics in China A History of Chinese Law: The Present Condition and Theory,* Nihonhyoronsha, 1966.

Masao, Kimura, *The Formation of Ancient Chinese Empire, — Specially it's Basic Conditions,* Fumaisha, 1965.

Masaru, Mabuchi, *Revival 'a Theory of Institution' in American Politics,* SHIHO, Iwanami Shoten, October, 1987.

Masaru, Maruyama, *A account of 'Spiritual Pollution Campaign' in China,* This is YOMIURI, Yomiuri Shinbunsha, April 1984.

Masataka, Sakano, *A History of Political Diplomacy in Modern China,* University of Tokyo Press, 1973.

Masato, Yamamura, *Nation and Form village in Contemporary Soviet,* Ochanomizu Shobo, 1990.

Masnori, Kikuchi (eds.) *Socialism and Modern World,* Yamakawa Shuppansha, 1989.

Midori, Kisaki, *The Roles of the Enterprises in China1, 2—The Side of their Lives : Asian Economics,* The Research Institute of Asian Economy, March, April 1988.

——, *State owned Enterprises in Contemporary China : An Essay in Inside Structure,* Study Series of Contemporary China 32, Academy of Asian Politics and Economics, 1995.

Mineo, Nakajima (eds.) *History of Contemporary China,* Yuhikaku, 1981.

Minoru, Nanbu, *Financial Policy in Contemporary China*, Taga Shuppansha, 1991.

Minoru, Takeuchi (eds./ trans.) *The Constitutions in People's Republic of China* ,Sososha, 1991.

Mitsuo, Hoshi, *Great Canal: An Encounter of China,* Kondo Shuppansha, 1977.

Mitsunori, Takehana, *An Introduction of A Theory of Chinese Constitution,* Seibundo, 1991.

Mitsuru, Hashimoto, *An Undercurrent of Contemporary China,* Gyorosha, 1990.

Moore, B. / Takatsugu Miyazaki (trans.) *The Social Origin of Dictatorship and Democratic Politics*, Iwanami Shoten, 1986.

Naoshi, Sekiguchi, *Reform of Economic System in China,* University of Tokyo Press, 1992.

Noboru, Niida, *History of Chinese Law System,* Iwanami Shoten, 1963.

Nobuo, Shinotome, *Contemporary Politics of Soviet,* University of Tokyo Press, 1987.
Noriyuki Tokuda, *Political Dynamics of Mao Zedong Doctrine,* Keio Tsushin, 1977.
—— (eds.) *The Middle and Long Time View of Chinese Politics Centering around center-locality Relationships at S turning Point,* Japan Institute of International Affairs, 1986.
Padock, S. / Mineo Nakajima (comp.) / Katsumi Hnagami (trans.) *A Biography of Deng, Xiaoping*, Jijitsuushinnsha, 1989.
Reiitsu, Kojima, *Technology and Economics in China,* Keisou Shobo, 1975.
—— (eds.) *Economic Reform in China,* Keisou Shobo, 1988.
The Research Center for Chinese Economics of Kyushu University (eds.) *Economic System and Statistical Financial System in China,* University of Kyushu Press, 1991.
The Research Center for Chinese Modern History (eds.) *A Study of National Government' History,* Kyuko Shoin, 1986.
The Research Center for Socialist Law (eds.) *Some Aspects of 'Reform' in Socialism*, Houritsubunkasha, 1985.
Sai, Abe and Mitsuru Uchida (eds.), *Little Dictionary of Contemporary Politics,* Yuhikaku, 1978. Satoshi Amako, *China Revolution and the Basic Leaders,* Kenbun Shuppan, 1984.
——, *An Introduction to the Theory of Changes of Contemporary Politics in China—Political Process before and after founded New China,* Academy of Asian Politics and Economics' Study Series, 1984.
——, *China, Changing a Great Nation of Socialism,* University of Tokyo Press, 1992.
——, *A Period of Deng Xiaoping as History,* Toho Shoten, 1992.
——, *Possibilities of Authoritarianism in Cascade Type,* SEKAI, Iwanami Shoten, August 1994.
——, *Social Changes and Relations between Centers and Localities in Contemporary China,* Priority area Study of the Ministry of Education no.113 (eds.) China area studies no.7. 1998.
——, *Contemporary China, Political society at the Stage of shift,* University of Tokyo Press, 1998.
Sei-ichiro, Takagi and Akira Ishii (eds.) *International Relations and Chinese Politics,* University of Tokyo Press, 1984.
Shigeru, Ishikawa, *Capital Accumulation System in China,*

Hitotsubashi University Economic Study Series 11, Iwanami Shoten, 1960.

Shigeki, kaizuka, *Chinese History*, Iwanami Shoten, 1970.

Shigeko, hayashi, *China Unforgettable Days*, Aki Shobo, 1986.

Shigeaki, Uno, Koji Kobayashi and Shin Yabuki, *History of Contemporary China 1949- 1985,* Yuhikaku, 1987.

Shigeaki, Uno (eds.) *Iwanami Lecture Contemporary China 3: Silent Social Changes*, Iwanami Shoten,

Shigeo, Nishimura, *Democracy and Nationalism in China: The Twentieth Century New View of a History of Chinese Politics,* Kenbunsha, 1991.

Shinkichi, Etoh (eds.) *Political Structure of Contemporary China,* Japan Institute of International Affairs, 1982.

Shinichi, Kawai, *Chinese Enterprises and Soviet Model—A Study of Historical One- Leader- system,* Academy of Asian Politics and Economics' Study Series, 1990.

Shin-ichi, Tanigawa, *Study note: 'work unit' System in China A Consideration of Political System in Mao, Zedong Period,* A Monthly Report for Chinese Study, Research Institute of China, March, 1997.

Shin, Yabuki, *Important Documents for China Crisis,* All-3 volume, Sososha, 1989.

——, *The Truth of Tiananmen Incident,* The first and second volumes, Sososha, 1990.

——, *Destination of Huge- Nation-China,* Toho Shoten, 1996.

Shinji, Kojima (eds.) *Iwanami Lecture Contemporary China 4, History and Democratization,* Iwanami Shoten, 1989.

Skiner, W./Siichi Imai and the others (trans.) *Market and Social Structure of Rural Districts in China,* Houritsubunkasha, 1979.

Sousei, Iwata, *A Theory of Economical System 4: Contemporary Socialism,* Toyo Keizai Shinposha, 1981.

——, *Basic Problems of Developing Economics,* Iwanami Shoten, 1990.

State Council China Economic Reform Research Institute / Kensaku Ishikawa (comp / trans.) *Economic Reform in China,* Toyo Keizai Shinposha, 1988.

Susumu, Takahashi, *A Study of Political Regime of Authoritarianism ,* *SHISO,* Iwanami Shoten, July 1977.

Tadao, Ishikawa, *A Memorial essays of Prof. Tadao Ishikawa on his sixtieth Birthday: Contemporary China and the World—It's Political Development,* Keio Tsushin, 1982.

Tadashi, Miyamoto (eds.) *A Theory of World Constitution,* Gakuyo Shobo, 1982.

Tadayo, Watanabe and Yoshimi Sakurai (eds.) *A rice crop Culture of Jiaugnan in China: Learning Edge Study,* Nihon Hoso Shuppan Kyoukai, 1984.

Taisuke, Murakami, Hisao Kumagai and Shunpei Kumon, *Economic System*, Iwanami Shoten, 1973.

Takashi, Inokuchi, *Composition of Politics and Economics in Contemporary Japan- Government and Market,* Toyo Keizai Shinposha, 1983.

——, *Nation and Society,* University of Tokyo Press, 1988.

Tang, Liang, *'The Principle CCP Manage Cadres' and Personal Management of Public Administration*, A Study of Law and Politics, Keio University, no.15 December 1992.

——, *Party and Government Relationship in Contemporary China,* Keio University Press, 1997.

Taro, Kinoshita, *Worlds' Constitutions vol. 2,* Gyouin Shokan, 1985.

Tatsumi, Okabe (eds.) *Re-investigation of Socialism in China,* Japan Institute of International Affairs, 1986.

Tatsuo, Yamada (eds.) *Contemporary China in History,* Keiso Shobo, 1996.

Tetsuro, Kto, *A Theory of Nation in The Renaissance,* Aoki Shoten, 1986.

Tomo,shi Kuniya, *People's Tribunal and 'Direction of the Party Central' at a Turning Point in China,* An Annual Report for a Study of Law in Socialism, no.8, 1987.

——, *A Law of Industrial Enterprises of Peoples' owed System—Explanatory notes,* A Monthly Report for Chinese Study, Research Institute of China, May 1988.

Tomohiro, Sasaki, *Jiang, Zemin's Political Power Grope for 'Authrity of the Central'*, Ajiken world Trend, December 1995 and January 1996 combined number.

——, *The Relation between the City Authority of Beijing and the Center Concerning Re-development of City of Beijing,* Priority area Study of the Ministry of Education vol.113 (eds.) China Area Studies vol.6. 1997.

Tomokazu, Nishikawa (eds.) *A Frame Work for Analysis of*

Comparative Politics, Minerva Shobo, 1986.

Tomoyuki, Kojima, *Chinese Politics and Mass Line—Mass Movement and Mao, Zedong, The Political Movement between the center and locality,* Keio Tsushin, 1985.

Toshikazu, Hori, *A Study of Equal-field- System*, Iwanami Shoten, 1975.

Toshio, Tajima, *The Dividing Structure of State-run Industrial Enterprises in China,* A Quarterly Report for Chinese Study no.22, Research Institute of China, 1992.

——, *Financial Relation and Reform of State-owned Enterprises in China,* A Monthly Report for Chinese Study , Research Institute of China, April,1994.

Weber, M./Koushiro Sera (trans.) *Sociology of Control 1,* Soubunsha, 1960.

Xu, Jiatun / Masako Aoki, Hideyuki Osuda and Zhao Hongwei (trans.) *The Recovery Work for Hong Kong, the first and second volumes,* Chikuma Shobo, 1996.

Yang, Dongping / Masako Aoki and Zhao Hongwei (trans.) *Beijing's People and Shanghai's People. The twentieth Century in Offence and defense and Complication,* Nippon Hoso Kyoukai, 1997.

Yang, Zhongmei / Michiko Kono (trans.) Mu Yaobang, *A Chinese Leader's Dead or Alive,* Sososha, 1989.

Yasuhiro, Matsuda, *'Reconstruction' of China National Party, Domain, Party, Government,* Faculty of Law, Keio University (eds.) A Study of Law and Politics no.21, 1994.

Yeltsin, B.N/Toyoki Ogasawara (trans.) *The Confession,* Soushisha, 1990.

——, *Political Economy of Chinese Modernization,* PHP Institute, 1989.

——, *Political Changes of Greater China,* Keisou Shobo, 1995.

——, Masashi Ando (eds.) *Chinese Study Handbook: Original History of Contemporary China, Extra volume,* Iwanami Shoten, 1995.

——, Kazuko Mohri (eds.) *A Period of Reform and Opening-up in China: A Theory of Contemporary China 2,* Japan Institute of International Affairs, 1991.

Yoichi, Funabashi, *Inside One Chinese Report,* Asahi Shinbunsha, 1984.

Yoshiaki, Nishimura, *Consciousness Determination and Possession in Contemporary Socialism,* Iwanami Shoten, 1986.

Yoshifumi, Nakai (eds.) *Political Economics at a Ttransition Period in China,* Research Institute of Asian Economy, 1998.

Yoshihiro, Hatano, *A study of Chinese modern military clique,* Kawade Shobo Shinsha, 1973.

Yoshimi, Matsumoto, *A Historical Study of Chinese Village System,* Iwanami Shoten, 1977.

Yoshinari, Kokubu, *A Controversy in the Party Central concerning Grand Leap Forward* : A Study of Law vol.52 no.7, The Research Center for Law at Keio University, July 1979.

——, *A Controversy in the Party Central concerning Socialist Education Movement —former History of the Great Cultural Revolution 1962-1965*: Asian Studies, vol.27 no.3, Academy of Asian Politics and Economics, October 1980.

——, *An Analysis for the 8th National Congress of CCP concerning around the Leaders' Recognition of Situation, A Memorial Essays of Prof. Tadao Ishikawa on his sixtieth Birthday: Contemporary China and the World—It's Political Development,* Keio Tsushin, 1982.

——, *Democratization and Chinese Politics,* The Simul Press, Inc.1992.

Yoshiro, Matsda, *Chinese Statistics System,* The Research Institute of Asian Economy, 1989.

Yoshiro Togawa, *History of Confucianism*, Yamakawa Shuppansha, 1987.

Yuji, Muramatsu, *Social System of Chinese Economics,* Toyo Keizai Shinposha, 1949. Re-issue 1975.

Yujiro, Murata, *Power and Cultural Expression in the twentieth century China Empire Nation. Ethnicity,* Priority area Study of the Ministry of Education no.113 (eds.) China area studies no.7. 1998.

Yukio, Kumashiro, *A Theory of Comparative Agricultural Law,* Ochanomizu Shobo, 1969.

Yukio,Yamane (eds.) *A Guide for a study of Chinese History,* Yamakawa Shuppan, 1994.

Zhang, Youyu and Kazuo Amano (comp.) *An Outline of Contemporary Chinese Law*, Houritsubunkasha, 1989.

Zhao, Hongwei, *Chinese University Students' Structure of Consciousness The Consciousness of Politics Regarding Tiananmen Incident in1989,* A Monthly Report for Chinese Study, Research Institute of China, September, 1990.

——, *A Consideration of Political System in Contemporary China The Multi-layered Centralized Regime and Price Reform (1984-1989),* Contemporary China, An Annual Report of Academy of Contemporary China, Japan. No.65 1990. 1991.

——, *Discuss New Authoritarianism,* Zhao, Hongwei (eds.) Dongying Qiusuo, International Cultural Hall, 1991.

——, *A Consideration of Political System in Contemporary China, Analysis for Phenomenon of Lordship Economy,* Asian Study vol.38 no.4, Academy of Asian Politics and Economics, 1992.

——, *The Power of Provincial Party Secretary for center-locality relationship in China,* Priority area Study of the Ministry of Education vol.113 (eds.) China Area Studies no.6. 1997.

——, *Origin of 'bang' in Contemporary Politics in China,* Kyorin study of Social Science, Academy of Social Science at Kyorin University,vol.14 no.2 1998.

Zhou, Xiaomeng, *Market Economy as Necessary Conditions for Free Society—The Post of Public Post 'work unit' in China,* Yujyo Onitsuka (eds.) ' Library Correlative Social science 3 The Conditions for Free Society' Shinseisha, 1996.

Chinese Sources

All-China Federation of Trade Unions, *The Investigation of Chinese Working-class Situation,* (Beijing) Labor Publishing House, 1987.

An, Ziwen, *An Ziwen's Biography,* (Taiyuan) Shanxi People's Publishing House, 1985.

Auditing Rules of People's Republic of China, China Auditing, (Beijing) April 1988.

All-China Federation of Trade Unions International Division, *Structure of Chinese Labor Union,* 1988.

All-China Federation of Trade Unions Study Center for Political Policy, *Historical Documents of Enterprise Management System in China,* (Beijing) Economic Management Publishing House, 1986.

Association of Mayors (eds.) *Introduction of Urban Development Districts in China,* (Beijing) Urban Publishing House, 1994.

Buo, Yipo, *Memory of Some Serious Decisions and Affairs,* (Beijing) Central Party School of CCPCC Press, 1991.

Buo, Guili, *Economic Management of Town Government,* A Study of

Politics, March 1986.

China Biographical Dictionary Editing Committee (eds.) *China Biographical Dictionary 1994.*

CCPCC, *The Provisional Regulation Concerning Election of Party Administrative Leaders*, People's Daily, May 17 1995.

CCPCC Study Center for Documents, *After 3rd Plenum of the 11th CCPCC Important Documents,* (Beijing) People's Publishing House, 1982.

CCPCC Study Center for Documents, *After 12th National Congress of CCP Important Documents,* The first and second volumes, (Beijing) People's Publishing House, 1986.

Central Office of CCPCC (eds.) *The Climax of Socialism in Chinese Rural,* (Beijing) People's Publishing House, 1956.

Chen, Kulong, *Present Chinese Finance (the first volume)*, Chinese Academy of Social Sciences Publishing House, 1988.

Dao, Tianding, *A Study of Local State Organization in China,* (Wuhan) Qunzhong Publishing House, 1985.

Deng, Xiaoping, *A Selection of Dong Xiaoping,* People's Publishing House, vol.1 1984. vol.2 1983. vol.3 1993.

Deng, Yingtao, *Capital Analysis of Outside Budget in China,* (Beijing) People's University Press, 1990.

Ding, Shuimu, *Register Management and Social Control* , Society, (Beijing) 1989. The Third Term.

Economic Publishing House (eds.) *Chinese Economic Yearbook 1989*, (Beijing) 1989.

Fan, Gang and the others, *General Theory of Public –owned System,* Shanghai Sanlian Book Shop, 1990.

Fang, Jue, *Changes for New Demand and Opinion for Democratic outline,* Hong Kong magazine, Zhengming, January, March 1998.

Gu, Maoran, *Introduction for Legislation in New China,* (Beijing) Legal Publishing House, 1995.

Han, Guang, *An Outline of Reform and Development in Chinese Contemporary Political System,* (Beijing) CCP Historical Publishing House, 1988.

He, Guangyuan, *Arrangement for Enterprise Organization is Urgent Subject,* Economic Management, (Beijing) February 1983.

Hu, Rulei, *A Study of Chinese Feudalistic Social Form,* (Shanghai) Sanlian press, 1979.

Hua, Sheng and the others, *Reform 10 years; Recollection Reflection*

and Prospects, Economic Study, (Beijing) vol.9 1988.
Huang, Philip, *Crisis of Recognition: Standard of Chinese Study,* Ooxford University Press, 1994.
Jiang, Liu and the others (eds.) *An Social Blue Paper 1996-1997 The Analysis and Predict of Chinese Social Situation,* (Beijing) Chinese Academy of Social Sciences Publishing House, 1997.
Jiang, Zemin, *Brace ourself up for National Sprits*, People's Daily (Overseas Version), December 28 1994.
——, *Some Important Relations Which Treat in Right Way,* People's Daily, January 17 1996.
——, *Concerning Lecturing about politics,* CCP-organ, Qiushi, July 1996.
——, *The Political Report of The 14th National Congress of CCP,* People's Daily, October 21 1992.
——, *The Political Report of The 15th National Congress of CCP,* China Press, September 25 1997.
Li, Jingxiu, *A History of Political System in Modern China,* Beijing Qiushi Publishing House, 1988.
Li, Li, *Political System problems,* Xu, Ming (eds.) Turning Point, (Beijing) Today' China Press. 1997.
Li, Lulu and Li, Hanlin, *System Reform of Chinese Work Unit,* Chinese Social Science Quarterly, 1994. The Second Term.
Li, Rui, *An Authentic Record: Lushan Conference,* (Beijing) Chunqiu Publishing, 1989.
Li, Zhisui, *Reminiscences of Mao Zedong' Private Doctor,* (Taiwan) Shibao Wenhua Publishing, 1994.
Liu, Yishun and Zeng, Xisheng's 'Subcontract Field' in Anhui, CCP History Study, (Beijing) March,1987.
Lui, Jun and Li, Lin (eds.) *New Authoritarianism —Controversy of Reform Theory,* Beijing Academy of Economics Publishing House, 1989.
Ma, Junlei and Luo, Liqin, *The Important Policy of Reform for Financial and Tax System in China,* China Economics, no.339, March 1994.
Ma, Qi and the others, *Chinese Communist Party 40 years Administration (1949-1989)* (Beijing) CCP Material Data publishing House.1989.
Mo, Shuben (eds.) *Development of Wage for Both White and Blue Color in This-35-years,* China Labor Personnel Publishing House,

1986.

Mao, Zedong, *The Selected Works of Mao Zedong,* Vol.1-5, (Beijing) People's Publishing House.1977.

Ministry of Public Security, *Public Security Laws 1950-1979,* (Beijing) Qunzhong Publishing House, 1980.

Ministry of Personnel Law Section (eds.) *Personnel Work Documents,* (Beijing) China Personnel Press, 1991. No.13 China Statistical Bureau, *China Social Statistics Documents 1990.*

——, *China Statistical Yearbook,* Every Years.

——, *China Rural Statistical Yearbook,* Every Years.

——, *China Trade Prices Statistical Documents 1953-1983.*

People's Bank of China Personnel Section (eds.) *Personnel Work Documents,* (Beijing) China Financial Publishing House, 1985.

Qiu, Yongming, *A System History of Chinese Inspection*, (Shanghai) Huadong Educational University Press, 1992.

Song, Rufen, *Career of Participating Chinese Legislation*, The first and second volumes, (Beijing) Chinese Legal System Publishing House, 1994.

Tan, Shew, *Formation and Characteristic of Social Guarantee System by 'work unit' at Cities,* A Study of Socialism, (Beijing) May 1995.

Tian, Fu (eds.) *Posture of The Government Party and Objection of Liberalized Capitalism,* Central Party School of CCPCC Press, 1990.

Tsai, Keru, A Consideration of Reform for Auditing Organization in China, China Auditing, (Beijing) October 1986.

Villager's Autonomous System in Chinese Rural Districts Study Group, *Election System of Village Committee in Chinese Rural,* Villager's Autonomous System in Chinese Rural Districts Study Report.1993. Research Center for Lower Political power Construction in China.

Wang, Haibo, *New History of Chinese Industrial Economy*, (Beijing) Economic Management Publishing House, 1986.

Wang, Zhongtian, *Investigation for Separation Party from Public Administration*, (Beijing) Chunqiu Publishing House, 1988.

Wang, Ying and the others, *Social Middle Class Reform and Chinese Social organization,* (Beijing) China Fazhan Publishing House, 1993.

Wei, Liqun (eds.) *The Center-Locality Economic Relationship in Market-oriented Economy,* (Beijing) China Economic Publishing

House, 1994.
Wu, Guoguang and Zheng, Yongnian, *A Theory of center-locality Relationship,* (Beijing) Oxford University Press, 1995.
Yan, Jiaqi, *The Days with Baotong,* Yang, Zhongmei (eds. Chinese Magazine) Democratic China (Tokyo) no.40 November 1992.
Yang, Guoqiang, *Cause and Influence of Nation-Power-Deterioration in Modern China,* Priority area Study of the Ministry of Education no.113 (eds.) China area studies no.7. 1998.
Yang, Zhongmei, *Zunyi Conference and Yanan Rectification Movement,* Hong Kong Zunyi Publishing. 1989.
Zhang, Hongsheng (comp.) *A History of Chinese Law System,* (Beijing) Law Publishing House.1983.
Zhang, Jinfan, *A Theory of Chinese Law History,* (Beijing) Law Publishing House.1982.
Zhang, Mingzhao, *Reform of Financial Management System*, Financial News, (Beijing) September 1985.
Zhang, Qinwu, *The Register Note,* Qunzhong Publishing House, 1987.
Zhang, Zhijian (chief comp.) *Present Personnel Management in China,* (Beijing) Present China Press, 1994.
Zhao, Shenghui, *A History of Chinese Communist party Structure, (Hefei)* Anki People's Publishing House. 1988.
Zhao, Ziyang, *The Political Report of 13rd National Congress of CCP,* People's Daily, November 4 1987.
Zhong, Chengxun (eds.) *A Study of Local Government's Investment,* (Beijing) China Financial Economic Publishing House, 1993.
Zhou, Yuming and Shao,Yong, *History of Banghui in China,* Shanghai People's Publishing House, 1993.

English Sources

Almond, Gabriel. "Corporatism, Pluralism and Professional Memory," *World Politics,* (1983).
Almond, G. and Powell, G., *Comparative Politics: A Developmental Approach*, Boston: Little, Brown, 1966.
Barnett, Doak, "Ten Years After Mao." *Foreign Affairs*, Fall 1986.
Bianco, Lucian, *Origins of the Chinese Revolution, 1915-1949*, Stanford: Stanford University Press, 1971.
Butterfield, Fox, *China: Alive in the Bitter Sea,* New York: Random House Inc, 1990.

Chamberlain, Heath, B., "Party-management relations in Chinese Industries; some political dimension of economic reform," *The China Quarterly*, No 112, dec (1987).

Chan, Anita, & Madsen, R.& Ungar, J., *Chen Village*, Berkley: University of Colifornia Press, 1984.

Chang, Chung Li, *The Chinese Gentry: Studies on their Role in Nineteenth Century Chinese Society*. University of Washington Press, 1955.

Chang, Parris, *Power and Policy in China*, 2nd enl. ed., Pennsylvania: Pennsylvania State University Press, 1978.

Cohen, Paul, A., *Discovering History in China: American Historical Writing on the Recent Past*, New York: Columbia University Press, 1984.

Easton, David, *The Political System An Inquiry into the State of Political Science*, New York: Alfred A. Knopf, 1953.

——, "An Approach to the Analysis of Political System," *World Politics*, No. 9, (1957).

Fairbank, John, K., *The United States and China*, New York: The Viking Press, 1971.

——, "Why China's Rulers Fear Democracy," The New York: *Review of Books*, vol. 28, (September, 1989).

——, "From the Ming to Deng, Xiaoping." *New York: Review of Books*, Vol. 31 (May, 1989).

——, " 'Preface,' Children of the Dragon, dy Human Rights in China, " New York: *Collier Books*, Macmillan Publishing Company, 1990.

Friedrich, Carl, J., and Zbigniew, K. Brzezinski, *Totalitarian Dictatorship and Totalitarian Dictatorship and Autocracy*. Second ed. Revised by Carl J, Friedrich, Cambridge, Mass.: Harvard University Press, 1965

Gill, G., *The Collapse of a Single-Party System*, Cambridge: Cambridge University Press, 1994.

Goodman, David, *Groups and Politics in the People's Republic of China*, Cardiff: University College Cardiff Press, 1984.

——, *Centre and Province in the People's Republic of China,Sichuan and Guizhou 1955-1965*, Cambridge: Cambridge University Press, 1986.

Granick, David, *Chinese State Enterprises*, Chicago: The University of Chicago Press, 1990.

Harding, Harry, "The Study of Chinese Politics: Toward a Third Generation of Scholarship," *World Politics*, (January 1984).

Held, D, "Democracy and the New International Order," in Held, D., and Archibugi, D (eds.), *Cosmopolitan Democracy: An Agenda for a New World Order*, Polity Press, 1955.

Henderson, Gail, E., and Cohen, Myron, S., *The Chinese Hospital: A Socialist Work Unit*, New Haven: Yale University Press, 1984.

Huang, Philip, *The Peasant Economy and Social Change in North China*, Stanford: Stanford University Press, 1985.

——, *The Peasant Family and Rural Development in the Yangzi Delta, 1350-1988*, Stanford: Stanford University Press, 1990.

Huntington, S., and Crozier, M., and Watanuki, J., "The Governability of Democracies," *World Politics,* (1975).

James, Cole, *Competition and Cooperation in Nineteenth Century China*, Arizona: University of Arizona Press, 1986.

Jia, Hao and Li, Zhimin, *Changing Central-Local Relations in China*, Cambridge: Westview Press, 1994.

Johnson, Chalmers, *Peasant Nationalism and Communist Power: The Emergence of Revolutionary China 1937-1945*,Stanford: Stanford University Press, 1962.

——, "What's Wrong with Chinese Political Studies?." *Issues & Studies*, June 1982, Asian Suruey, October 1982.

Johnson, Graham, E., "The Production Responsibility System in Chinese Agriculture: Some Examples from Guangdong," *Pacific Affairs*, Fall 1982.

Joseph, Esherick, and Mary Rankin, eds., *Chinese Local Elites and Patterns of Dominance*, California: University of California Press, 1990.

Katzenstein, Peter,. "Introduction: Domestic and International Forces and Strategies of Foreign Economic Policy," Peter, Katzenstein. ed. in *Between Power and Plenty; Foreign Economic Policies of Advanced Industrial States*. Madison: University of Wisconsin Press, 1978.

Lampton, D. M., *The Politics of medicine in China: The Policy Prosess, 1949-1977*, Boulder: Westview Press, 1977.

——, *Policy Implementation in Post-Mao China*, Berkeley: University of California Press, 1987.

Lieberthal, Kenneth, and Oksenberg, Michel, *Policy Making in China: Leaders, Structures, and Processes*, Princeton: Princeton

University Press, 1988.
——, *Governing China: From Revolution Through Reform*, W. W. Norton & Company Inc., 1995.
Linz, Juan J., "An Authoritarian Regime: Spain," in Erik, Allard, and Stein, Rokkan, eds. *Mass Politics: Studies in Political Sociology*, New York: Free Press, 1970.
——, "Totalitarian and Authoritarian Regimes," in Greenstein, F. I., and Plsby, N. W., eds. *Handbook of Political Science*, vol.3, Reading, Mass: Addison Wesley Pub.Co, 1975.
Linz, Juan J., and Stepan, Alfred, *The Breakdown of Democratic Regimes*, 3 vols. Baltimore: The Johns Hopkins University, Press, 1978.
Liu, Alan, P. L., *Communications and National Integration in Communist China*, Berkley: University of California Press, 1971.
——, *Political Culture and Group Conflict in Communist China*, Santa Barbara: Clio Books, 1976.
Louis, Putterman, "Effort, Productivity, and Incentives in a 1970s Chinese People's Commune," *Journal of Comparative Economics*, Vol. 14 (1), 1990.
Madsen, Richard, *Morality and Power in a Chinese Village*, Berkeley: University of California Press, 1984.
Mary, Rankin, *Elite Activism and Political Transformation in China: Zhejiang Province, 1865-1911*, Stanford: Stanford University Press, 1986.
Metzger, Thomas, A., and Myers, Ramon, H., "inological Shadows: The State of Modern China Studies in the U. S.," in Amy, Auerbacher, Wilson, and Sidney, Leonard, Greenblatt, and Richard, Wilson, eds. *Methodological Issues in Chinese Studies*, New York: Praeger Publishers, 1983.
Nee, Victor, and Mozingo, David, eds. *State and Society in Contemporary China*, Ithaca and London: Cornell University Press, 1983.
Nove, Alec, *The Soviet Economic System*. George Allen and Unwin Ltd., WCIA ILU, England, 1977, 1980.
Oi, Jean, C., "Communism and Clientelism: Rural Policy in China," *World Politics*, Vol. 37, No. 2 (January 1985).
——, "Commercializing Chinese Rural Cardres," *Problems of Communism*, Vol. 35, No, 5 (Sept- Oct. 1986).
——, *State and Peasant in Contemporary China: The Political*

Economy of Village Government, Berkley: University of California Press, 1989.

Oksenberg, M., and Bush, R., " China's Political Evolution: 1972-1982, " *Problems of Communism*, (September-October 1982).

Oksenberg, M., and Steven, Goldstein, " The Chinese Political Spectrum." *Problems of Communism*, (March-April 1974).

Parish, W. L., and M. K. Whyte, *Village and Family in Contemporary China*, Chicago: University of Chicago Press, 1978.

Penny, Kane, *Famine in China 1959-1961: Demographic and Social Implications*, New York: Macmillan Press, 1988.

Perr, J. Elizabeth, "State and Society in Contemporary China." In *World Politics*, 41 July 1989.

Pye, Lucian, W., *The Spirit of Chinese Politics: A Psychocultural Study of the Authority Crisis in Political Development*, Cambridge, Mass: M. I. T., Press, 1968.

— — , *The Dynamics of Chinese Politics*, Cambridge, Mass: Odgeschlager, Gunn & Hain, Publishers, 1981.

——, "Tiananmen and Chinese Political Culture: the Escalation of Confrontation," in George, Hicks, ed., *The Broken Mirror: China After Tiananmen*. Essex, United Kingdom: Longman Group, 1990.

Rowe, William, *HanRow: Commerce and Society in a Chinese City, 1796-1889*. Stanford: Stanford University Press, 1984.

Schoppa, Keith, *Chinese Elites and Political Change: Zhejiang Province in the Early Twentieth Century*, Harvard University Press, 1982.

Schurmann, Franz, *Ideolgy and Organization in Communist China*, Second Edition, Enlarged. Berkeley, Los Angels, London: University of California Press, 1968.

Selden, Mark, *The Yenan Way in Revolutionary China*, Cambridge Mass: Harvard University Press, 1971.

Shue, Vivienne, *The Reach of the State*, Stanford: University of Stanford Press, 1988.

Skinner, William, eds., *The Chinese City between Two World*. Stanford University Press, 1974.

——, *The City in the Late Imperial China*. Stanford University Press, 1977.

Skocpol, Theda, "Bringing the State Back In: Strategies of Analysis in Current Research," in Skocpol, Theda, eds., *Bringing the State*

Back in, Cambrige: Cambrige University Press, 1985.

Solinger, Dorothy, *Three Visions of Chinese Socialism*, Boulder: Westview Press, 1984.

Stephen, Endicott, *Red Earth Revolution in a Sichuan Village*, London: Tauris, 1988.

Sulamith, Potter, and Jack, Potter. *China's Peasants The Anthropology of Revolution*, Cambridge: Cambridge University Press, 1990.

Suleiman, Ezra N, *Politics Power and Bureaucracy in France: The Administrative Elite,* Princeton: Princeton University Press, 1974.

Sutton, Donald, *Provincial Militarism and the Chinese Republic:The Yunnan Army, 1905-1925*, Michigan: University of Michigan Press, 1980.

Townsend, James, R., *Politics in China*, Boston: Little Brown and Company, 1974.

— — , " Back from the Brink of Revolutionary `Feudal' Totalitaraianism." Victor Nee, and David Mozingo, eds., *State and Society in Contemporary China*. Ithaca and London: Cornell University Press, 1983.

——, *The Cultural Revolution and Post-Mao Reforms: A Historical Perspective*, Chicago and London: The University of Chicago Press, 1986.

Tsou, Tang. "Prolegomenon to the Study of Informal Groups in CCP Politics." *The China Quarterly*, January 1976.

Vogel, Ezra F., *Canton under Communism: Programs and Politics in a Provincial Capital, 1949-1968*, Cambridge, Mass: Harvard University Press, 1969.

——, *Guangdong under Reform: One Step Ahead in China*, the President and Fellows of Harvard College, 1989.

Walder, Andrew, G., *Communist Neo-Traditionalism: Work and Authority in Chinese Industry*, Berkley: University of California Press, 1986.

——, "Wage Reforms and the Web of Factory Interests," *China Quarterly*, no. 109, March 1987.

——, "Factory and Manager in an Era of Reform," *The China Quarterly*, no.118, June 1989.

——, "The Political Sociology of the Beijing Upheaval of 1989," *Problems of Communism*, September-October 1989.

Weir, Margaret, and Skocpol, Theda, "State Structures and Possibilities for [Keynesian] Responces to Great Depression in Sweden, Britain and the United States." in Skocpol, Theda, eds., *Bringing the State Back in*, Cambrige: Cambrige University Press, 1985.

Wilson, Amy, Auerbacher, and Greenblatt, Sidney, Leonard, and Wilson, Richard, W., eds., *Methodological Issues in Chinese Studies*, New York: Praeger Publishers, Auerbacher, 1983.

Wittfogel, Karl, A., *Oriental Despotism: A Comparative Study of Total Power* New York: G. L. Ulmen, 1981.

Wolken, L. C., "The Restructuring of China's Banking System Under the Economic Reforms 1979-1989," New York: *Columbia Journal of World Business*, vol. 25, no. 1 & 2, Spring /Summer, 1990.

Xie, Weizhi, "The Semihierarchical Totalitarion Nature of Chinese Politics," *Comparative Politics*, 25, April, 1993.